the new
pressure
cooker
cookbook

the new
pressure
cooker
cookbook

*150 Delicious, Fast,
and Nutritious Dishes*

Ellen Brown

STERLING EPICURE
New York

STERLING EPICURE
New York

An Imprint of Sterling Publishing Co., Inc.
1166 Avenue of the Americas
New York, NY 10036

ISBN 978-1-4549-2175-2

Library of Congress Cataloging-in-Publication Data

Names: Brown, Ellen, author.
Title: The new pressure cooker cookbook : 150 delicious, fast, & nutritious dishes / Ellen Brown.
Description: New York, NY : Sterling Epicure, [2016] | Includes index.
Identifiers: LCCN 2016022341 | ISBN 9781454921752 (alk. paper)
Subjects: LCSH: Pressure cooking. | LCGFT: Cookbooks.
Classification: LCC TX840.P7 B76 2016 | DDC 641.5/87--dc23 LC record available at
https://lccn.loc.gov/2016022341

Distributed in Canada by Sterling Publishing Co., Inc.
c/o Canadian Manda Group, 664 Annette Street
Toronto, Ontario, Canada M6S 2C8
Distributed in the United Kingdom by GMC Distribution Services
Castle Place, 166 High Street, Lewes, East Sussex, England BN7 1XU
Distributed in Australia by NewSouth Books
45 Beach Street, Coogee, NSW 2034, Australia

For information about custom editions, special sales, and
premium and corporate purchases, please contact Sterling Special Sales
at 800-805-5489 or specialsales@sterlingpublishing.com.

Manufactured in Canada

2 4 6 8 10 9 7 5 3 1

www.sterlingpublishing.com

Photography by Bill Milne
Food styling by Diane Vezza

contents

PREFACE

There's always been a need to get food onto the table in a hurry. Long before we had a panoply of specialized pots and pans, there were basic cast iron skillets and copper sauté pans that cooked food over high heat for a short period of time.

For the better part of a century, before the first microwave oven "nuked" a frozen meal in minutes in the 1970s, there were pressure cookers sputtering puffs of steam into kitchens around the world. When cooks walked in with a bag of groceries after a day at work, their dinner—one that was actually assembled and cooked from real foods called *ingredients*—could be on the table in the amount of time it took to watch the evening news.

But this popularity came with a warning label flashing in neon. Most people still believe—even today—that pressure cookers are dangerous, sort of like culinary roadside bombs. Pressure cookers were the Loch Ness Monster of the kitchen. Everyone knew of someone who had either a) wiped marinara sauce off the kitchen cabinets or b) chipped away at the stalactites of corned beef and cabbage that had formed on the ceiling. The dish might change, depending on the cook's ethnic heritage, but the pressure cooker's potential for disaster remained constant.

All of these stories—most of which were apocryphal—are from the same era as *I Love Lucy*. We've now had three decades of refining pressure cookers to maximize the number of safety features. And now they come in electric as well as stovetop models. While old pressure cookers may have had the equivalent of a seatbelt, the models today have air bags and computers that put on the brakes for you.

That's why I want to give this wonder pot a name change. If used cars are now billed as "previously owned vehicles" then pressure cookers should be called "fast cookers," especially because they're vying for popularity against "slow cookers," aka Crock-Pots.®

I'm not saying that the pressure cooker is a universal helpmate, although any food that can be boiled, braised, or steamed is a good candidate for its assistance. I would never use it for foods like spinach or thin fish fillets because they would be overcooked by the time the pot reached pressure. And while some authors tout pressure-cooked cheesecakes and bread puddings, I find that certain categories of dishes are superior when baked in the dry heat of a conventional oven. Time doesn't trump results in my book.

The biggest hurdle for me to jump when I was adjusting to using a pressure cooker was that it's counterintuitive to the way we normally cook: the cooking is behind the scenes, literally hidden by the lid.

We use all of our senses when we cook. But with a pressure cooker there's no aroma in the air because there's hardly any evaporation. Water vapors don't carry the smells around the house. There's no sound and little to see, except for a few wisps of steam; you don't hear the sizzle of meat browning or the noise from the furious ring of bubbles that forms when you drop a morsel of food into hot oil to fry.

And perhaps most frustrating to cooks is that you can't give food a "poke test." Whether it's testing spears of asparagus with tongs in a skillet or peeking inside a grilled steak with the tip of a paring knife, most cooks like to get up close and personal with the food they cook. With a pressure cooker, that becomes an exercise in deferred gratification. But, because it works so rapidly, the gratification need not be deferred for too long.

And just think about these delicious rewards! You can have meltingly tender lamb shanks or short ribs of beef that take just a half hour to cook, compared with five times that long in the oven or ten times that long in a slow cooker. And the gravy has a richer

and more concentrated flavor, because the pressure cooker squeezes every bit of flavor out of those bones.

How would you like a bowl of creamy risotto, with just the right al dente texture to the rice, that literally makes itself in 7 minutes rather than taking half an hour of continual stirring? With the pressure cooker you can have it anytime. You can also enjoy artichokes in 10 minutes and a meatloaf too.

When you make these delectable dishes in a pressure cooker, the pressure is off about promptly getting dinner on the table.

Happy Cooking!

Ellen Brown
Providence, Rhode Island

INTRODUCTION

Lots of Generation Xers and Millennials know the phrase "work is like a pressure cooker," but choosing one from a shelf of random pots in a housewares store would stump them. That's because the generations that matured in the Era of the Microwave watched the supermarket frozen food aisle expand from a few shelves holding ice cream and TV dinners to every conceivable food group and cuisine. Even things that can be cooked quickly—like scrambled eggs—can be purchased, premade and at a high cost, and then reheated in this emission-producing device that gives everything the unappealing texture of foam rubber.

The science behind pressure cooking, on the other hand, goes back to the seventeenth century; it's hardly a new technology. That means it's been around long enough to be trustworthy. But in the spirit of songwriter Peter Allen's lyrics "everything old is new again," the pressure cooker is undergoing a surge in popularity with cutting-edge cooks and chefs.

Indeed the pressure cooker has a dual personality. On one side, it's the workhorse of the working person who has hungry mouths to feed at the end of the day. And then there are the sophisticated foodies, who have spent countless hours meticulously testing procedures and crowned the pressure cooker the victor in challenges like making stock— the backbone of cooking—and tenderizing various and sundry cuts of inexpensive meat. Their focus is not on survival, but on superior results and how they can be achieved.

The first time I became aware of the affinity of upper-echelon chefs for the pressure cooker was when English superstar Heston Blumenthal of The Fat Duck restaurant fame touted its virtues for producing the best chicken stock ever. Period. End of discussion. I then noticed the really savvy contestants on Bravo's *Top Chef* (my dive into reality television), who were using them for the very time-limited "Quickfire Challenges." Some chefs would create ethereally rich stews or dishes made with long-cooking beets in the allotted 20 minutes to watch their competitors get voted off.

These anecdotal observations were followed by delving into the work of Nathan Myhrvold, a retired Microsoft scientist, who wrote *Modernist Cuisine* with Chris Young and Maxime Bilet in 2011. While he advocated the use of *sous vide* (the ultimate in slow cooking), his work also lauded all the virtues of the pressure cooker.

Pressure Cooker History

The father of the pressure cooker was French physicist Denis Papin, whose reputation was made in the 1670s with his studies of steam and how to best use it. While working in London, a few years later in the early 1680s, he prepared a whole meal for members of the Royal Society, to show how food could be cooked much faster if the boiling point of water is raised by trapping its steam in a tightly closed pot. One guest at the dinner marveled at how the actual bones of beef and mutton were rendered as soft as cheese.

Papin's contraption was known as the Steam Digester or Papin's Digester, and it is credited as the foundation for the development of the steam engine, fitted with pistons and cylinders. But it was hardly an overnight sensation.

It was almost two centuries later, in 1864, when cast iron pressure cookers made their debut in Germany, and it was Spain that led the pressure-cooker pack by granting a patent in 1919. It was called *olla expres*, literally "express cooking pot," and the patent holder, José Alix Martínez of Zaragoza, wrote a book to support the cooker in 1924.

There were other iterations of the device put out by European manufacturers in the decades leading up to World War II, and the pressure cooker gained great visibility in the United States at the 1939 World's Fair. National Presto Industries, then called the National Pressure Cooker Company, introduced the machine to rave reviews.

In 1950, almost half of American homes contained pressure cookers, but that figure had dropped to 20 percent by 2011, according to a study by NPD Group, a consumer research firm. This reduced figure included electric pressure cookers, which were first patented in 1991. Pressure cookers remained popular in Europe, however, and now sales of these workhorse machines are growing in the United States again too.

How the Pressure Cooker Works

Some of us had never heard the acronym psi (pounds per square inch) until the New England Patriots were accused of deflating footballs in the championship game against the Indianapolis Colts in January of 2015. But be it inside a football or inside a closed pot, it's the pounds per square inch that make things happen. (For the sake of simplicity, this explanation is given for pressure at sea level. See page 9 for the discussion of pressure cooking at high altitudes.)

What maintains cooking in the slow lane is the low temperature at which water boils, 212°F (100°C). The steam produced escapes to the open air. But when you lock the lid on a specially designed pressure cooker, you take an open space and turn it into a closed space. As the steam can no longer escape, pressure builds up *and* the temperature of the boiling water rises.

So why does this happen? As heat is applied to any liquid, its constituent molecules move more rapidly and move farther apart. When the liquid boils, it changes state: that is, a portion of the liquid vaporizes. For water, this means that steam is produced at 212°F (100°C). In a pot virtually open to the air, the steam escapes to the atmosphere. But if the pot is tightly closed, the transformation of water to steam is delayed, because the increased steam pressure delays vaporization. As more and more heat is applied to the pot, the water temperature rises, and the trapped steam pressure rises above atmospheric pressure.

There are tables that list what the water temperature is for various steam pressures. Most modern pressure cookers are set to run at 15 psi. The corresponding water temperature is about 250°F (120°C). When using these heat/pressure relationships for cooking, the heat under the pot is reduced once the desired pressure (and corresponding temperature) is reached.

So what pressure cookers do on the cooking superhighway is to raise the speed limit. It's not just the water molecules around the food that gets heated to far beyond 212°F (100°C), it's also the water molecules *inside* the food. That's why cuts of meat reach an ethereal state of meltingly tender so quickly in a pressure cooker. The water molecules inside of it are not strolling along at 212°F (100°C), they are jogging for the finish line at 250°F (120°C).

The general rule is that for every 5°C that the boiling point of water is increased, cooking time is cut in half. So a stew that would take 3 hours of conventional simmering will be pressure-cooked to perfection in 20 minutes.

Reasons to Believe

Conventional wisdom, in addition to the belief that pressure cookers are innately dangerous, is that cooking at high temperatures is not healthful. That's what they say about the potential carcinogens produced when grilling food, so cooking under pressure must have some caveats too. Nothing could be further from the truth. Here is why.

Pressure Cooking Preserves Nutrients

A study in *The Journal of Food Science* stated that pressure cooking preserved

90 to 95 percent of the nutrients in food, while steaming came in second at 75 to 90 percent; way down the list was boiling at 40 to 75 percent. Despite cooking at higher temperatures, pressure cookers reduce leaching of nutrients into the cooking liquid, because of shorter cooking times. Certain nutrients such as vitamin C, for example, are easily broken down by oxidation. But because the interior of the pressure cooker is filled with superheated steam, it is purged of oxygen, so many more of the nutrients are retained.

Cooking Grains and Legumes in a Pressure Cooker Delivers More Nutrients

Phytic acids are the culprits found in the bran layer of nuts, seeds, and legumes that wear black hats; they are anti-nutrients. Phytic acids are the storage form of phosphorous, an important mineral used for energy production as well as in the formation of structural elements like cell membranes. Whereas a small amount of phytic acids are important, there's a serious downside: they bind minerals and other nutrients such as iron, zinc, calcium, and magnesium in our digestive tract and keep them from being absorbed. Pressure cooking removes twice the amount of phytic acid as boiling.

Pressure Cooking Saves Energy

Because the cooking times in a pressure cooker are so much shorter than conventional cooking, you end up using less energy from the burner on your stove or less electricity, if your pressure cooker is plugged into a wall socket. Because beef stew in a pressure cooker takes one-fifth the amount of time that would be needed to simmer it on a burner, energy saving is significant. And its cooking time is only one-tenth of what it would take to make the stew in a slow cooker.

So there are many reasons to believe in the benefits that come from using a pressure cooker—not the least of which is that so many more options are available now to help get midweek dinners onto the table quickly.

CHAPTER 1

Pressure Cooker Pointers

You should think of your pressure cooker as a Dutch oven with benefits. Like a Dutch oven (or a stockpot), it's big; it can boil up a ton of pasta for a crowd. Like other big pots, you can use it first to make a richly flavored, thick and satiny Bolognese Ragù to top that pasta. But—and here's the benefit—instead of 3 hours, your sauce can be ready in 20 minutes.

If you're trying out a pressure cooker for the first time you may feel a bit apprehensive. Few pots come with such a long and detailed instruction booklet or one that contains so many caveats. But by the time you've read through this chapter you'll be ready to confidently test-drive your cooker.

The most important thing you can do is to *read the instruction manual from cover to cover.* I cannot stress this enough. While each blender model has bells and whistles, all of them are pretty much the same. The same cannot be said about pressure cookers; they even vary as to the pressure level they reach.

And when you're reading the manual, look for the answers to these questions:

What is the minimal amount of liquid needed? To increase pressure you need steam, and to make steam you need liquid. Each manufacturer tells you what the minimum amount of liquid should be.

How do you lock the lid? Are there marks to line up?

What and where are the safety features? Most cookers today are constructed with at least two ways to ensure that the pot cannot accidentally open while under pressure. Find them and know how they work.

How do you know you've reached high pressure? Once again this is not standardized for stovetop cookers, although electric cookers start their built-in timer automatically when pressure is reached.

Stovetop Pressure Cooker

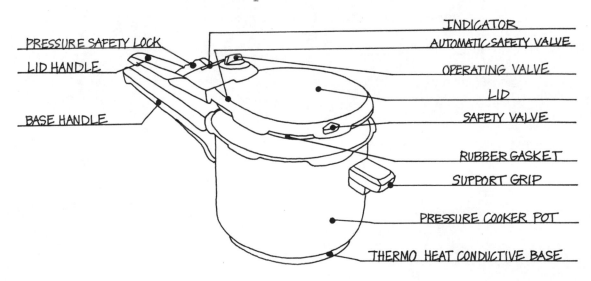

PRESSURE SAFETY LOCK

LID HANDLE

BASE HANDLE

INDICATOR

AUTOMATIC SAFETY VALVE

OPERATING VALVE

LID

SAFETY VALVE

RUBBER GASKET

SUPPORT GRIP

PRESSURE COOKER POT

THERMO HEAT CONDUCTIVE BASE

The diagram on page 2 may look nothing like your actual pressure cooker, because it seems that every manufacturer has its own engineering strategy for reaching the finish line, which is to produce pressure at 15 psi. But there are some common features:

The pot: I recommend stainless steel, rather than aluminum, because cooking certain acidic foods like tomatoes in aluminum can give them a bitter and metallic flavor. The bottom of the pot is usually a thicker sheet of metal so that food doesn't scorch when you're building pressure over high heat.

When you look inside you should see a line indicating the maximum level to which you can fill the pot. I believe that your fill level should always remain an inch below that line.

The pot always has a handle with a flat top that will match up with a similar handle on the lid when the lid is properly locked in place. Most manufacturers also provide a smaller handle on the opposite side of the pot that helps when moving it, although it doesn't serve a function in operating the cooker.

The lid: The lid is where the action is. On the inside of the lid there's a round rubber gasket at the edge; that's what seals the pot airtight so pressure can build. The lid always has a notched edge that will slide over the notched edge of the pot so it can be closed securely. The lid is where you'll find the safety locks that make it impossible to accidentally open the cooker when it's under pressure, as well as the release valve that brings the pressure down rapidly.

Stovetop Heat Sources

Your stove is the yin to the pressure cooker's yang, and the most powerful of its burners is what you want to use to build the pressure. That's really the most important thing to remember. It takes a lot of BTUs to generate the psi needed to cook under pressure. It's not that your simmer burner would just take more time to increase the psi inside your cooker; it might not do it successfully at all. You really need to put the pressure cooker on the burner that goes into overdrive.

But once you have reached high pressure, it's time to turn the heat down. You want to maintain high pressure using the least amount of energy necessary to do so. And how you accomplish this balancing act is different, according to how your stove functions.

Until you get to know your cooker and how long it generally takes to reach pressure, it's a good idea to stay in the kitchen. If a large quantity of food is being cooked, you know it will take a few minutes for the pressure to start building, but once that process begins, it's good to be around and ready to take action.

GAS STOVES

The reason why most food professionals endorse gas stoves is exactly the reason they work so well with a stovetop pressure cooker. You have instant and total control over the size and intensity of the flame. Put the pot in place and turn it on. There are no hot spots to worry about, so there's no need for a heat diffuser, and when the pot reaches pressure, you can fiddle with the flame to reach that Zen moment when the flame is as low as you can get it while still maintaining high pressure.

ELECTRIC STOVES AND HALOGEN COOKTOPS

Electric stoves and halogen cooktops are slow to heat up, and what's equally important for regulating a pressure cooker is that they're slow to cool down. Set your most powerful burner to high, with a heat diffuser on top of it, as you are slicing and dicing food to put in the pressure cooker. Put your cooker on top of the now very hot diffuser, and wait for the results.

As soon as the pot goes onto the hot burner, turn on a second burner and set it at medium heat. After using your cooker a few times you'll know exactly where to set the maintenance burner, but start with medium. When the cooker reaches pressure, move it physically to the cooler burner and turn off the hot burner.

Basic Techniques and Tips

Once you've used a pressure cooker a few times, all of this will come naturally. There are only three steps to follow: build the pressure, release the pressure, and clean the cooker. You may even discover, as I have, that a number of equivalent-sized pans can be retired to the basement, and the pot of your cooker can double as a soup pot or saucepan.

BUILDING THE PRESSURE

I'm always amused by the infomercials you see on television for pressure cookers. The claim is that "all of this is ready in 5 minutes!" That's technically true, but there's time on either side of that number that must be factored in.

The amount of time listed in a recipe is

how long a dish needs to cook *once the pressure level is reached*. That's when the countdown begins and you set the timer. But how long each recipe takes to reach high pressure is different. That's why cookbooks can't calculate it for you.

The amount of food in the cooker, the temperature of that food, and the power of your burner are all variables that factor into how long a cooker takes to reach pressure. For example, when making Fluffy Mashed Potatoes (page 245) there are just a few sliced potatoes in the 6-quart cooker with 1 cup of water. That will reach high pressure on my stove in about 4 minutes, whereas an 8-quart cooker with the fixings for Chicken Stock (page 15) with liquid close to the maximum line will probably take close to 30 minutes to reach high pressure.

RELEASING THE PRESSURE

Other than reading the instruction manual, the key to success in using a pressure cooker is to release the pressure using the method specified in the recipe. Keep in mind that the food is really cooking both before and after the pressure cooker reaches high pressure. In order to start forming pressure, the liquid has to have reached the temperature of boiling, and it will remain at that temperature for a variable time after the official cooking time is over.

There are only a few options, so it's not a difficult subject to master, and if you're not following a specific recipe, my advice is to consult a similar recipe or one of the many category charts contained in this book, to determine both the duration for cooking under pressure and the suggested release method.

Natural release: *This couldn't be easier. Turn off the heat source and wait until the pot's safety features unlock or give you the signal that it's safe to open the pot. For a gas stove, turning off the burner is all you need to do, and for an electric or halogen stove, you turn off the burner, slide the pot onto a cool burner, and let it sit there. If you're using an electric cooker, unplug it from the wall so that it doesn't automatically go into its "keep warm" mode.*

With natural release, the food actually continues to cook, because it takes some time for the pressure to fall. There is no hard-and-fast rule, but as a general guideline it takes about as much time for the natural release of pressure as it took to build the pressure. If it was a long time before you turned down the burner, it will be a long time before the pressure drops.

This is the release method used for most types of meat to ensure maximum tenderness. Even if the buttons have lowered, I still suggest turning the valve to its release position to make sure there's no pressure remaining in the cooker before removing the lid.

Timed natural release: *One variation on natural release is that occasionally you're instructed to use it for a finite amount of time and then quick-release any pressure that remains. The most common variable is a 10-minute natural release, so when you remove the cooker from the heat source, or unplug it, you set your timer again.*

Quick release: *This is the method to use for foods that cook relatively fast to prevent overcooking. The important thing to remember is to point the steam valve away from you, because when you open it the steam will come out very powerfully at first. During the winter it's nice to get some humidity in the house, but in warm months, I frequently place the cooker on a table in front of a window to let the steam escape outside.*

Cold water release: *This is the quick release method used for old-fashioned jiggle-top pressure cookers because they don't have a valve to open. I really do not recommend it because the trip from the stove to the sink can be a dangerous one, and it's possible to damage the pot if the metal warps from the temperature change. The only time this is an acceptable way to release the pressure is if you forgot to set a timer and fear the food will be woefully overcooked, because this is the fastest way to release pressure. Note that it's also impossible to use this method with an electric cooker.*

CLEANING THE COOKER

The pot in which the food is cooked gets scrubbed, just as you would any pot or pan, and it's safe to put it in the dishwasher, too. It's the lid that needs tender care.

Because of the equilibrium inside the cooker, as it reaches pressure, the inside of the lid is never really grubby the way a cover gets when you're braising food in the oven. But certain foods, like beans and rice, tend to foam, which is why some oil or butter is added to those recipes; it holds the foam down.

The machine is made of metal, but the gasket that turns a saucepan into a pressure cooker is rubber, which means it's delicate.

Remove the gasket each time you use the cooker, wash it with warm soapy water, and then rub it with a few drops of vegetable oil, once it has dried, to keep it pliable. If you use your pressure cooker a lot, order extra gaskets in advance and have them around. The last thing to do to the lid is to make sure the valves are not blocked, especially after cooking foods that tend to foam.

If you are using an electric cooker, use a damp soapy cloth to clean the inside of the housing, especially around the upper rim, where the lid attaches. But never fill the outer housing with water.

Electric Pressure Cooker

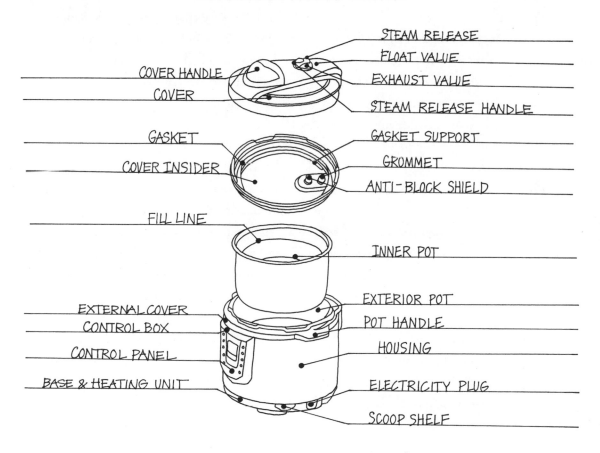

STEAM RELEASE
FLOAT VALVE
COVER HANDLE
EXHAUST VALVE
COVER
STEAM RELEASE HANDLE
GASKET
GASKET SUPPORT
COVER INSIDER
GROMMET
ANTI-BLOCK SHIELD
FILL LINE
INNER POT
EXTERNAL COVER
EXTERIOR POT
CONTROL BOX
POT HANDLE
CONTROL PANEL
HOUSING
BASE & HEATING UNIT
ELECTRICITY PLUG
SCOOP SHELF

In all candor, I tested hundreds of recipes in both electric and stovetop pressure cookers, and hands down I prefer the stovetop models.

Electric cookers have three parts rather than two. The actual cooking takes place in the inner pot, which is really just a metal cylinder. One problem is that the inner pot doesn't have a handle, so removing it to pour off liquid is quite a challenge. The inner pot merely rests inside the housing unit, so it doesn't sit firmly, either, if you're trying to brown food in it.

The lids of electric pots attach to the housing in the same way that the handle of a stovetop pot clicks onto the pot itself, and the lid contains the safety features as well as the steam release valve. An additional safety feature is that if the lid is not locked properly the machine will not turn on.

The real brains of the electric cooker are in the outer housing. That's where you'll find the heating element, the temperature sensor, and the pressure sensor, plus any programmable features that change, depending on the model.

When the heating element is turned on, the machine builds to pressure, at which time the pressure sensor will drop until the heat is needed again to rebuild the pressure level. The machine does all the monitoring, so that you really can go and read a book instead of hovering over your machine.

Once the cooking time is over, however, personal intervention is needed. The computer will automatically switch to its "keep warm" mode. While eventually the pressure will decrease naturally, there is no way for the machine to quick release itself.

Most electric cookers have a similar one-touch programming system, as do microwave ovens. But what I've found is that you're better off following the timing given in specific recipes.

You'll notice that it always takes longer to prepare food in electric cookers than it does in stovetop models. That is because the ultimate pressure in an electric cooker is 12.2 psi rather than 15 psi.

Adapting Favorite Recipes for Pressure Cooking

If you're like most people, your goal in using a pressure cooker is to redefine "fast food" and speed up the cooking time of some of your family's favorite dishes—and achieve better results, too. One of the great benefits of cooking under pressure is that flavor really penetrates food, rather than just coating the surface. It's as if you marinated it first, and then cooked it; there's flavor in every bite.

The way to start adapting recipes is to find a similar one in this book. Keep in mind that there's a minimum amount of liquid that's needed to build the pressure, and that it's not wise to use more than ½ cup of oil in a pressure cooker.

Because there's so little evaporation from a pressure cooker, cut back on the quantity of liquid by 20 percent, assuming the reduction will not put you below the minimum.

Look for recipes in which all the food is cooked at the same time, rather than adding it in stages. There are a few dishes, such as Corned Beef and Cabbage (page 134), in which pressure is reached to cook the meat and then released, so the vegetables can be cooked in the flavorful water. But those are the exceptions and not the rule.

The charts in this book give cooking times and release methods for many foods. You may have to consult a few of them to see if a recipe can be adapted. One trick I've learned when combining meats with vegetables is to cut the vegetables into larger pieces than usual. For example, sliced carrots cook in 1 to 2 minutes, while carrots cut into 1-inch chunks take 4 to 5 minutes.

Another way of adapting recipes is to cook the long-cooking steps under pressure and then add quick-cooking ingredients after the pressure has been released. The short-cooked elements are simmered conventionally on the stove. If you're using a stovetop cooker, you can leave it in the pot, but if you're using an electric cooker, I suggest transferring the contents to a saucepan.

FOODS NOT COMPATIBLE WITH PRESSURE COOKING

You'll notice that the cooking charts in the various chapters are not comprehensive and all-inclusive. That's because I've omitted certain foods that have such a short cooking time that they would be overcooked by the time pressure was reached. For example, you will not find spinach or green peas on the vegetable chart or filet mignon on the meat chart. If you don't see a food on the chart, check to see if it's included in the index. If not, save it to cook when you're using a sauté pan or conventional saucepan.

Pressure Cooking at High Altitudes

High altitudes change all the rules of cooking, including pressure cooking. At a few thousand feet above sea level there is less oxygen and atmospheric pressure, which means that water boils at a temperature lower than 212°F. When you are using traditional cooking methods it's important to increase the time a dish cooks, because water cannot be heated hotter than its boiling point.

The pressure cooker's ability to save time is even more important at high altitudes, but some minor adjustment is needed. The basic formula is to increase cooking times by 5 percent for every 1,000 feet above the first 2,000 feet above sea level; below the 2,000-foot level, the difference in cooking times is so negligible that you can ignore altitude as a factor. At a height of 5,000 feet, 12.2 psi is the maximum that can be achieved, so food will cook under pressure, but it will take it 20 percent longer to do so. If soaked beans cook for 10 minutes in Boston, they'll need 12 minutes in Denver.

Useful Equipment

You probably have all the utensils and gadgets you need already, but here's a list of the ones I use most often:

Immersion blender: *These are fabulous for pureeing soups and sauces right in the pot, but I suggest removing the insert from an electric cooker before using it, to make sure the food being pureed doesn't splash into the housing.*

Wire mesh spoons: *These large spoons are intended to be used to swirl food around in a wok. I like their shape and size more than traditional slotted spoons.*

Colanders and wire mesh strainers: *You'll use these frequently, especially for draining vegetables and beans.*

Straining lid: *This looks like a half-moon made of perforated metal. For draining small quantities of food, like potato slices that are going to be mashed right in the cooker, you can hold the straining lid against the edge of the cooker and keep the food from falling into the sink when you drain it.*

Steamers: *While most cookers come with a steamer basket, I've frequently used a smaller steamer set on top of the steamer basket to contain smaller quantities of food.*

Silicone pinch grips: *These are essential to use with an electric pressure cooker. They are thin but sturdy sheets of heavy silicone that protect your thumb and forefinger so that you can lift out the insert without burning yourself. I also use them for lifting hot lids from conventional pots.*

ACCESSORIES

Most pressure cookers today come with some sort of steamer insert and a triangular trivet that goes under the basket to keep it above the level of the water for steaming food. If your cooker does not include these items, go on the manufacturer's website and purchase them.

MAKING AN ALUMINUM FOIL SLING

If you need to lift a pan out of a pressure cooker, it can be cumbersome. However, some old-fashioned ingenuity using aluminum foil—a product that most everyone always has on hand—can help. When I bake bar cookies, I also use this system to remove them from the pan.

To create a "sling" for your cooker insert, cut two pieces of heavy-duty aluminum foil 18 inches long and fold each into thirds lengthwise. Lay them perpendicular to each other on a counter, crossing them at their centers, and then place the insert on the center. Pull the foil up along the outsides of the insert, and fold over the excess to create handles. Place the sling and insert into the pressure cooker. After the food has cooked, use hot mitts to gather two foil handles in each hand to help lift the insert out of the cooker.

Provençal Vegetable Soup with *Pistou*, page 22

CHAPTER 2

Stocks and Soups

In this chapter you'll find some wonderful soups that range from light broths to serve as a first course, to hearty and filling options that need just a loaf of crusty bread to make a great dinner. But the chapter begins with recipes for the essential building blocks of all great cooking—stocks.

Perhaps you never equated buying commercial stocks—many of which are loaded with sodium—as a "convenience food," but that's what they are. Starting dishes with homemade stocks, on the other hand, immediately elevates them. The depth of flavor and body achieved in stocks made with a pressure cooker is what made me into an aficionado. What made me a convert wasn't getting the same results in 1 hour that would normally take 5 hours with the conventional method of simmering stock. The results were simply better when the stocks were pressure-cooked.

The intense heat in pressure cooking promotes the extraction of flavor from both meats and vegetables. Also the conversion of collagen to gelatin, a process that creates the body in meat stocks, is achieved in record time in the pressure cooker. At first I was concerned that this method of cooking stocks would make them cloudy because they can't be skimmed, but the pressure cooker prevents the liquid from boiling, so stocks are perfectly clear.

Stocks are also a great way to make use of food destined for the compost bin. Reserve onion and carrot peels, the bottom of celery ribs, and the stems from which you've stripped the leaves of fresh parsley. Keep them in a bag in the freezer and use them for making stock.

If you take the time to bone your own chicken breasts or cut up your own beef stew meat from a roast, you have everything you need to make stock. I make stock on a weekly basis and usually buy the necessary ingredients for the recipe, as well as use any scraps I may have reserved in the freezer.

I do not add salt to stocks—an omission that makes them versatile, for example, when you want to drastically reduce a stock to form a sauce. When you reduce a salted stock, the salinity rises as the water evaporates, making the liquid impossibly salty for use in whatever sauce you planned to make.

But there is one negative aspect to making stocks in the pressure cooker. I really miss the aroma that fills the house when a stockpot simmers all day on the stove.

Chicken Stock

This is the most important stock, because it's used for pork and vegetable soups (assuming you're not a strict vegetarian), as well as with poultry.

MAKES **3 quarts**

SIZE **6-quart or larger pressure cooker**

TIME **80 to 90 minutes at high pressure; then allow the pressure to release naturally**

3 pounds chicken pieces (backs, giblets, leg quarters, wings)

2 tablespoons vegetable oil

3 celery ribs, cut into thick slices

2 onions, quartered

2 carrots, cut into thick slices

2 tablespoons whole black peppercorns

6 garlic cloves, peeled

4 sprigs fresh parsley

3 sprigs fresh thyme

2 bay leaves

Hack the chicken into 2-inch pieces with a sharp knife or cleaver.

Heat the oil in the cooker over medium-high heat or use the browning function of an electric cooker. Add some of the chicken parts, skin side down, and brown it well. Add 3 quarts of water to the cooker along with the celery, onions, carrots, peppercorns, garlic, parsley, thyme, and bay leaves. Close and lock the lid of the cooker.

STOVETOP: Place the cooker over high heat, and bring it to high pressure. Once high pressure is reached, reduce the heat as much as possible while retaining the high-pressure level. Cook for 80 minutes. Then take the pot off the heat and allow it to return to normal pressure naturally. Remove the lid, tilting it away from you, to allow the steam to escape.

OR

ELECTRIC: Set the machine to cook at high pressure for 90 minutes. After 90 minutes, unplug the pot so that it does not go into warming mode. Allow the pressure to return to normal naturally. Remove the lid, tilting it away from you, to allow the steam to escape.

Strain the stock through a fine-meshed sieve, pushing with the back of a spoon to extract as much liquid as possible. Discard the solids, spoon the stock into smaller containers, and refrigerate when the stock reaches room temperature. Remove and discard the fat layer from the surface of the stock once chilled.

The stock can be refrigerated and used within 3 days, or frozen for up to 6 months.

NOTE The giblets—the neck, heart, liver, and gizzard—are in that little bag inside a whole chicken. Save all these pieces, minus the bag, for making the stock. Separate out the chicken liver, and freeze it separately.

VARIATIONS

⋆ **Turkey Stock:** Substitute 3 pounds of turkey giblets for the chicken pieces and add 2 sprigs of fresh sage to the cooker.

⋆ **Chinese Chicken Stock:** Substitute 2 bunches of scallions for the onions and cilantro for the parsley and thyme, omit the carrots and bay leaves, and add ½ cup thickly sliced fresh ginger to the cooker.

⋆ **Ham Stock:** Substitute 3 pounds of smoked ham hocks for the chicken parts (there is no need to brown them).

Beef Stock

Although beef stock is not specified as often as chicken stock in recipes, it is nevertheless the backbone of certain dishes. Beef shank is probably the least expensive cut of beef that makes good stock, but I urge you to get a chuck roast and cut the meat off it to make beef stew and then use the bones to make stock.

MAKES **3 quarts**

SIZE **6-quart or larger pressure cooker**

TIME **80 to 90 minutes at high pressure; then allow the pressure to release naturally**

2 **pounds beef trimmings (bones, fat) or inexpensive beef shank**
1 **celery rib, sliced**
1 **medium onion, sliced**
1 **carrot, trimmed, scrubbed, and cut into thick slices**
1 **tablespoon whole black peppercorns**
3 **sprigs fresh parsley**
2 **sprigs fresh thyme**
4 **garlic cloves, peeled**
2 **bay leaves**

Preheat the oven broiler and line a broiler pan with heavy-duty aluminum foil. Broil the beef bones for 3 minutes on each side, or until browned. Transfer the beef to the pressure cooker and add 3 quarts of water, the celery, onion, carrot, peppercorns, parsley, thyme, garlic, and bay leaves.

Close and lock the lid of the cooker.

STOVETOP: Place the cooker over high heat, and bring it to high pressure. Once high pressure is reached, reduce the heat as much as possible while retaining the high-pressure level. Cook for 80 minutes. Then take the pot off the heat and allow it to return to normal pressure naturally. Remove the lid, tilting it away from you, to allow the steam to escape.

OR

ELECTRIC: Set the machine to cook at high pressure for 90 minutes. After 90 minutes, unplug the pot so that it does not go into warming mode. Allow the pressure to return to normal naturally. Remove the lid, tilting it away from you, to allow the steam to escape.

Strain the stock through a fine-meshed sieve, pushing with the back of a spoon to extract as much liquid as possible. Discard the solids and spoon the stock into smaller containers. Refrigerate once the stock reaches room temperature; then remove and discard the layer of fat from the surface of the stock.

The stock can be refrigerated and used within 3 days, or it can be frozen for up to 6 months.

NOTE Most really good restaurants make veal stock instead of beef stock, but they have access to veal bones, which would cost a fortune for most of us. The least expensive cut of veal is the shank, used in cooking osso buco. Another option is breast of veal, but it is difficult to find in most supermarkets.

VARIATION

★ **Veal Stock:** Substitute pounds of veal shank or veal breast for the beef parts.

Vegetable Stock

You may think it not necessary to use vegetable stock if making a vegetarian dish that includes the same vegetables as in the stock, but that's not the case. Using stock creates a much more richly flavored soup that can't be replicated by increasing the quantity of vegetables cooked in it.

MAKES **3 quarts**

SIZE **6-quart or larger pressure cooker**

TIME **60 to 70 minutes at high pressure; then allow the pressure to release naturally**

2 carrots, scrubbed, trimmed, and thinly sliced
2 celery ribs, sliced
2 leeks, white part and pale green parts only, thinly sliced and rinsed well
1 small onion, peeled and thinly sliced

1 tablespoon whole black peppercorns
4 sprigs fresh parsley
3 sprigs fresh thyme
2 sprigs fresh rosemary
2 garlic cloves, peeled
1 bay leaf

The stock can be refrigerated and used within 3 days, or it can be frozen for up to 6 months.

NOTE While it's fine to save carrot peelings or parsley stems to use in stocks, always discard the dark green tops of leeks, because they make stock taste bitter and somewhat grassy. They're good for composting, however.

Pour 3 quarts of water into the cooker, and add the carrots, celery, leeks, onion, peppercorns, parsley, thyme, rosemary, garlic, and bay leaf.

Close and lock the lid of the cooker.

STOVETOP: Place the cooker over high heat, and bring it to high pressure. Once high pressure is reached, reduce the heat as much as possible while retaining the high-pressure level. Cook for 60 minutes. Then take the pot off the heat and allow it to return to normal pressure naturally. Remove the lid, tilting it away from you, to allow the steam to escape.

OR

ELECTRIC: Set the machine to cook at high pressure for 70 minutes. After 70 minutes, unplug the pot so that it does not go into warming mode. Allow the pressure to return to normal naturally. Remove the lid, tilting it away from you, to allow the steam to escape.

Strain the stock through a fine-meshed sieve, pushing with the back of a spoon to extract as much liquid as possible. Discard the solids and spoon the stock into smaller containers. Refrigerate once the stock reaches room temperature.

Corn Stock

This stock is a relatively new addition to my repertoire, but all it took to convince me that it was worth the trouble was a side-by-side comparison of two corn soups, one made with chicken stock and the other made with corn stock. There's lots of sweet corn flavor in the cobs we toss out, and they really add to corn soups.

MAKES **3 quarts**

SIZE **6-quart or larger pressure cooker**

TIME **60 to 70 minutes at high pressure; then allow the pressure to release naturally**

10 **fresh corncobs (kernels removed and reserved for other use)**

3 **quarts Vegetable Stock (page 17) or Chicken Stock (page 15), or purchased stock**

First use a knife and scrape as much of the milky liquid as possible from the corncobs right into the cooker. Then cut the cobs into 2-inch pieces with a sharp serrated knife. Add the stock.

Close and lock the lid of the cooker.

STOVETOP: Place the cooker over high heat, and bring it to high pressure. Once high pressure is reached, reduce the heat as much as possible while retaining the high-pressure level. Cook for 60 minutes. Then take the pot off the heat and allow it to return to normal pressure naturally. Remove the lid, tilting it away from you, to allow the steam to escape.

OR

ELECTRIC: Set the machine to cook at high pressure for 70 minutes. After 70 minutes, unplug the pot so that it does not go into warming mode. Allow the pressure to return to normal naturally. Remove the lid, tilting it away from you, to allow the steam to escape.

Strain the stock through a fine-meshed sieve, pushing with the back of a spoon to extract as much liquid as possible. Discard the solids and spoon the stock into smaller containers. Refrigerate the stock once it reaches room temperature.

The stock can be refrigerated and used within 3 days, or it can be frozen for up to 6 months.

NOTE If you don't have time to make the stock the same day you buy the corn, it's better to freeze the cobs rather than refrigerate them. The sugars in corncobs start to convert to starch as soon as the ears are picked (the same is true of the kernels). But freezing the cobs, and making the stock later, produces a better product than using them after they've been refrigerated a few days.

Seafood Stock

Be it for a sublime and silky sauce or a hearty chowder, the key to the depth of flavor of all fish and seafood dishes is a reduced stock. Seafood is more delicate than other forms of protein, so a stock really enhances the flavor of dishes.

MAKES **3 quarts**

SIZE **6-quart or larger pressure cooker**

TIME **60 to 70 minutes at high pressure; then allow the pressure to release naturally**

2 pounds bones and skin from firm-fleshed white fish, such as halibut, cod, or sole
Shells from 3 pounds raw shrimp (optional)
1 cup dry white wine
2 (3-inch) pieces lemon zest
1 carrot, trimmed, and cut into 1-inch chunks
1 medium onion, peeled and sliced
1 celery rib, sliced
1 tablespoon whole black peppercorns
3 sprigs fresh parsley
2 sprigs fresh thyme
2 sprigs fresh tarragon
2 garlic cloves, peeled
1 bay leaf

Place the fish trimmings in the cooker and add the shrimp shells, if using. Add 3 quarts of water, along with the wine, lemon zest, carrot, onion, celery, peppercorns, parsley, thyme, tarragon, garlic, and bay leaf.

Close and lock the lid of the cooker.

STOVETOP: Place the cooker over high heat, and bring it to high pressure. Once high pressure is reached, reduce the heat as much as possible while retaining the high-pressure level. Cook for 60 minutes. Then take the pot off the heat and allow it to return to normal pressure naturally. Remove the lid, tilting it away from you, to allow the steam to escape.

OR

ELECTRIC: Set the machine to cook at high pressure for 70 minutes. After 70 minutes, unplug the pot so that it does not go into warming mode. Allow the pressure to return to normal naturally. Remove the lid, tilting it away from you, to allow the steam to escape.

The stock can be refrigerated and used within 3 days, or it can be frozen for up to 6 months.

NOTE It can be tricky to make seafood stock if you don't live near the coast or have access to a supermarket that has a good seafood department. Fortunately, seafood stock is now available in more stores, but if you can't find it, bottled clam juice is a good substitute. Use it in place of the water, and simmer it with vegetables and wine to intensify and round out its flavor.

Strain the stock through a fine-meshed sieve, pushing with the back of a spoon to extract as much liquid as possible. Discard the solids and spoon the stock into smaller containers. Refrigerate the stock once it reaches room temperature.

Garbure
(Basque Bean and Cabbage Soup)

The clear broth of this soup, which hails from the Pyrenees Mountains, gets its rich flavors from hearty vegetables and aromatic smoked paprika. For a light supper, enjoy this soup with a platter of Spanish meats and cheeses or as an appetizer before serving Braised Lamb Shanks (page 152).

SERVES **6 to 8**

SIZE **6-quart or larger pressure cooker**

TIME **6 to 8 minutes at high pressure; then allow the pressure to release naturally**

The soup can be prepared up to 2 days in advance and refrigerated, tightly covered. Reheat it over low heat, covered, until hot, stirring occasionally.

1½ cups dried white navy beans
2 tablespoons olive oil
1 medium onion, diced
3 garlic cloves, minced
1 carrot, diced
1 celery rib, diced
2 tablespoons sweet smoked Spanish paprika (*pimentón de la vera dulce*)
6 cups Vegetable Stock (page 17), Chicken Stock (page 15), or purchased stock

¾ pound redskin potatoes, scrubbed and cut into 1-inch cubes
6 cups firmly packed thickly sliced green cabbage
¼ cup chopped fresh parsley
2 teaspoons fresh thyme leaves
1 bay leaf
Salt and freshly ground black pepper to taste

Rinse the beans in a colander and place them in a mixing bowl covered with cold salted water. Allow the beans to soak for a minimum of 6 hours, or overnight. Or place the beans into a saucepan of salted water and bring to a boil over high heat. Boil 1 minute. Turn off the heat, cover the pan, and soak the beans for 1 hour. After using either of these soaking methods, drain the beans, discard the soaking water, and cook or refrigerate the beans as soon as possible.

Heat the oil in the cooker over medium-high heat or use the browning function of an electric cooker. Add the onion, garlic, carrot, and celery. Cook, stirring frequently, for 3 minutes, or until the onion is translucent. Add the paprika and cook for 1 minute, stirring constantly. Add the beans, stock, potatoes, cabbage, parsley, thyme, and bay leaf.

Close and lock the lid of the cooker.

STOVETOP: Place the cooker over high heat, and bring it to high pressure. Once high pressure is reached, reduce the heat as much as possible while retaining the high-pressure level. Cook for 6 minutes. Then take the pot off the heat and allow it to return to normal pressure naturally. Remove the lid, tilting it away from you, to allow the steam to escape.

OR

ELECTRIC: Set the machine to cook at high pressure for 8 minutes. After 8 minutes, unplug the pot so that it does not go into warming mode. Allow the pressure to return to normal naturally. Remove the lid, tilting it away from you, to allow the steam to escape.

Remove and discard the bay leaf, season to taste with salt and pepper, and serve immediately.

NOTE It's only in the past decade that I've discovered the wonders of smoked, sweet Spanish paprika, *pimentón de la vera dulce*. The peppers are smoked over oak fires that really permeate them before they are ground. Using this spice adds an instant grilled flavor and aroma to foods.

Provençal Vegetable Soup with Pistou

This soup is the Provençal version of Italian minestrone. It's enriched at the end with a dollop of garlicky basil pistou, a sauce that is similar to Italian pesto, but made without pine nuts. This soup is a great winter dish because it's made with dried herbes de Provence rather than a panoply of fresh herbs, and like minestrone, it's filling.

SERVES **4 to 6**

SIZE **6-quart or larger pressure cooker**

TIME **5 to 6 minutes at high pressure; then allow the pressure to release naturally**

The soup can be prepared up to 2 days in advance and refrigerated, tightly covered, but it is better not to stir in the cooked pasta until just before serving. Reheat the soup over low heat, stirring it occasionally, and add the cooked pasta. The *pistou* can be prepared up to 1 day in advance and refrigerated. Press a sheet of plastic wrap directly onto the surface of the *pistou* to prevent discoloration.

SOUP

- 1 cup dried cannellini or navy beans
- 2 tablespoons kosher salt
- 1 small zucchini, diced
- 1 small yellow squash, diced
- 3 tablespoons olive oil
- 1 large onion, diced
- 2 leeks, white parts only, thinly sliced and rinsed well
- 6 garlic cloves, minced
- 6 cups Vegetable Stock (page 17), Chicken Stock (page 15), or purchased stock
- 1 large carrot, diced
- ½ fresh fennel bulb, trimmed and diced
- 1 celery rib, diced
- 1 (14.5-ounce) can petite diced tomatoes, undrained
- 3 tablespoons chopped fresh parsley
- 1 tablespoon herbes de Provence
- 1 bay leaf
- 1 cup ditalini or other small pasta shape such as orzo
- ¼ pound green beans, trimmed, cut into ¾-inch pieces
- Salt and freshly ground black pepper to taste

PISTOU

- 3 garlic cloves, peeled
- 3 cups firmly packed fresh basil leaves
- ⅓ cup olive oil
- ¾ cup freshly grated Parmesan cheese
- Salt and freshly ground black pepper to taste

Rinse the beans in a colander and place them in a mixing bowl covered with cold salted water. Allow the beans to soak for a minimum of 6 hours, or overnight. Or place the beans into a saucepan of salted water and bring to a boil over high heat. Boil 1 minute. Turn off the heat, cover the pan, and soak the beans for 1 hour. After using either of these soaking methods, drain the beans, discard the soaking water, and cook or refrigerate the beans as soon as possible.

Place 4 cups of cold water in a mixing bowl and stir in the kosher salt. Add the diced zucchini and yellow squash, and soak them for 15 minutes. Drain, and rinse well.

Heat the oil in the cooker over medium-high heat or use the browning function of an electric cooker. Add the onion, leeks, and garlic. Cook, stirring frequently, for 3 minutes, or until the onion is translucent. Add the beans, stock, carrot, fennel, celery, tomatoes, parsley, herbes de Provence, and bay leaf.

Close and lock the lid of the cooker.

STOVETOP: Place the cooker over high heat, and bring it to high pressure. Once high pressure is reached, reduce the heat as much as possible while retaining the high-pressure level. Cook for 5 minutes. Then take the pot off the heat, and allow it to return to normal pressure naturally. Remove the lid, tilting it away from you, to allow the steam to escape.

OR

ELECTRIC: Set the machine to cook at high pressure for 6 minutes. After 6 minutes, unplug the pot so that it does not go into warming mode. Allow the pressure to return to normal naturally. Remove the lid, tilting it away from you, to allow the steam to escape.

NOTE Herbes de Provence, found in the spice section of many supermarkets and gourmet stores, is a dried blend of many herbs associated with the sunny cuisine of Provence, including basil, thyme, fennel, lavender, rosemary, sage, and marjoram.

While the soup cooks, bring a small pan of salted water to a boil over high heat. Cook the ditalini according to package directions until al dente. Drain, and set aside.

Add the green beans, zucchini, and yellow squash to the soup, and cook over medium-high heat or use the browning function of an electric cooker, for 3 to 4 minutes, or until the vegetables are tender. Remove and discard the bay leaf, stir in the cooked pasta, and season to taste with salt and pepper.

While the soup cooks, make the *pistou*. Combine the garlic and basil in a food processor fitted with a steel blade, and chop it finely, using on-and-off pulsing. Slowly add the olive oil, and puree until smooth. Add the cheese, and blend well. Season to taste with salt and pepper.

To serve, ladle the soup into low bowls and place 1 tablespoon of *pistou* in the center. Pass around the remaining *pistou* separately.

Potage Saint-Germain
(French Split Pea Soup)

While I think of thick and filling split pea soup as a hearty winter dish, this version is light enough to serve in the spring and summer, too. The combination of split peas with cream, fresh peas, and other vegetables truly lightens both the color and flavor.

SERVES **6 to 8**

SIZE **6-quart or larger pressure cooker**

TIME **5 to 6 minutes at high pressure; then allow the pressure to release naturally**

The soup can be prepared up to 2 days in advance and refrigerated, tightly covered. Reheat it over low heat, covered, until hot, stirring occasionally.

3 tablespoons unsalted butter
2 medium onions, chopped
1 carrot, chopped
2 celery ribs, chopped
1 cup firmly packed shredded romaine lettuce
1 cup green peas (fresh or frozen)
2 cups dried split peas, rinsed
6 cups Vegetable Stock (page 17), Chicken Stock (page 15), or purchased stock

2 tablespoons chopped fresh parsley
1 teaspoon fresh thyme leaves
1 bay leaf
¾ cup heavy cream
Salt and freshly ground black pepper to taste

GARNISH

4 to 6 tablespoons crème fraîche
¼ cup chopped fresh watercress leaves

Heat the butter in the cooker over medium heat or use the browning function of an electric cooker. Add the onions, carrot, and celery, and cook, stirring frequently, for 3 minutes, or until the onions are translucent. Add the lettuce, peas, split peas, stock, parsley, thyme, and bay leaf.

Close and lock the lid of the cooker.

STOVETOP: Place the cooker over high heat, and bring it to high pressure. Once high pressure is reached, reduce the heat as much as possible while retaining the high-pressure level. Cook for 5 minutes. Then take the pot off the heat and allow it to return to normal pressure naturally. Remove the lid, tilting it away from you, to allow the steam to escape.

OR

ELECTRIC: Set the machine to cook at high pressure for 6 minutes. After 6 minutes, unplug the pot so that it does not go into warming mode. Allow the pressure to return to normal naturally. Remove the lid, tilting it away from you, to allow the steam to escape.

NOTE Lentils and split peas are legumes that do not benefit from any presoaking. They cook very quickly, but you make sure the heat is as low as possible, while the pot retains high pressure, because they have a tendency to scorch.

Remove and discard the bay leaf. Stir in the cream and allow the soup to cool for 5 minutes. Puree the soup with an immersion blender, or if you are using a food processor fitted with a steel blade, puree the soup in batches. Season the soup to taste with salt and pepper and serve immediately, garnishing each serving with 1 tablespoon of crème fraîche and a sprinkling of watercress.

Coconut Carrot Soup

Carrots have a place in almost all of the world's cuisines, although the ones I've seen on trips to Asia have a far more vivid hue than the typical orange ones in the United States. The innate sweetness of carrots takes to myriad seasonings— in this case the creaminess of coconut, plus a slight kick from crystallized ginger. This soup is an elegant way to begin any dinner and is inspired by one that I enjoyed a few years ago at Kevin Binkley's restaurant, Binkley's, in Arizona. Serve it before Pork in Black Bean Sauce with Bok Choy (page 170).

SERVES **6 to 8**

SIZE **6-quart or larger pressure cooker**

TIME **7 to 8 minutes at high pressure; then allow the pressure to release naturally**

The soup can be prepared up to 2 days in advance and refrigerated, tightly covered. Reheat it over low heat, stirring occasionally.

4 tablespoons (½ stick) unsalted butter
1½ pounds carrots, sliced
2 celery ribs, sliced
1 small onion, diced
¼ cup cream sherry
3 cups Vegetable Stock (page 17) or purchased stock
1 (14-ounce) can light coconut milk
½ cup grated unsweetened coconut

3 tablespoons chopped crystallized ginger
2 tablespoons firmly packed light brown sugar
1 cup heavy cream
Salt and freshly ground black pepper to taste

GARNISH
¼ cup toasted unsweetened coconut

Heat the butter in the cooker over medium heat or use the browning function of an electric cooker. Add the carrots, celery, and onion. Cook, stirring frequently, for 3 minutes, or until the onion is translucent. Add the sherry and cook for 2 minutes. Add the stock, coconut milk, coconut, ginger, and brown sugar to the cooker.

Close and lock the lid of the cooker.

STOVETOP: Place the cooker over high heat, and bring it to high pressure. Once high pressure is reached, reduce the heat as much as possible while retaining the high-pressure level. Cook for 7 minutes. Then take the pot off the heat and allow it to return to normal pressure naturally. Remove the lid, tilting it away from you, to allow the steam to escape.

—OR—

ELECTRIC: Set the machine to cook at high pressure for 8 minutes. After 8 minutes, unplug the pot so that it does not go into warming mode. Allow the pressure to return to normal naturally. Remove the lid, tilting it away from you, to allow the steam to escape.

Allow the soup to cool for 5 minutes. Puree the soup with an immersion blender, or if you're using a blender or a food processor fitted with a steel blade, puree the soup in batches.

Stir in the cream. Bring the soup back to a simmer over medium heat or use the browning function of an electric cooker. Season to taste with salt and pepper, and serve immediately. Garnish each serving with a sprinkle of toasted coconut.

NOTE There's some confusion about coconut products today. Low-calorie coconut water has never been so popular, and many people confuse it with coconut milk. Coconut milk is the result of pureeing high-fat coconut meat with water and gives dishes an incredibly creamy and rich texture without adding a dairy product. Light coconut milk does the same, but with a fraction of the calories.

Cream of Winter Vegetable Soup

This soup, which is a blushing orange color, combines root vegetables and winter squash. It's filling without being very rich and is a wonderful prelude to Coq au Vin (page 94).

SERVES **4 to 6**

SIZE **6-quart or larger pressure cooker**

TIME **8 to 9 minutes at high pressure; then allow the pressure to release naturally**

The soup can be prepared up to 2 days in advance and refrigerated, tightly covered. Reheat it over low heat, stirring occasionally. Add milk or cream if the soup needs thinning after reheating.

3 tablespoons unsalted butter
2 large leeks, white and light green parts
2 garlic cloves, minced
1 large carrot, sliced
1 large parsnip, sliced
1 large sweet potato, peeled and diced
½ butternut or acorn squash, peeled and diced
6 cups Vegetable Stock (page 17), Chicken Stock (page 15), or purchased stock

1 tablespoon fresh thyme leaves
1 bay leaf
2 tablespoons freshly squeezed lemon juice
¾ cup heavy cream
Salt and freshly ground black pepper to taste

GARNISH
1 cup croutons
2 tablespoons toasted pumpkin seeds

Heat the butter in the cooker over medium heat or use the browning function of an electric cooker. Add the leeks and garlic, and cook, stirring frequently, for 3 minutes, or until the leeks are translucent. Add the carrot, parsnip, sweet potato, squash, stock, thyme, bay leaf, and lemon juice.

Close and lock the lid of the cooker.

STOVETOP: Place the cooker over high heat, and bring it to high pressure. Once high pressure is reached, reduce the heat as much as possible while retaining the high-pressure level. Cook for 8 minutes. Then take the pot off the heat and allow it to return to normal pressure naturally. Remove the lid, tilting it away from you, to allow the steam to escape.

OR

ELECTRIC: Set the machine to cook at high pressure for 9 minutes. After 9 minutes, unplug the pot so that it does not go into warming mode. Allow the pressure to return to normal naturally. Remove the lid, tilting it away from you, to allow the steam to escape.

Remove and discard the bay leaf. Allow the soup to cool for 5 minutes. Puree the soup with an immersion blender; or if you are using a food processor fitted with a steel blade, puree the soup in batches. Stir the cream into the soup, and season it to taste with salt and pepper. Bring it back to a simmer over medium heat or use the browning function of an electric cooker. Serve hot, garnishing each serving with croutons and pumpkin seeds.

NOTE Leeks are the like the character named Pigpen in "Peanuts." They leave a trail of grime and dirt wherever they go. Leeks are very labor intensive to grow because the soil must constantly be piled up at the base of the leek to encourage the growth of a long white stalk. I've decided that the best way to get rid of all the grit and sand is to rinse leeks well. I then slice the leeks and place them in a large bowl of cold water and swish them around. Be sure to remove the sliced leeks from the water with a slotted spoon, because if you drain them in a colander, all the grit goes right back onto them.

Cuban Black Bean Soup

This is by far one of my favorite soups for cold weather because it's so thick and earthy, and yet it's vibrantly spiced. Serve it for supper with some crusty bread and a plate of sliced jicama drizzled with lime juice, or serve a small bowl of it before enjoying Picadillo (page 138).

SERVES 6 to 8

SIZE 6-quart or larger pressure cooker

TIME 7 to 8 minutes at high pressure; then allow the pressure to release naturally

The soup can be prepared up to 2 days in advance and refrigerated, tightly covered. Reheat it over low heat, stirring occasionally. Add stock or water if the soup needs thinning after reheating.

1 pound dried black beans
¼ cup olive oil
1 large onion, diced
1 red bell pepper, seeds and ribs removed, and finely chopped
6 garlic cloves, minced
1 or 2 jalapeño or serrano chiles, seeds and ribs removed, and finely chopped

2 tablespoons ground cumin
1 tablespoon ground coriander
5 cups Vegetable Stock (page 17) or purchased stock
Salt and freshly ground black pepper to taste
¼ cup chopped fresh cilantro
Sour cream for serving (optional)
Lime wedges for serving (optional)

Rinse the beans in a colander and place them in a mixing bowl covered with cold salted water. Allow the beans to soak for a minimum of 6 hours, or overnight. Or place the beans into a saucepan of salted water and bring to a boil over high heat. Boil 1 minute. Turn off the heat, cover the pan, and soak the beans for 1 hour. After using either of these soaking methods, drain the beans, discard the soaking water, and cook or refrigerate the beans as soon as possible.

Heat the oil in the cooker over medium-high heat or use the browning function of an electric cooker. Add the onion, red bell pepper, garlic, and chiles. Cook, stirring frequently, for 3 minutes, or until the onion is translucent. Reduce the heat to low, and stir in the cumin and coriander. Cook for 1 minute, stirring constantly. Stir in the beans and stock.

Close and lock the lid of the cooker.

STOVETOP: Place the cooker over high heat, and bring it to high pressure. Once high pressure is reached, reduce the heat as much as possible while retaining the high-pressure level. Cook for 7 minutes. Then take the pot off the heat and allow it to return to normal pressure naturally. Remove the lid, tilting it away from you, to allow the steam to escape.

OR

ELECTRIC: Set the machine to cook at high pressure for 8 minutes. After 8 minutes, unplug the pot so that it does not go into warming mode. Allow the pressure to return to normal naturally. Remove the lid, tilting it away from you, to allow the steam to escape.

Remove 2 cups of the beans with a slotted spoon, and puree them in a food processor fitted with a steel blade or in a blender. Be careful not to fill the container too full when blending hot ingredients. Return the beans to the soup, stir in the cilantro, season to taste with salt and pepper, and ladle the soup into bowls. Top each serving with a dollop of sour cream and serve with lime wedges, if desired.

NOTE There's no question that chiles contain potent oils; however there's no need to wear rubber gloves when handling them. I cut the chiles on a glass plate rather than on my cutting board, so the volatile oils do not penetrate the cutting surface. What's most important is that you wash your hands thoroughly after handling chiles.

Curried Red Lentil Soup

Hearty lentils come in a variety of colors and are part of many of the world's cuisines, including India's, where they are called dal. *This vividly colored and aromatic soup was developed by my friend, Bruce Tillinghast, who was formerly the chef and owner at New Rivers restaurant in Providence. It is thickened with a number of fresh vegetables in addition to the lentils.*

SERVES **6 to 8**

SIZE **6-quart or larger pressure cooker**

TIME **6 to 7 minutes at high pressure with quick pressure release**

The soup can be prepared up to 2 days in advance and refrigerated, tightly covered. Reheat it over low heat, stirring occasionally. Add stock or water if the soup needs thinning after reheating.

3 tablespoons olive oil
1 large red bell pepper, seeds and ribs removed, and chopped
1 medium onion, chopped
3 garlic cloves, minced
1 large carrot, chopped
1 celery rib, chopped
1 parsnip, chopped
2 tablespoons garam masala
2 tablespoons sweet paprika
1 tablespoon ground cumin
1 teaspoon crushed fenugreek seeds
1 teaspoon ground turmeric

½ teaspoon cayenne
10 cups Vegetable Stock (page 17) or purchased stock
3 tablespoons tomato paste
1 bay leaf
3 tablespoons chopped fresh cilantro or parsley
3 cups red lentils, rinsed well
Salt and freshly ground black pepper to taste

GARNISH
¾ cup plain Greek yogurt

Heat the oil in a cooker over medium-high heat or use the browning function of an electric cooker. Add the red bell pepper, onion, garlic, carrot, celery, and parsnip. Cook, stirring frequently, for 3 minutes, or until the onion is translucent. Stir in the garam masala, paprika, cumin, fenugreek, turmeric, and cayenne. Cook for 1 minute, stirring constantly. Add the stock, tomato paste, bay leaf, cilantro, and lentils. Stir well to dissolve the tomato paste. Bring to a boil, stirring occasionally.

Close and lock the lid of the cooker.

STOVETOP: Place the cooker over high heat, and bring it to high pressure. Once high pressure is reached, reduce the heat as much as possible while retaining the high-pressure level. Cook for 6 minutes. Then take the pot off the heat and quick release the pressure according to the instructions provided by the manufacturer. Remove the lid, tilting it away from you, to allow the steam to escape.

OR

ELECTRIC: Set the machine to cook at high pressure for 7 minutes. After 7 minutes, unplug the pot so that it does not go into warming mode. Quick release the pressure according to the instructions provided by the manufacturer. Remove the lid, tilting it away from you, to allow the steam to escape.

NOTE Aromatic fenugreek seeds, grown on the Indian subcontinent, are an integral part of most curry powder formulations and can usually be found in Indian and Middle Eastern markets, and increasingly in general supermarkets. If you can't find them, substitute yellow mustard seeds.

Allow the soup to cool for 5 minutes. Puree half of the soup with an immersion blender, or if you're using a food processor fitted with a steel blade, puree half the soup in batches.

Season the soup to taste with salt and pepper, and serve immediately, garnishing each serving with a dollop of the yogurt.

Roasted Garlic Vichyssoise

Vichyssoise is actually an American invention, despite the French name. This chilled leek and potato soup was created in the early 1900s by Chef Louis Diat, during his tenure at The Ritz-Carlton Hotel in New York City. Diat named the soup after Vichy, the resort town near his boyhood home in France. The combination of delicate leeks with creamy potatoes can't be beaten, except by adding the nutty sweetness of roasted garlic.

SERVES **6 to 8**

SIZE **6-quart or larger pressure cooker**

TIME **5 to 6 minutes at high pressure with quick pressure release**

The soup can be prepared up to 2 days in advance and refrigerated, tightly covered. Stir well before serving.

2 heads fresh garlic
1 tablespoon olive oil
3 tablespoons unsalted butter
6 leeks, white parts only, chopped, and rinsed well
2 pounds russet potatoes, peeled and diced

7 cups Chicken Stock (page 15) or purchased stock
1 cup heavy cream
Salt and freshly ground white pepper to taste

GARNISH
¼ cup snipped fresh chives

Preheat the oven to 350°F. Cut 1 inch off the top of each garlic head, and rub the heads with the olive oil. Wrap the heads tightly in foil, and place them on a baking sheet. Roast the garlic for 45 minutes, or until tender. When cool enough to handle, break the heads apart into cloves and squeeze the roasted garlic cloves out their skins. Set them aside.

Melt the butter in the cooker over medium heat or use the browning function of an electric cooker. Add the leeks and cook, stirring frequently, for 3 minutes, or until the leeks are translucent. Add the potatoes, stock, and roasted garlic.

Close and lock the lid of the cooker.

STOVETOP: Place the cooker over high heat, and bring it to high pressure. Once high pressure is reached, reduce the heat as much as possible while retaining the high-pressure level. Cook for 5 minutes. Then take the pot off the heat and quick release the pressure according to the instructions provided by the manufacturer. Remove the lid, tilting it away from you, to allow the steam to escape.

OR

ELECTRIC: Set the machine to cook at high pressure for 6 minutes. After 6 minutes, unplug the pot so that it does not go into warming mode. Quick release the pressure according to the instructions provided by the manufacturer. Remove the lid, tilting it away from you, to allow the steam to escape.

Stir in the cream and allow the soup to cool for 5 minutes. Puree the soup with an immersion blender, or if you are using a food processor fitted with a steel blade, puree the soup in batches. Season the soup to taste with salt and pepper. Refrigerate the soup until cold, at least 4 hours but preferably overnight. Adjust the seasoning if necessary. To serve, ladle the soup into bowls and top with some chopped chives.

NOTE You can always substitute finely chopped green scallion tops for chives in any recipe. It's rare that you ever use a whole scallion, so most of the green tops frequently go to waste.

VARIATIONS

★ **Classic Vichyssoise:** Omit the garlic from the recipe.

★ **Leek and Potato Soup:** Omit the cream, and increase the chicken stock by ¾ cup. Instead of pureeing the soup, mash some of it with a potato masher and serve it hot.

Seafood Minestrone with Herb Oil

We think of minestrone as primarily being a vegetable soup, but the vegetables used in minestrone can also be a wonderful foil for delicate cubes of fresh fish. An aromatic, lusty herb oil drizzled over the soup adds richness to this lean dish. Serve it with a loaf of hot garlic bread.

SERVES **4 to 6**

SIZE **6-quart or larger pressure cooker**

TIME **3 to 4 minutes at high pressure with quick pressure release**

The pressure-cooked base can be prepared up to 2 days in advance and refrigerated, tightly covered. Reheat it in a saucepan over low heat until simmering, and then cook the fish cubes.

SOUP

1 medium zucchini

2 tablespoons kosher salt

¼ pound small shells or other small pasta

3 tablespoons olive oil

1 large onion, diced

2 garlic cloves, minced

1 large carrot, sliced

½ fennel bulb, cored and diced

3 cups firmly packed sliced green cabbage

4 cups Seafood Stock (page 19) or purchased stock

1 (14.5-ounce) can diced tomatoes, undrained

3 tablespoons chopped fresh parsley

1 tablespoon chopped fresh oregano

2 teaspoons fresh thyme leaves

1 bay leaf

1 (4-inch) Parmesan rind (optional)

1 cup canned white cannellini beans, drained and rinsed

1 pound thick, white, firm-fleshed fish fillets, such as cod, halibut, monkfish, or swordfish, cut into ¾-inch cubes

Salt and freshly ground black pepper to taste

½ cup freshly grated Parmesan cheese, for serving

HERB OIL

½ cup firmly packed parsley leaves

½ cup firmly packed basil leaves

2 tablespoons fresh rosemary

3 garlic cloves, minced

⅓ cup olive oil

Salt and freshly ground black pepper to taste

Cut the zucchini in half lengthwise and then into ⅓-inch slices. Place 4 cups of cold water in a mixing bowl, and stir in the kosher salt. Add the zucchini slices, and soak them for 15 minutes. Drain and rinse well.

Bring a large pot of salted water to a boil. Add the pasta, and cook according to package directions until al dente. Drain and set aside.

While the water heats, heat the olive oil in the cooker over medium-high heat or use the browning function of an electric cooker. Add the onion, garlic, carrot, fennel, and cabbage. Cook, stirring frequently, for 3 minutes, or until onion is translucent. Add the zucchini, stock, tomatoes, parsley, oregano, thyme, bay leaf, and Parmesan rind, if using.

Close and lock the lid of the cooker.

STOVETOP: Place the cooker over high heat, and bring it to high pressure. Once high pressure is reached, reduce the heat as much as possible while retaining the high-pressure level. Cook for 3 minutes. Then take the pot off the heat and quick release the pressure according to the instructions provided by the manufacturer. Remove the lid, tilting it away from you, to allow the steam to escape.

OR

ELECTRIC: Set the machine to cook at high pressure for 4 minutes. After 4 minutes, unplug the pot so that it does not go into warming mode. Quick release the pressure according to the instructions provided by the manufacturer. Remove the lid, tilting it away from you, to allow the steam to escape.

NOTE While it's still difficult to find fresh fennel in some supermarkets, it's becoming easier to find than in the past. I adore its slightly licorice taste and use it for cole slaw, in place of cabbage, many times. But if you can't find it, you can always substitute 2 celery ribs for each ½ fennel bulb specified in a recipe

Remove and discard the bay leaf and Parmesan rind, if used. Add the beans and fish to the cooker, and bring to a simmer over medium heat or use the browning function of an electric cooker. Cover the cooker without locking the lid in place and turn off the heat. Allow the fish to sit in the hot liquid for 5 minutes, or until cooked through.

While the soup cooks, prepare the herb oil. Combine the parsley, basil, rosemary, garlic, and oil in a food processor fitted with a steel blade or in a blender. Puree until smooth. Season to taste with salt and pepper, and scrape the mixture into a bowl.

To serve, ladle soup into bowls. Pass around the herb oil and the grated Parmesan cheese separately.

Manhattan Clam Chowder

Both tomato-based Manhattan and creamy New England clam chowders have their coterie of devoted fans, and in all honesty, I don't think one should have to decide between these two styles of mollusk-based bliss. My version has some crispy bacon as a garnish and a number of hearty vegetables in an aromatic broth. Serve it before Shrimp Creole (page 84).

SERVES **6 to 8**

SIZE **6-quart or larger pressure cooker**

TIME **3 to 4 minutes at high pressure with quick pressure release**

The chowder can be prepared up to 2 days in advance and refrigerated, tightly covered. Reheat it over low heat, stirring occasionally.

1 **pound chopped fresh clams**
3 **slices thick-cut bacon, diced**
2 **tablespoons olive oil**
3 **large onions, diced**
4 **celery ribs, diced**
3 **garlic cloves, minced**
½ **green bell pepper, seeds and ribs removed, chopped**
1½ **tablespoons fresh thyme leaves, divided**
3 **(8-ounce) bottles clam juice**

2 **russet potatoes, peeled and cut into ½-inch dice**
2 **bay leaves**
3 **(14.5-ounce) cans petite diced tomatoes, undrained**
Salt and freshly ground black pepper to taste
Hot red pepper sauce to taste

GARNISH
¼ **cup fresh chopped parsley**

Drain the clams, reserving the liquor. Refrigerate the clams until ready to use.

Cook the bacon in the cooker over medium-high heat or use the browning function of an electric cooker for 5 to 7 minutes, or until crisp. Remove the bacon from the cooker with a slotted spoon and drain on paper towels. Set it aside.

Add the olive oil, onions, celery, garlic, and green pepper to the cooker. Cook, stirring frequently, for 3 minutes, or until the onions are translucent. Add the reserved clam juice, half of the thyme, bottled clam juice, potatoes, bay leaves, and tomatoes to the cooker. Stir well.

Close and lock the lid of the cooker.

STOVETOP: Place the cooker over high heat, and bring it to high pressure. Once high pressure is reached, reduce the heat as much as possible while retaining the high-pressure level. Cook for 3 minutes. Then take the pot off the heat and quick release the pressure according to the instructions provided by the manufacturer. Remove the lid, tilting it away from you, to allow the steam to escape.

OR

ELECTRIC: Set the machine to cook at high pressure for 4 minutes. After 4 minutes, unplug the pot so that it does not go into warming mode. Quick release the pressure according to the instructions provided by the manufacturer. Remove the lid, tilting it away from you, to allow the steam to escape.

NOTE Cans of petite cut diced tomatoes began appearing in stores about 5 years ago. They are such a boon when cooking foods like this soup, because they are the perfect size to fit on a soup spoon. If you can't find them, chop and dice larger diced tomatoes.

Remove and discard the bay leaves. Bring the soup back to a simmer over medium-high heat or use the browning function of an electric cooker. Add the clams and remaining thyme, and simmer for 2 minutes, or until the clams are cooked through. Season to taste with salt, pepper, and hot red pepper sauce.

To serve, ladle the soup into bowls and top each with a sprinkling of bacon and parsley.

Mulligatawny

Mulligatawny, which means "pepper water" in Tamil, is a creamy Anglo-Indian chicken soup that became popular in Britain during the Raj. It's thickened with rice and contains some sweet apples as a foil to the spices. It's a lovely lunch dish served with a crunchy slaw and some naan (Indian flatbread).

SERVES **6 to 8**

SIZE **6-quart or larger pressure cooker**

TIME **6 to 7 minutes at high pressure with quick pressure release**

The soup can be prepared up to 2 days in advance and refrigerated, tightly covered. Reheat it over low heat, stirring occasionally. Add milk or cream if the soup needs thinning after reheating.

- 4 tablespoons (½ stick) unsalted butter
- 1¼ pounds boneless, skinless chicken thighs, cut into ¾-inch cubes
- 1 medium onion, diced
- 2 carrots, diced
- 1 celery rib, diced
- 3 garlic cloves, minced
- 2 tablespoons grated fresh ginger
- 3 tablespoons garam masala, or to taste
- 1 teaspoon ground cumin
- 7 cups Chicken Stock (page 15) or purchased stock
- 1 cup light coconut milk
- 2 Golden Delicious apples, peeled, cored, and diced
- ½ cup short-grain sushi rice
- 1 tablespoon cider vinegar
- ⅔ cup heavy cream
- Salt and freshly ground black pepper to taste

GARNISH
- ½ cup toasted chopped cashews
- ¼ cup chopped fresh cilantro

Heat the butter in the cooker over medium-high heat or use the browning function of an electric cooker. Add the chicken and cook, stirring frequently, for 2 minutes, or until the chicken is opaque. Remove the chicken from the cooker with a slotted spoon and set it aside. Add the onion, carrots, celery, garlic, and ginger to the cooker. Cook, stirring frequently, for 3 minutes, or until the onion is translucent. Stir in the garam masala and cumin, and cook for 1 minute, stirring constantly.

Return the chicken to the cooker and add the stock, coconut milk, apples, and rice.

Close and lock the lid of the cooker.

STOVETOP: Place the cooker over high heat, and bring it to high pressure. Once high pressure is reached, reduce the heat as much as possible while retaining the high-pressure level. Cook for 6 minutes. Then take the pot off the heat and quick release the pressure according to the instructions provided by the manufacturer. Remove the lid, tilting it away from you, to allow the steam to escape.

OR

ELECTRIC: Set the machine to cook at high pressure for 7 minutes. After 7 minutes, unplug the pot so that it does not go into warming mode. Quick release the pressure according to the instructions provided by the manufacturer. Remove the lid, tilting it away from you, to allow the steam to escape.

NOTE There is virtually no difference in flavor or consistency between regular coconut milk and the reduced-fat version. However, there is a big difference in calories and fat. Changing the heavy cream to half-and-half truly diminishes the soup, but you can save some fat calories by using lighter coconut milk.

Stir in the vinegar and cream, and bring the soup back to a simmer. Season to taste with salt and pepper, and serve immediately. Garnish each serving with cashews and cilantro.

Cháo (Vietnamese Rice Chowder)

Vietnamese cuisine is known for its soups, especially pho, *which has a flavorful clear broth. But I prefer this thick and comforting rice chowder, similar to a congee. It's subtle, and the nuances of flavor from fried shallots, ginger, and scallions add complexity to the dish. Serve it with Steamed Clams in Chinese Black Bean Sauce (page 65) or Asian Beef Stew with Star Anise (page 126).*

SERVES **6 to 8**

SIZE **6-quart or larger pressure cooker**

TIME **12 to 14 minutes at high pressure; then allow the pressure to release naturally for 10 minutes, and quick release any remaining pressure**

The soup can be prepared up to 2 days in advance and refrigerated, tightly covered. Reheat it over low heat, stirring occasionally. Add stock or water if the soup needs thinning after reheating.

- 3 **scallions**
- ½ **cup vegetable oil**
- 2 **shallots, diced**
- ½ **pound ground pork, turkey, or veal**
- 3 **tablespoons fish sauce, preferably Vietnamese**
- 2 **teaspoons granulated sugar**
- 1 **cup short-grain sushi rice, rinsed well in a sieve**

- 3 **tablespoons fresh ginger, julienned**
- 2 **quarts Chicken Stock (page 15), Chinese Chicken Stock (page 15), or purchased stock**
- ¼ **cup firmly packed individual fresh cilantro leaves, divided**
- **Additional fish sauce and freshly ground black pepper to taste**

Thinly slice the white parts of the scallions. Slice 4 inches of the green tops into ¼-inch slices. Set aside the white rings and green tops separately.

Heat the oil in the cooker over medium-high heat or use the browning function of an electric cooker. Add the shallots and cook, stirring occasionally, for 4 to 6 minutes, or until the shallots are browned. Remove the shallots from the cooker with a slotted spoon and drain on paper towels. Set them aside.

Discard all but 1 tablespoon of the oil from the cooker. Place the cooker back over medium-high heat or use the browning function of an electric cooker. Crumble the meat into the cooker and sprinkle with the fish sauce and sugar. Cook, stirring constantly, for 2 minutes, or until the meat loses its raw color. Add the rice, ginger, stock, and white scallion rings to the cooker.

Close and lock the lid of the cooker.

STOVETOP: Place the cooker over high heat, and bring it to high pressure. Once high pressure is reached, reduce the heat as much as possible while retaining the high-pressure level. Cook for 12 minutes. Then take the pot off the heat and allow it to return to normal pressure naturally for 10 minutes. Quick release any remaining pressure according to the instructions provided by the manufacturer. Remove the lid, tilting it away from you, to allow the steam to escape.

—OR—

ELECTRIC: Set the machine to cook at high pressure for 14 minutes. After 14 minutes, unplug the pot so that it does not go into warming mode. Allow the pressure to return to normal naturally for 10 minutes. Quick release any remaining pressure according to the instructions provided by the manufacturer. Remove the lid, tilting it away from you, to allow the steam to escape.

Add half of the scallion greens, half of the fried shallots, and half of the cilantro leaves to the soup, and simmer over low heat for 2 minutes. Season to taste with additional fish sauce and pepper. Ladle the soup into bowls, garnishing each serving with the remaining scallions, cilantro, and shallots.

NOTE There are literally thousands of different species of rice grown around the world. Usually, rice is grouped by the length of the grain, and it is important to use the type of rice specified—or one from the same family—in a recipe. Brown rice has become more popular than white rice (from which the germ and bran layers have been removed), because of its greater nutritional value, but it also takes far longer to cook. This soup calls for short-grain sushi rice, because it leaches starch into the soup and thickens it. While jasmine rice is also used extensively in Asian cooking, it has a far longer grain and will not achieve the same results in this recipe.

Cauliflower Soup with Bacon

*This soup has a luxurious, satiny mouthfeel because the bulk of it is pureed cauliflower.
Herbs add a nuanced flavor, and bacon gives a smoky undertone to the soup, but
the real star of this show is the snowy white cruciferous vegetable.*

SERVES **6 to 8**

SIZE **6-quart or larger pressure cooker**

TIME **5 to 6 minutes at high pressure; then allow the pressure to release naturally**

The soup can be prepared up to 2 days in advance and refrigerated, tightly covered. Reheat it over low heat and thin it with additional stock or cream if necessary.

¼ pound bacon, cut into 1-inch lengths
1 large onion, diced
1 celery rib, diced
2 medium russet potatoes, peeled and cut into ¾-inch chunks
1 (1½- to 2-pound) head cauliflower, leaves discarded, trimmed, and diced

5 cups Chicken Stock (page 15) or purchased stock
1 sprig fresh thyme
1 bay leaf
½ cup heavy cream
Salt and freshly ground white pepper to taste

GARNISH
½ cup grated sharp cheddar cheese

Cook the bacon in the cooker over medium-high heat or use the browning function of an electric cooker for 5 to 7 minutes, or until crisp. Remove the bacon from the cooker with a slotted spoon and drain on paper towels. Set it aside.

Discard all but 2 tablespoons of the bacon grease from the cooker. Add the onion and celery, and cook, stirring frequently, for 3 minutes, or until the onion is translucent. Add the potatoes, cauliflower, stock, thyme, and bay leaf to the cooker.

Close and lock the lid of the cooker.

STOVETOP: Place the cooker over high heat, and bring it to high pressure. Once high pressure is reached, reduce the heat as much as possible while retaining the high-pressure level. Cook for 5 minutes. Then take the pot off the heat and allow it to return to normal pressure naturally. Remove the lid, tilting it away from you, to allow the steam to escape.

OR

ELECTRIC: Set the machine to cook at high pressure for 6 minutes. After 6 minutes, unplug the pot so that it does not go into warming mode. Allow the pressure to return to normal naturally. Remove the lid, tilting it away from you, to allow the steam to escape.

Remove and discard the thyme sprig and bay leaf from the cooker and allow the soup to cool for 5 minutes. Puree the soup with an immersion blender, or if you're using a food processor fitted with a steel blade, puree the soup in batches.

Stir in the cream and season to taste with salt and pepper. Reheat the soup to a simmer over low heat or use the browning function of an electric cooker. Ladle the soup into bowls and serve, garnishing each serving with the reserved bacon and a sprinkling of cheese.

NOTE When selecting a head of cauliflower, look for one that is creamy white and shiny with no spots showing or a dull finish. If you see brown spots, yellowing leaves, or small flowers growing out of the florets, the head is past its prime. The size of a cauliflower is not related to its quality, so choose a head that fits your needs or your recipe.

Caldo Verde
(Kale Soup with Linguiça)

There's no question that kale is a nutritional nirvana. A member of the cabbage family, kale is now considered a superfood because of its high level of phytonutrients, especially a group called the glucosinolates. This traditional Portuguese soup features kale along with spicy sausage. All you need to do to make it into a meal is add a loaf of crusty bread and a tossed salad.

SERVES **4 to 6**

SIZE **6-quart or larger pressure cooker**

TIME **3 to 4 minutes at high pressure with quick pressure release**

The soup can be prepared up to 2 days in advance and refrigerated, tightly covered. Reheat it over low heat, stirring occasionally. Add stock or water if the soup needs thinning after reheating.

1 tablespoon olive oil
½ pound linguiça, chouriço, or smoked kielbasa, diced
1 large onion, diced
2 garlic cloves, minced
1½ pounds boiling potatoes, peeled and diced
5 cups Chicken Stock (page 15) or purchased stock
1 pound fresh kale
Salt and freshly ground black pepper to taste

Heat the oil in the cooker over medium-high heat or use the browning function of an electric cooker. Add the sausage and cook, stirring frequently, for 3 to 5 minutes, or until browned. Remove the sausage from the cooker with a slotted spoon, and set it aside. Discard all but 2 tablespoons of grease from the cooker.

Add the onion and garlic, and cook, stirring frequently, for 3 minutes, or until the onion is translucent. Add the potatoes and stock to the cooker.

Close and lock the lid of the cooker.

STOVETOP: Place the cooker over high heat, and bring it to high pressure. Once high pressure is reached, reduce the heat as much as possible while retaining the high-pressure level. Cook for 3 minutes. Then take the pot off the heat and quick release the pressure according to the instructions provided by the manufacturer. Remove the lid, tilting it away from you, to allow the steam to escape.

OR

ELECTRIC: Set the machine to cook at high pressure for 4 minutes After 4 minutes, unplug the pot so that it does not go into warming mode. Quick release the pressure according to the instructions provided by the manufacturer. Remove the lid, tilting it away from you, to allow the steam to escape.

NOTE Whenever starchy vegetables or legumes—like potatoes and dried beans—are added to a soup, the broth may thicken when the mixture is refrigerated. It's best to reheat and then evaluate if additional liquid is needed to thin it out to a more pleasing texture.

While the soup cooks, prepare the kale. Rinse the kale and discard the stems and center of the ribs. Cut the leaves crosswise into thin slices.

Allow the soup to cool for 5 minutes. Puree ¾ of the soup with an immersion blender, or if you're using a food processor fitted with a steel blade, you may need to puree the soup in batches. You want to leave some of the potatoes in pieces.

Bring the soup to a boil over medium heat or use the browning function of an electric cooker, stirring occasionally. Return the sausage to the cooker and stir in the kale. Reduce the heat to low and simmer the soup with the cover on the cooker, but not locked, for 10 to 15 minutes, or until the kale is cooked and tender. Season to taste with salt and pepper, and serve immediately.

Barley Mushroom Soup

We can thank Eastern European Jewish immigrants for bringing this hearty and warming winter soup, as well as borscht, to our shores in the nineteenth century. Barley grew well in the cold climates of Russia and Poland, and mushrooms could be harvested in the fall and dried for use all winter. This is truly a meal in a bowl, with little needed, except perhaps a loaf of crusty pumpernickel.

SERVES **6 to 8**

SIZE **6-quart or larger pressure cooker**

TIME **35 to 40 minutes at high pressure; then allow the pressure to release naturally**

The soup can be prepared up to 2 days in advance and refrigerated, tightly covered. Reheat it over low heat, stirring occasionally. Add stock or water if the soup needs thinning after reheating.

- ½ cup chopped dried porcini mushrooms
- 2 quarts Beef Stock (page 16) or purchased stock, divided
- 2 tablespoons vegetable oil
- 1 pound beef chuck or brisket, cut into ½-inch cubes
- 1 large sweet onion, such as Vidalia or Bermuda, diced
- 2 carrots, sliced
- 2 celery ribs, sliced
- 2 garlic cloves, minced
- 1 pound fresh crimini mushrooms, wiped with a damp paper towel, trimmed, and sliced
- 1 cup whole-grain hulled barley, rinsed well
- ¼ cup chopped fresh parsley, divided
- 2 teaspoons fresh thyme
- 1 bay leaf
- Salt and freshly ground black pepper to taste

Combine the dried mushrooms and ¾ cup of the stock in a microwave-safe container. Microwave on high (100 percent power) for 1 to 1½ minutes, or until the stock boils. Soak the mushrooms in the stock for 10 minutes, pushing them down into the liquid with the back of a spoon. Drain the mushrooms, reserving the stock. Strain the stock through a sieve lined with a paper coffee filter or paper towel. Set aside.

Heat the oil in the pressure cooker over medium-high heat or use the browning function of an electric cooker. Add the beef and brown it on all sides. Remove the beef from the cooker with a slotted spoon and set it aside. Add the onion, carrots, celery, and garlic to the cooker. Cook, stirring frequently, for 3 minutes, or until the onion is translucent. Add the fresh mushrooms and cook them, stirring frequently, for 3 minutes, or until the mushrooms begin to soften.

Add the beef, remaining stock, reserved mushroom stock, soaked dried mushrooms, barley, 2 tablespoons of the parsley, thyme, and bay leaf to the cooker.

Close and lock the lid of the cooker.

STOVETOP: Place the cooker over high heat, and bring it to high pressure. Once high pressure is reached, reduce the heat as much as possible while retaining the high-pressure level. Cook for 35 minutes. Then take the pot off the heat and allow it to return to normal pressure naturally. Remove the lid, tilting it away from you, to allow the steam to escape.

OR

ELECTRIC: Set the machine to cook at high pressure for 40 minutes. After 40 minutes, unplug the pot so that it does not go into warming mode. Allow the pressure to return to normal naturally. Remove the lid, tilting it away from you, to allow the steam to escape.

Remove and discard the bay leaf, season to taste with salt and pepper, and ladle the soup into bowls, sprinkling each serving with the remaining parsley.

NOTE The difference between whole-grain hulled barley and pearled barley is the same as that between brown rice and white rice. Pearled barley is milled to remove the outer coating, so it is not as nutritious as whole-grain hulled barley, nor does it contain as much fiber. Pearled barley also keeps a broth thin, because starch does not leech out of it. If you are substituting pearled barley in this or any other recipe, the cooking time will be about 18 minutes in a stovetop cooker and 20 minutes in an electric cooker.

Beet Borscht, page 51

Beet Borscht

This soup, originating in Eastern Europe, uses three ingredients that can easily be stored for the winter—beets, cabbage, and potatoes. With a slight hint of both sweet and sour flavors, it's a homey and warming soup that can also be pureed and served cold in the summer months. Serve it before Sweet and Sour Stuffed Cabbage (page 140).

SERVES **6 to 8**

SIZE **6-quart or larger pressure cooker**

TIME **6 to 7 minutes at high pressure; then allow the pressure to release naturally**

The soup can be prepared up to 2 days in advance and refrigerated, tightly covered. Reheat it over low heat, stirring occasionally.

SOUP

- 2 tablespoons vegetable oil
- 1 large onion, diced
- 1 large carrot, chopped
- 2 garlic cloves, minced
- 6 cups firmly packed shredded green cabbage
- 1½ pounds fresh beets, scrubbed, trimmed, and cut into ½-inch dice (peeling is not necessary)
- 6 cups Vegetable Stock (page 17) or purchased stock
- 1 (28-ounce) can diced tomatoes, undrained
- 2 tablespoons tomato paste
- 3 tablespoons chopped fresh parsley
- 2 teaspoons fresh thyme leaves
- 2 bay leaves
- 3 tablespoons freshly squeezed lemon juice
- 3 tablespoons granulated sugar
- 1 pound russet potatoes, peeled and cut into 1-inch cubes
- Salt and freshly ground black pepper to taste

SAUCE

- ¾ cup sour cream
- 3 tablespoons chopped fresh dill
- ¼ cup finely chopped cucumber
- 3 tablespoons finely chopped onion

GARNISH

- 1 cup croutons, preferably made from rye bread

Heat the oil in the cooker over medium-high heat or use the browning function of an electric cooker. Add the onion, carrot, and garlic to the pot, and cook, stirring frequently, for 3 minutes, or until the onion is translucent. Add the cabbage and cook for 2 minutes, or until the cabbage wilts.

Add the beets, stock, tomatoes, tomato paste, parsley, thyme, bay leaves, lemon juice, sugar, and potato cubes. Stir well to dissolve the tomato paste.

(continued on the following page)

(continued from the previous page)

Close and lock the lid of the cooker.

STOVETOP: Place the cooker over high heat, and bring it to high pressure. Once high pressure is reached, reduce the heat as much as possible while retaining the high-pressure level. Cook for 6 minutes. Then take the pot off the heat and allow it to return to normal pressure naturally. Remove the lid, tilting it away from you, to allow the steam to escape.

—OR—

ELECTRIC: Set the machine to cook at high pressure for 7 minutes. After 7 minutes, unplug the pot so that it does not go into warming mode. Allow the pressure to return to normal naturally. Remove the lid, tilting it away from you, to allow the steam to escape.

While the soup cooks, prepare the sauce. Combine the sour cream, dill, cucumber, and onion in a small mixing bowl and stir well. Season to taste with salt and pepper, and refrigerate until ready to serve.

Remove and discard the bay leaves. Season to taste with salt and pepper. Ladle the soup into bowls. Top each serving with a dollop of the sour cream mixture and garnish with a few croutons.

NOTE The pigment that gives beets their rich, purple-crimson color—betacyanin—is also a powerful cancer-fighting agent. Beets' potential effectiveness against colon cancer, in particular, has been demonstrated in several studies. Beets are also high in manganese and folate.

VARIATIONS

★ **Beef and Beet Borscht:** Brown 1 pound of beef chuck, cut into ½-inch cubes, in the cooker before cooking the onion mixture. Substitute Beef Stock (page 16) for the Vegetable Stock in the recipe.

★ **Cold Borscht:** Once the soup has cooled, puree it with an immersion blender, or if you are using a blender or food processor fitted with a steel blade, puree it in batches. Chill the soup well.

Asian-Scented Butternut Squash Bisque

I adore the seductive flavor and blushing color that winter squash brings to dishes, especially soups. In this easy-to-make bisque, butternut squash is blended with the Asian aromas and flavors of hoisin sauce and Chinese five-spice powder.

SERVES **4 to 6**

SIZE **6-quart or larger pressure cooker**

TIME **4 to 5 minutes at high pressure; then allow the pressure to release naturally**

The soup can be prepared up to 2 days in advance and refrigerated, tightly covered. Reheat it over low heat, covered, until hot, stirring occasionally.

NOTE Occasionally during the summer months prepeeled butternut squash disappears from the produce department and I'm faced with peeling a whole one. This can be done easily if you poke it with a sharp meat fork or skewer and microwave it on high (100 percent power) for 2 minutes, turning it after 1 minute. Then cut the squash in half, discard the seeds, and peel it. The short time in the microwave softens the flesh enough to make it easy to peel.

VARIATION

★ **Kentucky Butternut Squash Soup**: Substitute molasses for the hoisin sauce, bourbon for the rum, and cinnamon for the Chinese five-spice powder to create an American flavor profile.

3 pounds peeled butternut squash, cut into 1½-inch chunks
2½ cups Vegetable Stock (page 17), Chicken Stock (page 15), or purchased stock
2 scallions, white parts and 4 inches of green tops, chopped
3 tablespoons hoisin sauce
2 tablespoons dark rum
½ teaspoon Chinese five-spice powder
1 cup light cream
Salt and freshly ground black pepper to taste

GARNISH
4 to 6 tablespoons crème fraîche

Combine the squash, stock, scallions, hoisin sauce, rum, and five-spice powder in the cooker.

Close and lock the lid of the cooker.

STOVETOP: Place the cooker over high heat, and bring it to high pressure. Once high pressure is reached, reduce the heat as much as possible while retaining the high-pressure level. Cook for 4 minutes. Then take the pot off the heat and allow it to return to normal pressure naturally. Remove the lid, tilting it away from you, to allow the steam to escape.

OR

ELECTRIC: Set the machine to cook at high pressure for 5 minutes. After 5 minutes, unplug the pot so that it does not go into warming mode. Allow the pressure to return to normal naturally. Remove the lid, tilting it away from you, to allow the steam to escape.

Stir in the cream and allow the soup to cool for 5 minutes. Puree the soup with an immersion blender, or if you are using a food processor fitted with a steel blade, puree the soup in batches. Season the soup to taste with salt and pepper, and serve immediately, garnishing each serving with 1 tablespoon of crème fraîche.

Salmon en Papillote
with Tomatoes, Capers, and Olives, page 58

CHAPTER 3

Fish and Seafood

With a few exceptions, the recipes in this chapter are not about how to cook fish in a pressure cooker. Instead, they show you how to cook the stew base or sauce into which the fish is placed and then cooked conventionally for a few minutes, after the pressure is released. Those stew bases and sauces do take some time to cook, however, and your friend the pressure cooker will be there to help.

The growth in per capita consumption of fish in the United States has been skyrocketing for the past decade because of the health profile of some aquatic species. Fish are excellent sources of B vitamins, iodine, phosphorus, potassium, iron, and calcium.

The most important nutrient in fish may be omega-3 fatty acids. These are the primary polyunsaturated fatty acids found in the fat and oils in fish. They have been found to lower the levels of low-density lipoproteins (LDL), the "bad" cholesterol, and raise the levels of high-density lipoproteins (HDL), the "good" cholesterol that helps reduce risk factors for heart disease, including high cholesterol and high blood pressure. Fatty fish, such as mackerel and salmon, that live in cold water have the most omega-3 fatty acids, although all fish have some omega-3s.

Families of Fish

Although most of the recipes in this chapter were developed with a specific fish in mind, it's more important to use the *freshest* fish you can find in the market, rather than a particular species. All fin fish fall into three basic families, and you can easily substitute one species with another. Use the following table to make choices at the fish counter a lot easier.

A GUIDE TO FISH

DESCRIPTION	SPECIES	CHARACTERISTICS
FIRM, LEAN FISH	Black sea bass, cod family, flat fish (flounder, sole, halibut), grouper, lingcod, ocean perch, perch, porgy, red snapper, smelt, striped bass, turbot, some species of salmon, trout, drum family, tilefish	Low-fat, mild to delicate flavor, firm flesh, flake when cooked
MEATY FISH	Catfish, carp, eel, monkfish (anglerfish), orange roughy, some species of pike, salmon, shark, sturgeon, swordfish, some tuna varieties, mahi-mahi (dolphinfish), whitefish, pompano, yellowtail	Low to high fat, diverse flavors and textures, usually thick steaks or fillets
FATTY OR STRONG-FLAVORED FISH	Bluefish, mackerel, some tuna varieties	High fat, and pronounced flavor

Cooking Fish Correctly

There's no chart with cooking times in this chapter because each piece of fish is unique. With the power of the pressure cooker, even an extra 15 seconds can make a difference and result in overcooked fish.

Perfectly cooked fish is moist and has a delicate flavor, and overcooking is the most prevalent cooking error. Fish is done when the flesh has just begun to turn from translucent to opaque and is firm but still moist. If the piece of fish is thick enough to be tested with an instant-read thermometer, the internal temperature should be 145°F. It should flake easily when tested with a fork. Fish continues to cook after it's taken away from the heat, and it will become opaque in the center.

When cooking fish conventionally, the 10-Minute Rule, also known as the Canadian Cooking Method, is a good guideline. It was developed by the Canadian Department of Fisheries to try to boost consumption of fish in that country. While it is not perfect, it certainly makes for an easy rule of thumb: Cook fish for a total of 10 minutes per inch of thickness.

But in this book, we're using a pressure cooker, the Speedy Gonzales of cooking methods. So we've just invented the 3-Minute Rule, or 4-Minute Rule if you're using an electric pressure cooker. All of the cooking times given in the recipes assume that the fish you're cooking is about an inch thick, but if it's thicker or thinner, please adjust the time.

Salmon en Papillote
with Tomatoes, Capers, and Olives

Steaming food wrapped in parchment paper is one of the healthiest ways that it can be cooked. There is very little fat required, and the juices from the fish create a light and flavorful sauce. This dish, made with blushing pink salmon in a sauce of bright tomatoes, with flecks of herbs and the vibrant flavors of capers and olives, is also visually stunning. Serve it with crusty garlic bread and a tossed salad.

SERVES **4**

SIZE **6-quart or larger pressure cooker**

TIME **4 to 10 minutes at high pressure with quick pressure release**

The packets can be prepared for cooking up to 6 hours in advance and refrigerated.

⅓ cup olive oil, divided

4 garlic cloves, thinly sliced

1 shallot, minced

¼ teaspoon crushed red pepper flakes (optional)

4 (6-ounce) skinned salmon fillets or other species (see the chart on page 56)

Freshly ground black pepper to taste

1 cup ripe cherry tomatoes (preferably of different colors), halved

2 teaspoons fresh thyme leaves

2 teaspoons chopped fresh rosemary

2 tablespoons capers, drained and rinsed

¼ cup diced kalamata olives

¼ cup dry white wine

GARNISH

3 tablespoons chopped fresh parsley

Lemon wedges

Cut four 15-inch squares of parchment paper and fold them in half. Starting at the fold, draw half a large heart shape and cut out the hearts. Cut four 18-inch lengths of heavy-duty aluminum foil.

Using 2 tablespoons of the olive oil, brush the center seam of each heart. Heat an additional 2 tablespoons of oil in a small skillet over medium heat. Add the garlic, shallot, and crushed red pepper, if using. Cook, stirring frequently, for 2 minutes. Scrape the mixture into a mixing bowl.

Season the salmon to taste with pepper; do not use salt because there are salty ingredients in the topping. Place the salmon on the greased paper. Tuck under the thin end of each fillet to make a package of uniform thickness.

Add the tomatoes, thyme, rosemary, capers, olives, and remaining oil to the mixing bowl and toss to combine. Divide the mixture on top of the salmon fillets, and drizzle each fillet with 1 tablespoon of the wine.

Starting at the top of each parchment heart, make small, tight overlapping folds along the edge to seal the packet. Then enclose each packet in a sheet of aluminum foil, and crimp the foil to keep it closed.

Pour 1½ cups of water into the cooker, and place a steamer basket on a trivet so that it sits above the water. Arrange the fish packets inside the steamer.

Close and lock the lid of the cooker.

STOVETOP: Place the cooker over high heat, and bring it to high pressure. Once high pressure is reached, reduce the heat as much as possible, while still retaining the high-pressure level. Cook for 4 to 8 minutes, depending on the thickness of the fish fillets. Take the cooker off the heat, and quick release the pressure according to the instructions provided by the manufacturer. Remove the lid, tilting it away from you, to allow the steam to escape.

OR

ELECTRIC: Set the machine to cook at high pressure for 6 to 10 minutes. After the allotted time, unplug the pot so that it does not go into warming mode. Quick release the pressure according to the instructions provided by the manufacturer. Remove the lid, tilting it away from you, to allow the steam to escape.

Remove the fish packets from the steamer with tongs. Slide the parchment packets out of the aluminum foil, and carefully slit the paper to allow the steam to escape. Transfer the packets to shallow soup bowls, and serve immediately, sprinkling each portion with parsley. Pass the lemon wedges separately.

> **VARIATION**
>
> ⋆ **Provençal Salmon en Papillote:** Omit the capers. Substitute chopped, oil-cured black olives for the kalamata olives, and substitute orange juice for the white wine. Reduce the tomatoes to ½ cup, and add ½ cup chopped red bell pepper to the packets. Sprinkle ½ teaspoon grated orange zest on top of each fillet.

Lemon Herb Cod en Papillote

Garlic, lemon, and fresh herbs enliven the flavor of delicate white-fleshed fresh fish.
Serve the fish with Risotto alla Milanese (page 200) and Caponata (page 240).

SERVES **4**

SIZE **6-quart or larger pressure cooker**

TIME **4 to 10 minutes at high pressure with quick pressure release**

> The packets can be prepared for cooking up to 6 hours in advance and refrigerated.

2 tablespoons unsalted butter, softened

4 (6-ounce) cod fillets, or other species shown on the chart on page 56

Salt and freshly ground black pepper to taste

1 leek, white part only, halved horizontally, thinly sliced, and rinsed well

3 garlic cloves, minced

3 tablespoons chopped fresh dill

2 tablespoons chopped fresh parsley

1 tablespoon grated lemon zest

2 tablespoons freshly squeezed lemon juice

2 tablespoons dry white wine

Lemon wedges for serving

Cut four 15-inch squares of parchment paper and fold them in half. Starting at the fold, draw half a large heart shape and cut out the hearts. Cut off four 18-inch lengths of heavy-duty aluminum foil.

Using the 2 tablespoons of butter, coat the center seam of each heart. Sprinkle the cod with salt and pepper. Place a portion of the leeks on top of the butter and top it with a piece of cod. Tuck under the thin end of each fillet to make a package of uniform thickness.

Combine the garlic, dill, parsley, and lemon zest in a small bowl. Rub this mixture on each piece of cod and drizzle the cod with the lemon juice and wine.

Starting at the top of each parchment heart, make small, tight overlapping folds along the edge to seal the packet. Then enclose each packet in a sheet of aluminum foil and crimp the foil to keep it closed.

Pour 1½ cups of water into the cooker, and place a steamer basket on a trivet so that it sits above the water. Arrange the fish packets inside the steamer.

Close and lock the lid of the cooker.

STOVETOP: Place the cooker over high heat, and bring it to high pressure. Once high pressure is reached, reduce the heat as much as possible, while still retaining the high-pressure level. Cook for 4 to 8 minutes, depending on the thickness of the fish. Take the pot off the heat, and quick release the pressure according to the instructions provided by the manufacturer. Remove the lid, tilting it away from you, to allow the steam to escape.

OR

ELECTRIC: Set the machine to cook at high pressure for 6 to 10 minutes, depending on the thickness of the fish. After the allotted time, unplug the pot so that it does not go into warming mode. Quick release the pressure according to the instructions provided by the manufacturer. Remove the lid, tilting it away from you, to allow the steam to escape.

Remove the fish packets from the steamer with tongs. Slide the parchment packets out of the aluminum foil, and carefully slit the paper to allow the steam to escape. Transfer the packets to shallow soup bowls and serve immediately. Pass the lemon wedges separately.

NOTE The method of wrapping fish in both parchment paper and aluminum foil ensures success when cooking *en papillote* (pronounced *ahn-pah-pee-yoht*) in a pressure cooker. When acidic foods like wine and tomatoes come into contact with aluminum foil, they can react and create a bitter taste. Because the power of the pressure-cooking may cause parchment paper to tear apart and possibly block the steam vents, most pressure cooker manufacturers do **not** suggest using it. By sealing the parchment packet tightly and wrapping it securely in foil, both problems are avoided.

Moules Marinières
(French Sailor-Style Mussels), page 63

Moules Marinières
(French Sailor-Style Mussels)

The key to this almost instant dish is having lots of crusty toasted bread around to sop up the sauce. Moules Marinières are a staple along the coast of the Côte d'Azur, and a salad made with fresh fennel in a lemon vinaigrette is a nice contrast. Although cooking mussels conventionally is hardly a bother, you'll find that they are more plump and tender when pressure-cooked.

SERVES **2 to 3**

SIZE **6-quart or larger pressure cooker**

TIME **1 to 2 minutes at high pressure with quick pressure release**

The mussels must be cooked at the last minute; however, the vegetable and wine base can be prepared up to 2 hours in advance.

2 **pounds mussels**
2 **tablespoons unsalted butter**
1 **leek, white and light green parts, thinly sliced and rinsed well**
2 **shallots, thinly sliced**
6 **garlic cloves, thinly sliced**
Salt and freshly ground black pepper to taste

2 **sprigs fresh thyme**
2 **bay leaves**
1 **cup dry white wine**
3 **tablespoons mayonnaise**
3 **tablespoons chopped fresh parsley**
2 **tablespoons freshly squeezed lemon juice**
1 **teaspoon grated lemon zest**

Scrub the mussels well with a stiff brush under cold running water, and discard any mussels that are cracked or do not close tightly when tapped with your finger.

Heat the butter in the cooker over medium heat or use the browning function of an electric cooker. Add the leek, shallots, and garlic, and sprinkle with salt and pepper. Cook, stirring frequently, for 3 minutes, or until the leeks are translucent. Add the thyme, bay leaves, and wine, and bring to a boil over high heat. Cook the liquid for 2 minutes, or until it is is reduced by ⅓. Add the mussels to the cooker.

Close and lock the lid of the cooker.

(continued on the following page)

(continued from the previous page)

STOVETOP: Place the cooker over high heat, and bring it to high pressure. Once high pressure is reached, reduce the heat as much as possible while still retaining the high-pressure level. Cook for 1 minute. Then take the pot off the heat and quick release the pressure according to the instructions provided by the manufacturer. Remove the lid, tilting it away from you, to allow the steam to escape.

—OR—

ELECTRIC: Set the machine to cook at high pressure for 2 minutes. After 2 minutes, unplug the pot so that it does not go into warming mode. Quick release the pressure according to the instructions provided by the manufacturer. Remove the lid, tilting it away from you, to allow the steam to escape.

Remove the mussels from the cooker with a slotted spoon and set them aside. Discard any mussels that did not open. Remove and discard the thyme sprigs and bay leaves.

Stir the mayonnaise, parsley, lemon juice, and lemon zest into the cooker, and bring to a boil. Turn off the heat. Season to taste with salt and pepper. Return the mussels to the cooker and allow them to sit for 1 minute. Serve immediately.

NOTE Two families of mussels are sold in the United States. The Atlantic blue mussel is the most common—its dark shell is tinged with blue. Most Atlantic mussels are about 2 to 3 inches long. The lighter and larger New Zealand blue-lipped mussels are more commonly found on the Pacific Coast. This recipe was timed for the Atlantic mussels. Add about 30 seconds if you're using larger ones.

Steamed Clams in Chinese Black Bean Sauce

While most Americans associate clams with chowder and New England, these mollusks are popular in traditional Chinese cooking too. Serve these clams with some steamed rice and a crispy vegetable stir-fry.

SERVES **3 or 4**

SIZE **6-quart or larger pressure cooker**

TIME **1 to 2 minutes at high pressure with quick pressure release**

This dish must be cooked at the last minute; however you can prep for it up to 4 hours in advance.

3 pounds littleneck clams
2 tablespoons fermented black beans
¼ cup dry sherry
1 tablespoon toasted sesame oil
3 scallions, white parts and 4 inches of green tops, sliced
3 garlic cloves, minced

3 tablespoons grated fresh ginger
½ cup clam juice
3 tablespoons oyster sauce
2 tablespoons cornstarch

GARNISH
¼ cup chopped scallions

Scrub the clams well under cold running water. Discard any clams that do not shut tightly. Set them aside.

Place the black beans on a cutting board, and hit them with the bottom of a small skillet or the flat side of a meat mallet to crush them. Stir the black beans into the sherry to plump.

Heat the sesame oil in the cooker over medium-high heat or use the browning function of an electric cooker. Add the scallions, garlic, and ginger, and cook, stirring constantly, for 30 seconds. Stir in the sherry mixture, clam juice, and oyster sauce, and add the clams to the cooker.

Close and lock the lid of the cooker.

(continued on the following page)

(*continued from the previous page*)

STOVETOP: Place the cooker over high heat, and bring it to high pressure. Once high pressure is reached, reduce the heat as much as possible while retaining the high-pressure level. Cook for 1 minute. Then take the pot off the heat and quick release the pressure according to the instructions provided by the manufacturer. Remove the lid, tilting it away from you, to allow the steam to escape.

OR

ELECTRIC: Set the machine to cook at high pressure for 2 minutes. After 2 minutes, unplug the pot so that it does not go into warming mode. Quick release the pressure according to the instructions provided by the manufacturer. Remove the lid, tilting it away from you to allow the steam to escape.

Remove the clams from the cooker with a slotted spoon. Discard any clams that did not open. Place the cooker over medium-high heat or use the browning function of an electric cooker, and boil the liquid for 3 minutes.

Combine the cornstarch with 2 tablespoons of cold water in a small cup, stirring well to dissolve the cornstarch. Stir the mixture into the cooker, and bring to a boil over high heat or use the browning function with an electric cooker. Cook for 1 minute, or until the sauce thickens. Serve immediately, sprinkling the dish with the scallions.

NOTE While most of the mollusks you buy today have already been through a purging, I still think it's a good idea to do it yourself, to ensure that you're not chewing grit. After scrubbing clams or mussels well with a stiff brush, place them in a bowl of ice water mixed with 1 teaspoon of salt and 2 tablespoons of cornmeal to each quart of water. Refrigerate the mollusks for an hour or two, and then rinse them well.

VARIATIONS

★ **Clams with Spicy Black Bean Sauce:** Stir-fry 2 or 3 Chinese dried chiles, broken in half and seeded, with the scallions and garlic before cooking the clams. Remove and discard the chiles before serving the dish.

★ **Mussels with Black Bean Sauce:** Substitute mussels for the clams.

Caldo de Perro
(Spanish Fish Stew with Potatoes, Greens, and Aïoli)

Every cuisine that borders a body of water has a wonderful selection of fish stews created by fishermen with whatever they catch in their nets that day. This stew, from the region around Barcelona, features colorful escarole and potatoes and is topped with a garlicky mayonnaise sauce. A loaf of crusty bread is all you need as an accompaniment.

SERVES **4 to 6**

SIZE **6-quart or larger pressure cooker**

TIME **3 to 4 minutes at high pressure with quick pressure release**

The pressure-cooked base can be prepared up to 2 days in advance and refrigerated, tightly covered. Reheat it in a saucepan over low heat until it simmers, and then cook the fish cubes.

1½ pounds halibut, cod, monkfish, snapper, sea bass, or any firm-fleshed white fish
2 tablespoons olive oil
2 medium onions, diced
7 garlic cloves, minced, divided
4 cups Seafood Stock (page 19) or purchased stock
½ cup dry white wine
2 tablespoons freshly squeezed lemon juice

1 pound redskin potatoes, scrubbed and diced
2 tablespoons chopped fresh parsley
1 tablespoon fresh thyme
1 bay leaf
½ pound kale or escarole
½ cup mayonnaise
1 teaspoon grated lemon zest
Salt and freshly ground black pepper to taste

Rinse the fish and pat it dry with paper towels. Remove and discard any skin or bones. Cut the fish into 1-inch cubes and refrigerate, covered with plastic wrap, until ready to use.

Heat the oil in the cooker over medium-high heat or use the browning function of an electric cooker. Add the onion and 3 garlic cloves, and cook, stirring frequently, for 3 minutes, or until onion is translucent. Add the stock, wine, lemon juice, potatoes, parsley, thyme, and bay leaf to the cooker.

Close and lock the lid of the cooker.

(continued on the following page)

(continued from the previous page)

STOVETOP: Place the cooker over high heat, and bring it to high pressure. Once high pressure is reached, reduce the heat as much as possible while still retaining the high-pressure level. Cook for 3 minutes. Then take the pot off the heat and quick release the pressure according to the instructions provided by the manufacturer. Remove the lid, tilting it away from you, to allow the steam to escape.

—OR—

ELECTRIC: Set the machine to cook at high pressure for 4 minutes. After 4 minutes, unplug the pot so that it does not go into warming mode. Quick release the pressure according to the instructions provided by the manufacturer. Remove the lid, tilting it away from you, to allow the steam to escape.

While the stew cooks, prepare the escarole. Rinse the leaves and discard stems. Cut the leaves crosswise into ½-inch slices. Make the sauce by combining the mayonnaise, lemon zest, and remaining garlic. Refrigerate until ready to serve.

Remove and discard the bay leaf. Add the escarole and fish to the cooker, and bring it to a simmer over medium heat or use the browning function of an electric cooker. Cover the cooker, without locking the lid in place, and turn off the heat. Allow the fish to sit in the hot liquid for 5 minutes, or until it is cooked through. Season to taste with salt and pepper, and serve hot. Pass around the sauce separately.

NOTE A vegetable peeler and a pair of tweezers are the best ways to get rid of those pesky little bones in fish fillets. Run a peeler down the center of the fillet, starting at the tail end. It will catch the larger pin bones, and with a twist of your wrist, you can pull them out. For finer bones, use your fingers to rub the flesh lightly, and then pull out the bones with the tweezers.

VARIATIONS

★ Substitute Swiss chard or collard greens for the escarole.

★ Substitute boneless, skinless chicken for the fish, and substitute chicken stock for the seafood stock. Add the chicken to the cooker at the onset of the cooking time.

Caribbean Fish Stew

This is a subtle dish with flavor nuances from aromatic rosemary and orange zest, and a subtle spark from fresh ginger. The recipe works with any sort of fish or seafood, and it's on the table in minutes.

SERVES **4 to 6**

SIZE **6-quart or larger pressure cooker**

TIME **3 to 4 minutes at high pressure with quick pressure release**

The pressure-cooked base can be prepared up to 2 days in advance and refrigerated, tightly covered. Reheat it in a saucepan over low heat until it simmers, and then cook the fish cubes.

- 2 tablespoons olive oil
- 1 large onion, diced
- 1 large carrot, thickly sliced
- 1 celery rib, thickly sliced
- ½ fennel bulb, cored and diced
- 2 garlic cloves, minced
- 2 tablespoons fresh ginger, julienned
- ¾ cup dry white wine
- 3 cups Seafood Stock (page 19) or purchased stock
- 2 russet potatoes, peeled and cut into 1-inch cubes
- 2 tablespoons chopped fresh rosemary
- 2 teaspoons grated orange zest
- 2 bay leaves
- 1½ pounds thick white-fleshed fish fillets, such as cod, halibut, monkfish, or swordfish, cut into 1-inch cubes
- Salt and freshly ground black pepper to taste
- ¼ cup coarsely chopped fresh parsley for serving

Heat the oil in the cooker over medium-high heat or use the browning function of an electric cooker. Add the onion, carrot, celery, fennel, garlic, and ginger. Cook, stirring frequently, for 3 minutes, or until the onion is translucent.

Stir in the wine, stock, potatoes, rosemary, orange zest, and bay leaves.

Close and lock the lid of the cooker.

(continued on the following page)

(continued from the previous page)

STOVETOP: Place the cooker over high heat, and bring it to high pressure. Once high pressure is reached, reduce the heat as much as possible while retaining the high-pressure level. Cook for 3 minutes. Then take the pot off the heat and quick release the pressure according to the instructions provided by the manufacturer. Remove the lid, tilting it away from you, to allow the steam to escape.

—OR—

ELECTRIC: Set the machine to cook at high pressure for 4 minutes. After 4 minutes, unplug the pot so that it does not go into warming mode. Quick release the pressure according to the instructions provided by the manufacturer. Remove the lid, tilting it away from you, to allow the steam to escape.

Remove and discard the bay leaves. Add the fish to the cooker, and bring to a simmer over medium heat or use the browning function of an electric cooker. Cover the cooker without locking the lid in place, and turn off the heat. Allow the fish to sit in the hot liquid for 5 minutes, or until it is cooked through. Season the stew to taste with salt and pepper, and serve hot, sprinkling each serving with some of the parsley.

NOTE Some people who enjoy fish don't enjoy a "fishy" flavor. But there's a way around that for these recipes. Rather than using the seafood stock specified, substitute vegetable stock, if you're a vegetarian, or substitute chicken stock, if you're not. The "fishy" quotient will be greatly diminished.

VARIATION

★ Reduce the amount of fish by ½ pound, and add ½ pound shelled and deveined shrimp, bay scallops, or a combination of seafood.

Brazilian Fish Stew with Salsa, page 72

Brazilian Fish Stew with Salsa

This stew, from the Bahia region of Brazil, is only modestly spicy, but the combination of flavors from the vegetables and coconut milk makes it very special. It gets a topping of fresh tomato salsa that enlivens the cooked flavors of the dish.

SERVES **4 to 6**

SIZE **6-quart or larger pressure cooker**

TIME **3 to 4 minutes at high pressure with quick pressure release**

The pressure-cooked base can be prepared up to 2 days in advance and refrigerated, tightly covered. Reheat it in a saucepan over low heat until it simmers, and then cook the fish cubes.

STEW

- 3 tablespoons olive oil
- 1 large onion, sliced
- 4 garlic cloves, minced
- 1 red bell pepper, seeds and ribs removed, sliced
- 1 yellow or orange bell pepper, seeds and ribs removed, sliced
- 2 jalapeño or serrano chiles, seeds and ribs removed, chopped
- 2 tablespoons tomato paste
- 1 (14.5-ounce) can diced tomatoes, drained
- 1 cup light coconut milk
- ½ cup Seafood Stock (page 19) or purchased stock
- 1½ pounds thick, white-fleshed fish fillets, such as cod, halibut, monkfish, or swordfish, cut into 1-inch cubes
- 2 tablespoons dendê oil (optional)
  Salt and freshly ground black pepper to taste
- ¼ cup coarsely chopped cilantro
- 2 to 3 cups hot cooked rice, for serving

SALSA

- 2 ripe plum tomatoes, cored, seeded, and chopped
- 3 scallions, white parts and 4 inches of green tops, chopped
- 1 small jalapeño or serrano chile, seeds and ribs removed, chopped
- 2 garlic cloves, minced
- 2 tablespoons white wine vinegar
- 2 tablespoons olive oil
  Salt and freshly ground black pepper to taste

Heat the oil in a cooker over medium-high heat or use the browning function of an electric cooker. Add the onion, garlic, red bell pepper, yellow bell pepper, and jalapeño, and cook, stirring frequently, for 3 minutes, or until the onion is translucent. Stir in the tomato paste and cook for 1 minute, stirring constantly.

Add the tomatoes, coconut milk, and stock, and stir well to incorporate the tomato paste.

Close and lock the lid of the cooker.

STOVETOP: Place the cooker over high heat, and bring it to high pressure. Once high pressure is reached, reduce the heat as much as possible while retaining the high-pressure level. Cook for 3 minutes. Then take the pot off the heat and quick release the pressure according to the instructions provided by the manufacturer. Remove the lid, tilting it away from you, to allow the steam to escape.

OR

ELECTRIC: Set the machine to cook at high pressure for 4 minutes. After 4 minutes, unplug the pot so that it does not go into warming mode. Quick release the pressure according to the instructions provided by the manufacturer. Remove the lid, tilting it away from you, to allow the steam to escape.

While the pressure is building, make the salsa. Combine the tomatoes, scallions, jalapeño, garlic, vinegar, and oil in a bowl and mix well. Season to taste with salt and pepper, and allow it to sit at room temperature to blend the flavors.

When the pressure cooking is complete, add the fish to the cooker. Bring the stew to a simmer over medium heat or use the browning function of an electric cooker. Cover the cooker, without locking the lid in place, and turn off the heat. Allow the fish to sit in the hot liquid for 5 minutes, or until it is cooked through. Stir in the dendê oil, if using, and season to taste with salt and pepper. Serve the stew hot, on top of rice, and sprinkle each serving with cilantro. Pass around the salsa separately.

NOTE Bright orange dendê oil is an integral part of Brazilian cooking, as it is in African cooking. This oil is carried only by specialty markets that cater to African or Brazilian communities. If you don't have a specialty market near you, you can order the oil online. Although there is no exact substitute for dendê oil, the orange color can be replicated with Hispanic annatto oil, which is not difficult to find, or by grinding some annatto seeds into olive oil.

New England Seafood Stew
with Red Pepper Rouille

Portuguese influence is prominent in the cuisine of southern New England, dating back to the whaling era. Linguiça sausage is one of the manifestations of that heritage, and its seasoning flavors the broth of this hearty seafood stew. It's truly a meal in and of itself, perhaps with a tossed salad.

SERVES **6 to 8**

SIZE **6-quart or larger pressure cooker**

TIME **3 to 5 minutes at high pressure with quick pressure release**

The soup base, croutons, and rouille can be prepared up to 2 days in advance and refrigerated, tightly covered. Bring the soup to a boil, and cook the seafood just before serving.

STEW

- ¼ pound bacon, diced
- 1 medium onion, diced
- 1 carrot, diced
- 1 celery stalk, diced
- 3 garlic cloves, minced
- ½ pound mild linguiça or chorico sausage, diced
- 1 (14.5-ounce) canned diced tomatoes, undrained
- 2 oranges, zest grated and juiced
- ½ cup white wine
- 3 cups Seafood Stock (page 19) or purchased stock
- 2 tablespoons chopped fresh parsley
- 2 teaspoons fresh thyme leaves
- 1 bay leaf
- 3 tablespoons chopped fresh basil
- ½ pound peeled and deveined raw shrimp
- ¾ pound swordfish, cut into 1-inch cubes
- ½ pound bay scallops

Salt and freshly ground black pepper to taste

GARNISH

- ¼ pound cooked lobster meat

CROUTONS

- 6 to 8 (½-inch-thick) slices French or Italian bread
- 3 tablespoons olive oil
- ¼ to ⅓ cup freshly grated Parmesan cheese

ROUILLE

- 1 egg yolk
- 1 teaspoon Dijon mustard
- 1 tablespoon red wine vinegar
- 3 garlic cloves, peeled
- 2 tablespoons chopped fresh basil
- 1 teaspoon chili powder
- 1 red bell pepper, roasted, peeled, and seeded
- ½ cup olive oil
- ¼ cup fresh breadcrumbs

Cook the bacon in the cooker over medium-high heat or use the browning function of an electric cooker for 5 to 7 minutes, or until crisp. Remove the bacon from the cooker with a slotted spoon, and drain on paper towels. Set the bacon aside and discard all but

1 tablespoon of the bacon grease. Add the onion, carrot, celery, and garlic. Cook over medium-high heat, stirring frequently, for 3 minutes or until the onion is translucent. Add the linguiça and cook 3 minutes. Add the tomatoes, orange zest, orange juice, wine, stock, parsley, thyme, and bay leaf.

Close and lock the lid of the cooker.

STOVETOP: Place the cooker over high heat, and bring it to high pressure. Once high pressure is reached, reduce the heat as much as possible while retaining the high-pressure level. Cook for 3 minutes. Then take the pot off the heat and quick release the pressure according to the instructions provided by the manufacturer. Remove the lid, tilting it away from you, to allow the steam to escape.

OR

ELECTRIC: Set the machine to cook at high pressure for 5 minutes. After 5 minutes, unplug the pot so that it does not go into warming mode. Quick release the pressure according to the instructions provided by the manufacturer. Remove the lid, tilting it away from you, to allow the steam to escape.

For the croutons, preheat the oven to 375°F. Line a baking sheet with foil. Brush the bread slices with oil and sprinkle with the cheese. Bake the croutons for 10 minutes, or until the cheese is melted and the bread is crisp. Set the slices aside.

For the rouille, combine the egg yolk, mustard, vinegar, garlic, basil, chili powder, and red bell pepper in a blender or food processor fitted with a steel blade. Puree until smooth, and then drizzle the olive oil very slowly into the mixture with the motor running. Add the breadcrumbs to thicken, and season to taste with salt and pepper. Refrigerate the sauce.

To finish the stew, remove and discard the bay leaf. Add the basil, shrimp, swordfish, and scallops to the cooker, and bring to a simmer over medium heat or use the browning function of an electric cooker. Cover the cooker without locking the lid in place, and turn off the heat. Allow the fish to sit in the hot liquid for 5 minutes, or until it is cooked through. Season to taste with salt and pepper.

To serve, ladle the hot soup into bowls. Place a crouton in the center, and top with a few tablespoons of rouille. Garnish each bowl with lobster meat and bacon.

NOTE Fish and seafood do not freeze well—either before or after cooking. The reason is that when fish is frozen any liquid inside the cells expands to form ice. This expansion punctures delicate cell walls and makes the fish mushy when it is thawed. But fish cooks quickly; it's the base that takes the time. My suggestion is to double (or even triple) the recipe for the base and freeze the extra portions. Thaw it and add the fresh fish. Within 10 minutes, you'll be enjoying a delicious fish soup boasting a long-simmered base enlivened by perfectly cooked fresh fish.

Carolina Fish Muddle

It wasn't on the Outer Banks of North Carolina, but at Zingerman's Deli in Ann Arbor, Michigan, that I discovered this hearty and flavorful fish stew. A smoky undertone from bacon flavors the tomato broth, which is thickened with potatoes that literally fall apart as the base cooks.

SERVES **6 to 8**

SIZE **6-quart or larger pressure cooker**

TIME **18 to 20 minutes at high pressure; then allow the pressure to release naturally**

The pressure-cooked base can be prepared up to 2 days in advance and refrigerated, tightly covered. Reheat it in a saucepan over low heat until simmering, and then cook the fish cubes. Do not toast the bread until just before serving.

½ pound sliced bacon, diced
2 medium onions, diced
1 large leek, white part only, thinly sliced and rinsed well
1 large or 2 medium carrots, diced
2 celery ribs, diced
1 clove garlic, minced
1 bay leaf
4 cups Seafood Stock (page 19) or purchased stock
1 (28-ounce) can diced tomatoes, undrained
¼ pound slab bacon or salt pork
1 tablespoon fresh thyme leaves
¼ teaspoon crushed red pepper flakes or to taste
2 tablespoons chopped fresh parsley

½ pound pollock or other inexpensive white ocean fish, cut into 1-inch pieces
1½ pounds Yukon Gold or other waxy potatoes, peeled and cut into 1-inch dice
1 pound striped bass or other full-flavored ocean fish, cut into 1-inch chunks
1 pound cod or other flaky white ocean fish, cut into 1-inch chunks
Salt and freshly ground black pepper to taste
6 to 8 slices good crusty bread
3 to 4 tablespoons reserved hot bacon fat

Cook the diced bacon in a cooker over medium-high heat or use the browning function of an electric cooker for 5 to 7 minutes, or until crisp. Remove the bacon from the cooker with a slotted spoon and drain on paper towels. Set it aside. Reserve 3 to 4 tablespoons of the bacon fat and set aside.

Add the onions, leek, carrots, and celery to the bacon grease remaining in the cooker. Cook, stirring frequently, for 5 to 7 minutes, or until the vegetables soften. Add the garlic and bay leaf. Cook for 1 minute, stirring constantly.

Add the stock, tomatoes, bacon chunk, thyme, red pepper flakes, parsley, pollock, and potatoes to the cooker and stir well.

Close and lock the lid of the cooker.

STOVETOP: Place the cooker over high heat, and bring it to high pressure. Once high pressure is reached, reduce the heat as much as possible while retaining the high-pressure level. Cook for 18 minutes. Then take the pot off the heat and allow it to return to normal pressure naturally. Remove the lid, tilting it away from you, to allow the steam to escape.

OR

ELECTRIC: Set the machine to cook at high pressure for 20 minutes. After 20 minutes, unplug the pot so that it does not go into warming mode. Allow the pressure to return to normal naturally. Remove the lid, tilting it away from you, to allow the steam to escape.

NOTE Most supermarkets still display fish on chipped ice in a case, rather than prepackaging it, and they should. Fish should be kept at an even lower temperature than meat. Fish fillets or steaks should look bright, lustrous, and moist, with no signs of discoloration or drying.

Remove and discard the bay leaf and bacon chunk. Add the striped bass and cod to the cooker, and bring to a simmer over medium heat or use the browning function of an electric cooker. Cover the cooker without locking the lid in place, and turn off the heat. Allow the fish to sit in the hot liquid for 5 minutes, or until cooked through.

While the fish is cooking, toast the bread slices and rub each with some of the reserved bacon grease. To serve, ladle the muddle into low bowls and top each with a slice of toast. Sprinkle each bowl with some of the reserved bacon. Serve immediately.

Oyster Gumbo Z'herbes

Oyster gumbo is a hearty seafood entrée for a cold night. This vibrantly flavored version of the Louisiana classic is loaded with healthful greens and thickened with both fresh okra and filé powder, made by grinding sassafras root. Because of this gumbo's Southern heritage, I like to serve it with cornbread.

SERVES **6 to 8**

SIZE **6-quart or larger pressure cooker**

TIME **7 to 9 minutes at high pressure with quick pressure release**

The gumbo can be prepared up to 2 days in advance and refrigerated, tightly covered. Reheat it over low heat, stirring occasionally. Do not cook the oysters or add them to the gumbo until just prior to serving.

2 pints fresh oysters

½ cup vegetable oil or strained bacon grease, divided

¼ cup all-purpose flour

1 large onion, chopped

4 celery ribs, chopped

2 small green bell peppers, seeds and ribs removed, chopped

2 small turnips, peeled and chopped

8 scallions, white parts and 5 inches of green tops, chopped

4 garlic cloves, minced

4 cups firmly packed chopped fresh greens, some combination of collard greens, turnip greens, mustard greens, kale, spinach, escarole, or Swiss chard

4 teaspoons fresh thyme leaves

2 teaspoons filé powder

5 cups Seafood Stock (page 19) or purchased stock

1 tablespoon Worcestershire sauce

3 tablespoons chopped fresh parsley

2 bay leaves

½ pound fresh okra, trimmed and sliced (about 2 cups)

Salt and freshly ground black pepper to taste

Hot red pepper sauce to taste

3 to 4 cups hot cooked rice for serving

GARNISH

½ cup sliced scallion greens

Preheat the oven to 450°F. Drain the oysters, reserving the liquor. Strain the oyster liquor through a sieve lined with a double layer of cheesecloth or a paper coffee filter. Refrigerate the oysters and liquor separately.

Combine 6 tablespoons of the oil and the flour in an ovenproof pan. Bake the roux for 20 to 30 minutes, or until walnut brown, stirring occasionally.

Remove the pan from the oven and scrape the mixture into the pressure cooker. Add the onion, celery, green pepper, turnips, scallions, and garlic. Cook over medium heat or use the browning function of an electric cooker for 3 minutes, or until the onion is translucent. Add the greens and cook for 3 minutes, or until the greens wilt. Stir in the thyme and filé powder. Whisk in the stock gradually; then add the Worcestershire sauce, parsley, and bay leaves.

Close and lock the lid of the cooker.

STOVETOP: Place the cooker over high heat, and bring it to high pressure. Once high pressure is reached, reduce the heat as much as possible while retaining the high-pressure level. Cook for 7 minutes. Then take the pot off the heat and quick release the pressure according to the instructions provided by the manufacturer. Remove the lid, tilting it away from you, to allow the steam to escape.

OR

ELECTRIC: Set the machine to cook at high pressure for 9 minutes. After 9 minutes, unplug the pot so that it does not go into warming mode. Quick release the pressure according to the instructions provided by the manufacturer. Remove the lid, tilting it away from you, to allow the steam to escape.

While the soup base cooks, heat the remaining oil in a skillet over medium heat. Add the okra, and cook, stirring frequently, for 3 to 4 minutes, or until the okra is crisp-tender. Once the pressure is released on the cooker, add the okra to the gumbo, and simmer for 2 minutes over medium heat or use the browning function of an electric cooker. Remove and discard the bay leaves.

Place the oysters and the strained liquor in a deep skillet over low heat. Heat the oysters until the liquor begins to come to a simmer and the edges of the oysters are curled. Do not allow them to boil, or they will become rubbery.

Pour the oysters and their liquor into the cooker. Season to taste with salt, pepper, and hot red pepper sauce.

To serve, place ½ cup of rice into the bottom of each bowl. Ladle the gumbo over the top. Sprinkle each serving with scallion greens.

NOTE Roux, pronounced *roo*, as in kangaroo, is a mixture of fat and flour used as a thickening agent for soups and sauces. The first step in making roux is to cook the flour, so that the dish doesn't taste like raw flour. For white sauces, this is done over low heat, and butterfat is used. Many Creole and Cajun dishes, such as gumbo, use a fuller-flavored brown roux, made with oil or drippings and cooked until it turns a deep brown. Dark roux gives dishes an almost nutty flavor.

VARIATION

★ **Sausage and Oyster Gumbo:** Add ½ pound sliced Andouille or other spicy sausage to the pressure cooker with the vegetables.

Seafood Chili Blanco

Seafood is a natural for the robust seasoning of a traditional chili with beans, and this is one of my favorite renditions. There are no tomatoes, but don't let the pale color of this dish fool you. There's a lot of chile pepper power in the quickly cooked base.

SERVES **4 to 6**

SIZE **6-quart or larger pressure cooker**

TIME **6 to 7 minutes at high pressure; then allow the pressure to release naturally**

The pressure-cooked base can be prepared up to 2 days in advance and refrigerated, tightly covered. Reheat it in a saucepan over low heat until it simmers, and then cook the seafood.

½ pound dried cannellini or navy beans
3 tablespoons olive oil
1 medium yellow onion, diced
3 garlic cloves, minced
1 or 2 jalapeño or serrano chiles, seeds and ribs removed, finely chopped
2 celery ribs, diced
1 leek, white and light green parts, thinly sliced and rinsed well
1 green bell pepper, seeds and ribs removed, chopped
1 red bell pepper, seeds and ribs removed, chopped
2 tablespoons ground cumin
2 teaspoons dried oregano
1 tablespoon chopped chipotle chile in adobo sauce
1 tablespoon adobo sauce
1 (12-ounce) can or bottle of lager beer

3 cups Seafood Stock (page 19) or purchased stock
¾ pound jumbo (21 to 25 per pound) raw shrimp, peeled and deveined
¾ pound bay scallops
½ pound thick white-fleshed fish fillets such as cod, halibut, monkfish, or swordfish, cut into 1-inch cubes
½ cup chopped fresh cilantro
Juice of 1 lime
Salt and freshly ground black pepper to taste
2 to 3 cups hot cooked brown or white rice for serving

GARNISH
½ cup chopped scallion
½ cup grated Monterey Jack cheese
½ cup sour cream
1 cup diced avocado

Rinse the beans in a colander and place them in a mixing bowl covered with cold salted water. Allow the beans to soak for a minimum of 6 hours, or overnight. Or place the beans into a saucepan of salted water and bring to a boil over high heat. Boil 1 minute. Turn off the heat, cover the pan, and soak the beans for 1 hour. After using either of these soaking methods, drain the beans, discard the soaking water, and cook or refrigerate the beans as soon as possible.

Heat the oil in the cooker over medium-high heat or use the browning function of an electric cooker. Add the onion, garlic, chiles, celery, leek, green pepper, and red pepper. Cook, stirring frequently, for 3 minutes, or until the onion is translucent. Stir in the ground cumin and oregano, and cook for 1 minute, stirring constantly. Stir in the beans, chipotle chile, adobo sauce, beer, and stock.

Close and lock the lid of the cooker.

STOVETOP: Place the cooker over high heat, and bring it to high pressure. Once high pressure is reached, reduce the heat as much as possible while retaining the high-pressure level. Cook for 6 minutes. Then take the pot off the heat and allow it to return to normal pressure naturally. Remove the lid, tilting it away from you, to allow the steam to escape.

OR

ELECTRIC: Set the machine to cook at high pressure for 7 minutes. After 7 minutes, unplug the pot so that it does not go into warming mode. Allow the pressure to return to normal naturally. Remove the lid, tilting it away from you, to allow the steam to escape.

Add the shrimp, scallops, and fish to the cooker, and bring to a simmer over medium heat or use the browning function of an electric cooker. Cover the cooker, without locking the lid in place, and turn off the heat. Allow the mixture to sit in the hot liquid for 5 minutes, or until it is cooked through. Stir in the cilantro and lime juice. Season to taste with salt and pepper. Serve hot on top of rice, passing around the garnishes separately.

NOTE What really matters, when you're buying shrimp, is the number of shrimp per pound. This, in shrimp lingo, is called the "count." It's what you should look for, and if the count is not shown on the price tag, ask the person behind the counter. Ignore names such as Jumbo and Colossal; they're totally misleading. In my opinion, shrimp counts that are more than 26 to 30 per pound are too much work for not enough flesh, and it's best to save the huge ones that are a few ounces each for grilling or broiling.

VARIATION

★ **Chicken Chili Blanco:** Substitute 2 pounds boneless, skinless chicken breast halves, cut into 1-inch cubes, for the shrimp, scallops, and fish. Substitute Chicken Stock (page 15) for the seafood stock. While the beans are cooking, heat 2 tablespoons of olive oil in a skillet, and cook the chicken over medium-high heat for 2 minutes. Add the chicken to the cooker when the beans are done, and simmer the mixture, uncovered, for 5 minutes.

Southwestern Shrimp and Pinto Beans

Tender shrimp, poached in a bean stew flavored with garlic and spices, make this a wonderfully vibrant dish, and the level of spice can be adjusted to personal preference. Serve it with some Mexican Brown Rice (page 202) and some pico de gallo relish.

SERVES **4 to 6**

SIZE **6-quart or larger pressure cooker**

TIME **6 to 8 minutes at high pressure; then allow the pressure to release naturally**

The pressure-cooked base can be prepared up to 2 days in advance and refrigerated, tightly covered. Reheat it in a saucepan over low heat until it simmers, and then cook the shrimp.

¾ pound dried red kidney beans
¼ pound bulk raw chorizo sausage
2 medium onions, diced
5 garlic cloves, minced
2 jalapeño or serrano chiles, seeds and ribs removed, finely chopped
1 tablespoon paprika
1 tablespoon ground cumin
2 medium tomatoes, cored, seeded, and diced

2½ cups Seafood Stock (page 19) or purchased stock
2 tablespoons chopped fresh oregano
1 tablespoon fresh thyme leaves
1½ pounds extra-large (16 to 20 per pound) raw shrimp, peeled and deveined
3 tablespoons chopped fresh cilantro
Salt and freshly ground black pepper to taste

Rinse the beans in a colander and place them in a mixing bowl covered with cold salted water. Allow the beans to soak for a minimum of 6 hours, or overnight. Or place the beans into a saucepan of salted water and bring to a boil over high heat. Boil 1 minute. Turn off the heat, cover the pan, and soak the beans for 1 hour. After using either of these soaking methods, drain the beans, discard the soaking water, and cook or refrigerate the beans as soon as possible.

Heat the cooker over medium-high heat or use the browning function of an electric cooker. Crumble the sausage into the cooker, and cook, stirring frequently, for 3 minutes, or until the sausage browns. Add the onions, garlic, and chiles to the cooker, and cook, stirring frequently, for 3 minutes, or until the onions are translucent. Reduce the heat to low, and stir in the paprika and cumin. Cook for 1 minute, stirring constantly. Add the beans, tomatoes, stock, oregano, and thyme to the cooker.

Close and lock the lid of the cooker.

STOVETOP: Place the cooker over high heat, and bring it to high pressure. Once high pressure is reached, reduce the heat as much as possible while retaining the high-pressure level. Cook for 6 minutes. Then take the pot off the heat and allow it to return to normal pressure naturally. Remove the lid, tilting it away from, you to allow the steam to escape.

OR

ELECTRIC: Set the machine to cook at high pressure for 8 minutes. After 8 minutes, unplug the pot so that it does not go into warming mode. Allow the pressure to return to normal naturally. Remove the lid, tilting it away from you, to allow the steam to escape.

Add the shrimp to the cooker, and bring to a simmer over medium heat or use the browning function of an electric cooker. Cover the cooker, without locking the lid in place, and turn off the heat. Allow the shrimp to sit in the hot liquid for 5 minutes, or until cooked through. Stir in the cilantro, and season to taste with salt and pepper. Serve hot.

NOTE To devein a shrimp, you need to remove the black vein, actually the intestinal tract, from the shrimp. The first step is the easy part: pull off the shell. But do save and freeze your shrimp shells, because they're great for making stock. To devein the shrimp, hold it curved side up, so you can see the vein in its back. Cut a slit about halfway through the shrimp, with the tip of a sharp paring knife, and pull out the black vein. Depending on where the shrimp was caught, it may hardly need this process.

Shrimp Creole

Scallions, green bell pepper, and celery are the "holy trinity" of ingredients in Creole cooking. Above and beyond this trio, the cooks of Louisiana are not shy about including garlic and chiles. Shrimp Creole is a wonderful dish for a buffet party, because it does not require the use of a knife.

SERVES **6 to 8**

SIZE **6-quart or larger pressure cooker**

TIME **5 to 6 minutes at high pressure with quick pressure release**

> The pressure-cooked base can be prepared up to 2 days in advance and refrigerated, tightly covered. Reheat it in a saucepan over low heat until it simmers, and then cook the shrimp.

- 3 tablespoons olive oil
- 2 bunches of scallions, white parts and 4 inches of green tops, thickly sliced
- 6 garlic cloves, minced
- 1 large green bell pepper, seeds and ribs removed, diced
- 2 celery ribs, diced
- 1 jalapeño or serrano chile, seeds and ribs removed, chopped
  Salt and freshly ground black pepper to taste
- 2 tablespoons tomato paste
- 1 tablespoon paprika
- 1 teaspoon dried oregano
- 1 (28-ounce) can diced tomatoes, undrained

- 1 cup Seafood Stock (page 19) or purchased stock
- 2 tablespoons Worcestershire sauce
- 2 tablespoons chopped fresh parsley
- 2 teaspoons fresh thyme leaves
- 2 bay leaves
- 2 pounds extra-large (16 to 20 per pound) raw shrimp, peeled and deveined
- 3 to 4 cups hot cooked rice for serving

GARNISH
½ cup chopped scallions

Heat the oil in the cooker over medium-high heat or use the browning function of an electric cooker. Add the scallions, garlic, bell pepper, celery, and chile, and season to taste with salt and pepper. Cook, stirring often, for 3 minutes, or until the onion is translucent. Stir in the tomato paste, paprika, and oregano, and cook for 1 minute, stirring constantly. Add the tomatoes, stock, Worcestershire sauce, parsley, thyme, and bay leaves, and stir well.

Close and lock the lid of the cooker.

STOVETOP: Place the cooker over high heat, and bring it to high pressure. Once high pressure is reached, reduce the heat as much as possible while retaining the high-pressure level. Cook for 5 minutes. Then take the pot off the heat, and quick release the pressure according to the instructions provided by the manufacturer. Remove the lid, tilting it away from you, to allow the steam to escape.

—OR—

ELECTRIC: Set the machine to cook at high pressure for 6 minutes. After 6 minutes, unplug the pot so that it does not go into warming mode. Quick release the pressure according to the instructions provided by the manufacturer. Remove the lid, tilting it away from you, to allow the steam to escape.

Remove and discard the bay leaves. Add the shrimp to the cooker, and bring to a simmer over medium heat or use the browning function of an electric cooker. Cover the cooker without locking the lid in place, and turn off the heat. Allow the shrimp to sit in the hot liquid for 5 minutes, or until cooked through. Season to taste with salt and pepper, and serve hot on top of rice. Garnish each serving with a sprinkling of scallions.

VARIATION

★ **Fish Creole:** Substitute 2 pounds of thick, firm-fleshed, white fish fillets, such as cod or halibut, for the shrimp.

Moroccan Chicken with
Olives and Preserved Lemons, page 90

CHAPTER 4

Poultry

The famed nineteenth-century French gastronome Jean Anthelme Brillat-Savarin once wrote, "Poultry is for the cook what canvas is for the painter." Its inherently mild flavor takes to myriad methods of seasoning, and it is relatively quick to cook—especially with a pressure cooker at your side. And it's now the centerpiece of the American diet; American consumption averages more than 90 pounds of poultry per person—a figure that has almost doubled since 1970.

There's not a cuisine around the world that doesn't include a repertoire of poultry recipes, and so there is a great range of recipes in this chapter.

Cooking Poultry

When you are buying packaged chicken, look for containers that do not have an accumulation of liquid in the bottom. This could be a sign that the chicken has been frozen and thawed. Chicken should be stored in the coldest part of the refrigerator (40°F or below) in its original packaging and used within 2 or 3 days. Always put chicken in another plastic bag to ensure that any juices will not leak out of the packaging and spread to other fresh food in the refrigerator. When the chicken is removed from the wrapper, it should have absolutely no odor. If it has any off smells, take it back to the supermarket if it's before the expiration date, or discard it if it's after that date or came out of the freezer.

Illness-causing bacteria such as salmonella can grow in raw chicken. Many recipes call for seasoning raw chicken with salt and pepper before it is cooked. Touching other dishes or the pepper mill after you've handled raw chicken can cause cross-contamination. To minimize the risk, mix the necessary amount of salt and pepper in a small bowl so that you can move between the seasoning bowl and the chicken without touching anything else. Discard any leftover seasoning mix.

In addition to liking chicken seasoned, we also like the textural variation of the crispy skin and the succulent meat. And you can have that even though the poultry is being cooked in the closed environment of the pressure cooker with liquid. The pieces can be broiled either before or after the poultry is cooked.

If you're only browning the skin to add aesthetic richness to the sauce, broil it before its trip to the pressure cooker. But if you want to have the skin crispy, it should be browned after it is cooked.

COOKING TIMES (IN MINUTES)
FOR POULTRY IN THE PRESSURE COOKER

	STOVETOP	ELECTRIC	RELEASE METHOD
CHICKEN			
BREAST, BONELESS	1	2	NATURAL
BREAST, WITH BONE	10	12	NATURAL
GROUND	5	6	QUICK
LEG	12	14	NATURAL
THIGH, BONELESS	8	10	NATURAL
THIGH, WITH BONE	12	14	NATURAL
WHOLE, 4-POUND	25	30	NATURAL
WINGS	6	7	QUICK
TURKEY			
BREAST, BONE IN	25	30	NATURAL
BREAST, BONELESS	20	23	NATURAL
DRUMSTICKS	18	20	NATURAL
GROUND	5	7	QUICK
THIGHS	18	20	NATURAL
WINGS	15	18	NATURAL
OTHER			
CORNISH HEN	12	14	NATURAL
DUCK, LEG QUARTERS	30	35	NATURAL

Moroccan Chicken with Olives
and Preserved Lemons

Moroccan cuisine is known for its aromatic qualities and bright, clean flavors, and this chicken dish is emblematic of that style. The chicken is rendered meltingly tender in the pressure cooker, and the spices in the stock meld with the briny flavors from the olives and preserved lemons. Serve this with Quinoa Tabbouleh (page 212).

SERVES **4 to 6**

SIZE **6-quart or larger pressure cooker**

TIME **12 to 14 minutes at high pressure; then allow the pressure to release naturally**

The dish can be prepared up to 2 days in advance and refrigerated, tightly covered. Reheat it, covered, in a 350°F oven for 20 to 25 minutes, or until hot.

4 to 6 bone-in, skin-on chicken pieces of your choice (breasts cut in half, thighs, legs)
Salt and freshly ground black pepper to taste
2 tablespoons olive oil
1 large onion, diced
1 large carrot, thickly sliced
4 garlic cloves, minced
1 tablespoon ground coriander
1 tablespoon ground cumin
2 teaspoons ground ginger

1 cup Chicken Stock (page 15) or purchased stock
½ cup roughly chopped pitted green olives
2 small preserved lemons, rinsed well and thinly sliced with flesh discarded
2 to 3 cups hot couscous for serving

GARNISH

3 tablespoons chopped fresh cilantro

Preheat the oven broiler and line a broiler pan with heavy-duty aluminum foil. Sprinkle the chicken with salt and pepper. Broil the chicken pieces 6 inches away from the broiler element for 3 minutes on each side, or until browned. Set aside.

Heat the oil in the cooker over medium-high heat or use the browning function of an electric cooker. Add the onion, carrot, and garlic and cook, stirring frequently, for 3 minutes, or until the onion is translucent. Stir in the coriander, cumin, and ginger, and cook for 1 minute, stirring constantly. Stir in the stock. Add the chicken pieces to the cooker skin side down.

Close and lock the lid of the cooker.

STOVETOP: Place the cooker over high heat, and bring it to high pressure. Once high pressure is reached, reduce the heat as much as possible while retaining the high-pressure level. Cook for 12 minutes. Then take the pot off the heat and allow it to return to normal pressure naturally. Remove the lid, tilting it away from you, to allow the steam to escape.

OR

ELECTRIC: Set the machine to cook at high pressure for 14 minutes. After 14 minutes, unplug the pot so that it does not go into warming mode. Allow the pressure to return to normal naturally. Remove the lid, tilting it away from you, to allow the steam to escape.

Stir in the olives and slices of preserved lemon, and bring to a boil over medium heat or use the browning function of an electric cooker. Reduce the heat to low and simmer for 5 minutes. Season to taste with salt and pepper, and serve with couscous. Sprinkle each serving with some chopped cilantro.

NOTE Preserved lemons are an essential part of Moroccan cooking and are used in many tagine recipes. They're getting easier to find in supermarkets and online, but if you want to make them yourself, the traditional method takes a few weeks. However, there is a quicker way. Trim the ends off four lemons and cut each lemon into 8 long wedges. Toss the lemons with ¼ cup kosher salt and arrange them close together in a glass or porcelain baking dish. Add enough freshly squeezed lemon juice to cover them, and bake them, covered with foil, at 200°F for 4 hours, stirring them occasionally. After the lemons are cool, transfer them to a container and refrigerate them. They last for at least 6 months.

Chicken Provençal

This dish, hailing from sunny Southern France, is similar to that region's famed bouillabaisse, but it is made with chicken. The broth remains thin, but it's absorbed by thick slices of toast. A garlicky French aïoli tops the dish and adds to its richness.

SERVES **4 to 6**

SIZE **6-quart or larger pressure cooker**

TIME **12 to 14 minutes at high pressure; then allow the pressure to release naturally**

The dish can be prepared up to 2 days in advance and refrigerated, tightly covered. Reheat it, covered, in a 350°F oven for 20 to 25 minutes, or until hot. The bread and sauce can be prepared at the same time. Refrigerate the sauce and keep the toasted bread at room temperature in an airtight container.

CHICKEN

- 4 to 6 bone-in, skin-on chicken pieces of your choice (breasts cut in half, thighs, legs)
  Salt and freshly ground black pepper to taste
- 1 juice orange
- 2 tablespoons olive oil
- 1 large onion, diced
- 3 garlic cloves, minced
- ¾ cup dry white wine
- 2 cups Chicken Stock (page 15) or purchased stock
- 1 large pinch saffron
- 1 (14.5-ounce) can diced tomatoes, undrained
- 1 carrot, thickly sliced
- 1 parsnip, thickly sliced
- ½ fennel bulb, stalks and fronds removed, cored, and thickly sliced
- 3 tablespoons chopped fresh parsley
- 1 tablespoon fresh thyme leaves
- 1 bay leaf
  Salt and freshly ground black pepper to taste
  Vegetable oil spray
- 12 (¾-inch) slices French or Italian bread
- ½ cup freshly grated Parmesan cheese

SAUCE

- 2 garlic cloves, minced
- ½ teaspoon salt
- 1 tablespoon freshly squeezed lemon juice
- 1 teaspoon Dijon mustard
- ½ cup fruity olive oil
  Freshly ground black pepper to taste

Preheat the oven broiler and line a broiler pan with heavy-duty aluminum foil. Sprinkle the chicken with salt and pepper. Broil the chicken pieces 6 inches away from the broiler element for 3 minutes on each side, or until the pieces are browned.

Grate the zest from the orange and squeeze out the juice.

Heat the oil in the cooker over medium-high heat or use the browning function of an electric cooker. Add the onion and garlic and cook, stirring frequently, for 3 minutes, or until the onion is translucent. Add the wine, raise the heat to high, and cook for 3 minutes.

Add the orange zest, orange juice, stock, tomatoes, carrot, parsnip, fennel, parsley, thyme, and bay leaf to the cooker. Add the chicken pieces to the cooker skin side down.

Close and lock the lid of the cooker.

STOVETOP: Place the cooker over high heat, and bring it to high pressure. Once high pressure is reached, reduce the heat as much as possible while retaining the high-pressure level. Cook for 12 minutes. Then take the pot off the heat and allow it to return to normal pressure naturally. Remove the lid, tilting it away from you, to allow the steam to escape.

OR

ELECTRIC: Set the machine to cook at high pressure for 14 minutes. After 14 minutes, unplug the pot so that it does not go into warming mode. Allow the pressure to return to normal naturally. Remove the lid, tilting it away from you, to allow the steam to escape.

Remove and discard the bay leaf, and season to taste with salt and pepper.

While the chicken cooks, preheat the oven to 375°F. Cover a baking sheet with aluminum foil and spray the foil with vegetable oil spray. Arrange the bread slices on the baking sheet and sprinkle the bread with Parmesan cheese. Bake the bread for 15 to 18, minutes or until it is golden brown. Remove it from the oven and set it aside.

For the sauce, mash the garlic with the salt into a paste using a mortar and pestle. Combine the egg yolk, lemon juice, and mustard in a small bowl. Whisk together well and then whisk in the oil about 1 teaspoon at a time, whisking constantly. Whisk in the garlic paste and season to taste with pepper. Refrigerate until ready to serve. To serve, place toast slices on the bottom of shallow bowls and arrange chicken on top. Ladle the broth over the chicken and serve immediately, passing around the sauce separately.

NOTE It is true that saffron is the most expensive food in the world, and it has risen in price with all the conflict in the Middle East during the last decade. Iran produces about three-quarters of the world's saffron supply, and it takes the stamens from more than 150,000 crocus plants to make 1 kilo of this prized substance.

VARIATIONS

★ Substitute red wine for the white wine, omit the orange juice and zest, and substitute 2 teaspoons of Italian seasoning for the thyme.

★ You can substitute what I call Cheater's Aïoli for the sauce by mixing the garlic, lemon juice, and mustard into ½ cup of prepared mayonnaise.

Coq au Vin

All cooks need a good chicken in red wine recipe in their repertoire if for no other reason than to serve a hearty red wine with a white meat on a cold winter night. I like this rendition because the bacon gives it a smoky flavor. Serve it with some Cannellini Beans with Tomatoes and Sage (page 229).

SERVES **4 to 6**

SIZE **6-quart or larger pressure cooker**

TIME **6 to 7 minutes at high pressure; then allow the pressure to release naturally**

The dish can be prepared up to 2 days in advance and refrigerated, tightly covered. Reheat it, covered, in a 350°F oven for 20 to 25 minutes, or until hot.

- ¼ pound bacon, cut into 1-inch pieces
- 2 pounds boneless, skinless chicken breasts, cut into 1½-inch cubes
- Salt and freshly ground black pepper to taste
- ¼ cup all-purpose flour
- 1 onion, diced
- 4 garlic cloves, minced
- 2 cups dry red wine
- 2 tablespoons Cognac
- 1 cup Chicken Stock (page 15) or purchased stock

- 6 scallions, white parts and 3 inches of green tops, sliced
- 1 pound small mushrooms, wiped with a damp paper towel and trimmed
- 1 pound small redskin potatoes, scrubbed and halved
- 3 tablespoons chopped fresh parsley
- 1 tablespoon fresh thyme leaves
- 2 bay leaves
- 1 (1-pound) package frozen pearl onions, thawed and drained

Cook the bacon in the cooker over medium-high heat or use the browning function of an electric cooker for 5 to 7 minutes, or until crisp. Remove the bacon from the cooker with a slotted spoon and drain on paper towels. Set it aside.

Pat the chicken cubes dry with paper towels. Sprinkle the cubes with salt, pepper, and flour. Brown the cubes on both sides in the bacon grease and set them aside. Add the onion and garlic to the cooker and cook, stirring frequently, for 3 minutes, or until the onion is translucent. Add the wine and Cognac, and boil for 3 minutes.

Return the chicken and bacon to the cooker, and add the stock, scallions, mushrooms, potatoes, parsley, thyme, and bay leaves. Stir well.

Close and lock the lid of the cooker.

STOVETOP: Place the cooker over high heat, and bring it to high pressure. Once high pressure is reached, reduce the heat as much as possible while retaining the high-pressure level. Cook for 6 minutes. Then take the pot off the heat and allow it to return to normal pressure naturally. Remove the lid, tilting it away from you, to allow the steam to escape.

—OR—

ELECTRIC: Set the machine to cook at high pressure for 7 minutes. After 7 minutes, unplug the pot so that it does not go into warming mode. Allow the pressure to return to normal naturally. Remove the lid, tilting it away from you, to allow the steam to escape.

Remove and discard the bay leaves, and add the onions to the cooker. Simmer over medium heat or use the browning function of an electric cooker for 3 minutes. Then season to taste with salt and pepper, and serve immediately.

NOTE I no longer subscribe to the philosophy of not cooking with a wine that I wouldn't drink. I've discovered that the best way to buy "cooking wines"—both red and white—is in boxes. The box is equivalent to four bottles, and because the wine is dispensed through a spigot, the wine never touches air, and so it remains in prime condition for months.

Curried Chicken with Dried Currants
and Toasted Almonds

This flavor-filled dish, aromatic from curry and dotted with succulent dried currants, is actually American and dates from the Colonial period, when trade with southern Asia began. The toasted almonds on top add textural interest, and the dish traditionally is served over rice so that every drop of sauce can be enjoyed.

SERVES **4 to 6**

SIZE **6-quart or larger pressure cooker**

TIME **12 to 14 minutes at high pressure; then allow the pressure to release naturally**

The dish can be prepared up to 2 days in advance and refrigerated, tightly covered. Reheat it, covered, in a 350°F oven for 20 to 25 minutes, or until hot.

4 to 6 bone-in, skin-on chicken pieces of your choice (breasts cut in half, thighs, legs)
Salt and freshly ground black pepper to taste
2 tablespoons olive oil
1 large onion, diced
3 garlic cloves, minced
1 red bell pepper, seeds and ribs removed, thickly sliced
2 tablespoons curry powder
½ teaspoon ground ginger
1 tablespoon fresh thyme leaves

1 (14.5-ounce) can diced tomatoes, undrained
¼ cup dry sherry
1¼ cups Chicken Stock (page 15) or purchased stock
⅔ cup dried currants
2 tablespoons unsalted butter
½ cup slivered blanched almonds
1 tablespoon cornstarch
2 to 3 cups hot cooked rice for serving

GARNISH
3 tablespoons chopped fresh cilantro or parsley

Preheat the oven broiler and line a broiler pan with heavy-duty aluminum foil. Sprinkle the chicken with salt and pepper. Broil the chicken pieces 6 inches away from the broiler element for 3 minutes on each side, or until browned. Set aside.

Heat the oil in the cooker over medium-high heat or use the browning function of an electric cooker. Add the onion, garlic, and red bell pepper to the cooker and cook, stirring frequently, for 3 minutes, or until onion is translucent. Add the curry powder, ginger, and thyme to the cooker and cook for 1 minute, stirring constantly. Stir in the tomatoes, sherry, stock, and currants. Add the chicken pieces to the cooker skin side down.

Close and lock the lid of the cooker.

STOVETOP: Place the cooker over high heat, and bring it to high pressure. Once high pressure is reached, reduce the heat as much as possible while retaining the high-pressure level. Cook for 12 minutes. Then take the pot off the heat and allow it to return to normal pressure naturally. Remove the lid, tilting it away from you, to allow the steam to escape.

OR

ELECTRIC: Set the machine to cook at high pressure for 14 minutes. After 14 minutes, unplug the pot so that it does not go into warming mode. Allow the pressure to return to normal naturally. Remove the lid, tilting it away from you, to allow the steam to escape.

While the chicken cooks, heat the butter in a small skillet over medium heat. Add the almonds and cook for 3 to 5 minutes, stirring frequently, or until the almonds are brown.

Combine the cornstarch with 2 tablespoons of cold water in a small cup, stirring well to dissolve the cornstarch. Stir the mixture into the cooker, and bring to a boil over high heat or use the browning function of an electric cooker. Cook for 1 minute, or until the sauce thickens.

Season the chicken to taste with salt and pepper, and serve immediately over rice, sprinkling each serving with toasted almonds and cilantro.

NOTE Sherry and vermouth can be stored for months at room temperature after they're opened, but red and white wine soon turn to vinegar even if refrigerated. You can preserve them for future use in either of two ways: freeze them right out of the bottle or reduce and then freeze them—great for marinades later on.

VARIATION

★ Substitute 1½ pounds boneless pork loin for the chicken.

Chinese Red-Cooked Chicken with Plums

Red-cooking is the name given to braising in northern regional Chinese cooking, and although the addition of plums in this recipe is nontraditional, I love the fruity flavor they bring to the luscious sauce. Serve it over white or brown rice with some stir-fried bok choy on the side.

SERVES **4 to 6**

SIZE **6-quart or larger pressure cooker**

TIME **12 to 14 minutes at high pressure; then allow the pressure to release naturally**

The chicken can be cooked, up to the final broiling, 2 days in advance and refrigerated, tightly covered. Reheat it over low heat until it is hot and the sauce is simmering before broiling it.

1 tablespoon toasted sesame oil
1 tablespoon vegetable oil
½ small red onion, diced
3 garlic cloves, minced
3 tablespoons minced fresh ginger
1 teaspoon Chinese five-spice powder
½ cup dry sherry or Madeira
1½ cups Chicken Stock (page 15) or purchased stock
¼ cup soy sauce
¼ cup hoisin sauce
4 to 6 bone-in, skin-on chicken pieces of your choice (breasts cut in half, thighs, legs)
4 ripe plums, stoned and sliced
1½ tablespoons cornstarch

Heat the sesame oil and vegetable oil in the cooker over medium-high heat or use the browning function of an electric cooker. Add the onion, garlic, and ginger, and cook, stirring frequently, for 3 minutes, or until the onion is translucent. Add the five-spice powder and cook for 30 seconds, stirring constantly. Stir in the sherry and cook for 2 minutes. Stir in the stock, soy sauce, and hoisin sauce. Add the chicken pieces to the cooker skin side down.

Close and lock the lid of the cooker.

STOVETOP: Place the cooker over high heat, and bring it to high pressure. Once high pressure is reached, reduce the heat as much as possible while retaining the high-pressure level. Cook for 12 minutes. Then take the pot off the heat and allow it to return to normal pressure naturally. Remove the lid, tilting it away from you, to allow the steam to escape.

OR

ELECTRIC: Set the machine to cook at high pressure for 14 minutes. After 14 minutes, unplug the pot so that it does not go into warming mode. Allow the pressure to return to normal naturally. Remove the lid, tilting it away from you, to allow the steam to escape.

NOTE If you're trying to reduce the amount of saturated fat in your diet, discard the chicken skin once the chicken is cooked and don't broil it. But do cook the chicken pieces with the skin attached. It adds flavor to the sauce and helps retain moisture in the meat.

Preheat the oven broiler and line a broiler pan with heavy-duty aluminum foil. Remove the chicken from the cooker and transfer the pieces skin side up to the prepared pan. Tilt the cooker to spoon off as much fat as possible.

Add the plums to the cooker. Mix the cornstarch with 2 tablespoons of cold water in a small cup and stir well to dissolve the cornstarch powder. Bring the sauce to a boil over medium-high heat or use the browning function of an electric cooker. Stir in the cornstarch mixture and simmer for 5 minutes, or until the sauce is thickened and the plum slices are tender.

Broil the chicken 8 inches away from the broiler element for 2 minutes, or until the skin is crisp and browned. Serve immediately, spooning the sauce over the chicken.

Tarragon Chicken

The late and great James Beard once wrote that "chicken has no better friend than tarragon," and I agree; it's a classic in French bistros, and this dish will become a frequent visitor at your table, too. Serve it with White Vegetable Puree (page 253) and a tossed salad.

SERVES **4 to 6**

SIZE **6-quart or larger pressure cooker**

TIME **12 to 14 minutes at high pressure; then allow the pressure to release naturally**

The chicken can be cooked, up to the final broiling, 2 days in advance and refrigerated, tightly covered. Reheat it over low heat until it is hot and the sauce is simmering before broiling it.

2 tablespoons unsalted butter
1 tablespoon olive oil
5 shallots, minced
3 garlic cloves, minced
¾ cup dry white wine
1½ cups Chicken Stock (page 15) or purchased stock
½ cup firmly packed chopped fresh tarragon

2 tablespoons chopped fresh parsley
Salt and freshly ground black pepper to taste
4 to 6 bone-in, skin-on chicken pieces of your choice (breasts cut in half, thighs, legs)
1½ tablespoons cornstarch

Heat the butter and oil in the cooker over medium-high heat or use the browning function of an electric cooker. Add the shallots and garlic, and cook, stirring frequently, for 3 minutes, or until the shallots are translucent. Add the wine to the cooker and boil for 3 minutes. Stir in the chicken stock, tarragon, and parsley. Season to taste with salt and pepper. Add the chicken pieces to the cooker skin side down.

Close and lock the lid of the cooker.

STOVETOP: Place the cooker over high heat, and bring it to high pressure. Once high pressure is reached, reduce the heat as much as possible while retaining the high-pressure level. Cook for 12 minutes. Then take the pot off the heat and allow it to return to normal pressure naturally. Remove the lid, tilting it away from you, to allow the steam to escape.

OR

ELECTRIC: Set the machine to cook at high pressure for 14 minutes. After 14 minutes, unplug the pot so that it does not go into warming mode. Allow the pressure to return to normal naturally. Remove the lid, tilting it away from you, to allow the steam to escape.

NOTE When sautéing food you should always use a mixture of butter and oil, or all oil. The dairy solids in butter begin to burn at a relatively low temperature, but mixing butter with oil raises the temperature sufficiently to allow for sautéing.

Preheat the oven broiler and line a broiler pan with heavy-duty aluminum foil. Remove the chicken from the cooker and transfer the pieces skin side up to the prepared pan. Tilt the cooker to spoon off as much fat as possible.

Mix the cornstarch with 2 tablespoons of cold water in a small cup and stir well to dissolve the cornstarch. Bring the sauce to a boil over medium-high heat or use the browning function of an electric cooker. Stir in the cornstarch mixture and simmer for 1 minute, or until the sauce thickens.

Broil the chicken 8 inches away from the broiler element for 2 minutes, or until the skin is crisp and browned. Serve immediately, spooning the sauce over the chicken.

Korean Chicken Wings

I first encountered this supercrispy deliciousness at Federal Donuts in Philadelphia. Yes, that's right. Chicken at a doughnut shop, and Federal is not alone. Chicken that you eat before doughnuts is showing up as a trend at chic shops and restaurants all over the country. Pressure-cooking the wings before frying them gives them an enticing innate flavor that's perfect with the exterior crunch.

SERVES **4 to 6**

SIZE **6-quart or larger pressure cooker**

TIME **6 to 7 minutes at high pressure with quick pressure release**

The wings can be pressure-cooked up to 2 days in advance and refrigerated, and the batter can be made at the same time. They are best fried just before serving.

12 whole chicken wings, cut into 2 parts with tips reserved for making stock
3 tablespoons sliced fresh ginger
5 garlic cloves, sliced
3 scallions, white parts and 4 inches of green tops, cut into 1-inch lengths
¼ cup Korean or Japanese soy sauce

1 tablespoon kosher salt
¾ cup cornstarch
¾ teaspoon baking powder
⅓ cup all-purpose flour
Freshly ground black pepper to taste
¼ cup vodka
1 quart vegetable oil for frying

GARNISH
¼ cup chopped scallions
Sweet Thai chile sauce for serving

Place the wings in the pressure cooker and add the ginger, garlic, scallions, soy sauce, and 1 cup of water.

Close and lock the lid of the cooker.

STOVETOP: Place the cooker over high heat, and bring it to high pressure. Once high pressure is reached, reduce the heat as much as possible while retaining the high-pressure level. Cook for 6 minutes. Then take the pot off the heat and quick release the pressure according to the instructions provided by the manufacturer. Remove the lid, tilting it away from you, to allow the steam to escape.

OR

ELECTRIC: Set the machine to cook at high pressure for 7 minutes. After 7 minutes, unplug the pot so that it does not go into warming mode. Quick release the pressure according to the instructions provided by the manufacturer. Remove the lid, tilting it away from you, to allow the steam to escape.

Remove the wings from the cooker and arrange them on a wire rack. Cool them for 30 minutes at room temperature or refrigerate them for 15 minutes. Strain the cooking liquid, pressing with the back of a spoon on the solids. Pour the liquid into a measuring cup. Allow the liquid to sit, and spoon off as much fat from the top as possible.

Combine the salt, cornstarch, baking powder, flour, and pepper in a mixing bowl. Add the vodka and ¾ cup of the reserved chicken cooking liquid, and whisk until smooth.

Preheat the oven to 150°F, line a baking sheet with aluminum foil, and place a wire cooling rack on top of the foil.

Heat the oil in a wok or saucepan to a temperature of 375°F. Coat each piece of chicken with the batter, shaking it over the bowl to remove any excess. Fry a few pieces of chicken at a time, being careful not to crowd the pan. Fry the wings for 4 to 5 minutes, or until browned and crisp. Remove the wings from the pan with tongs and pat dry with paper towels. Keep the chicken warm in the oven while frying the remaining wings. Serve hot, garnished with scallions, if using. Pass around the sweet chile sauce separately.

NOTE Before finalizing this recipe I tried about a dozen different formulations, ranging from batter made only with cornstarch to one made with club soda. The cornstarch and the addition of baking powder create a light and somewhat bubbly coating, and then there's the vodka. All the alcohol evaporates when the chicken is fried at a high temperature, so don't worry about children eating it. The vodka functions the same way in the chicken batter as it does in pie crust, to keep gluten formation to a minimum.

Korean Chicken Wings, page 102

Turkey Tonnato

This is a riff on the classic refreshing Italian summer dish vitello tonnato, *except that here a lean and quickly cooked turkey breast is substituted for a veal loin, and it is napped with a sauce based on canned tuna. Serve it with Caponata (page 240) and Garbanzo Bean Salad Parmesan (page 227).*

SERVES **4 to 6**

SIZE **6-quart or larger pressure cooker**

TIME **20 to 22 minutes at high pressure; then allow the pressure to release naturally**

> The turkey can be cooked and the sauce can be made up to 2 days in advance and refrigerated, tightly covered.

TURKEY

- 2 tablespoons olive oil
- 1 (2-pound) boneless turkey breast half, with skin still attached
- Salt and freshly ground black pepper to taste
- 1 onion, diced
- 3 garlic cloves, minced
- ¼ cup dry white wine
- 1½ cups Turkey Stock (page 15), Chicken Stock (page 15), or purchased stock
- 5 sprigs fresh parsley
- 3 sprigs fresh thyme
- 2 sprigs fresh rosemary

SAUCE

- 2 (5-ounce) cans light tuna packed in olive oil, not drained
- 1 tablespoon anchovy paste
- 3 tablespoons freshly squeezed lemon juice
- 2 teaspoons grated lemon zest
- ½ cup mayonnaise
- Freshly ground black pepper to taste

GARNISH

- 2 tablespoons capers, drained and rinsed
- 3 tablespoons sliced black oil- or brine-cured olives

Heat the oil in the cooker over medium-high heat or use the browning function of an electric cooker. Sprinkle the turkey with salt and pepper. Brown the skin of the turkey breast well and set it aside. Add the onion and garlic to the cooker and cook, stirring frequently, for 3 minutes, or until the onion is translucent. Add the wine and boil for 2 minutes. Add the stock, parsley, thyme, and rosemary, and return the turkey to the cooker.

Close and lock the lid of the cooker.

STOVETOP: Place the cooker over high heat, and bring it to high pressure. Once high pressure is reached, reduce the heat as much as possible while retaining the high-pressure level. Cook for 20 minutes. Then take the pot off the heat and allow it to return to normal pressure naturally. Remove the lid, tilting it away from you, to allow the steam to escape.

OR

ELECTRIC: Set the machine to cook at high pressure for 22 minutes. After 22 minutes, unplug the pot so that it does not go into warming mode. Allow the pressure to return to normal naturally. Remove the lid, tilting it away from you, to allow the steam to escape.

NOTE What you're left with after preparing this dish is a few cups of incredibly rich turkey stock. Strain it and freeze it and you'll have the best turkey gravy you ever made.

Allow the turkey to cool to room temperature in the broth and then refrigerate it, tightly covered.

While the turkey chills, make the sauce. Combine the tuna, anchovy paste, lemon juice, and lemon zest in a food processor fitted with the steel blade or in a blender. Process until smooth. Scrape the mixture into a bowl, stir in the mayonnaise, and season to taste with pepper, adding more lemon juice as desired. Chill until ready to serve.

To serve, carve the turkey against the grain into thin slices. Spread each slice with some of the sauce and sprinkle each serving with capers and olives.

Turkey Mole

This dark and thick sauce is made with a combination of spices and unsweetened cocoa powder and thickened with peanut butter. It has a depth of flavor that's incredible. Serve the stew with Mexican Brown Rice (page 202) and add a tossed salad or some pico de gallo to round out the meal.

SERVES **4 to 6**

SIZE **6-quart or larger pressure cooker**

TIME **5 to 6 minutes at high pressure with quick pressure release**

> The dish can be prepared up to 2 days in advance and refrigerated, tightly covered. Reheat it, covered, over low heat until hot, stirring occasionally.

1½ pounds boneless skinless turkey breast meat
2 tablespoons olive oil
2 large onions, diced
3 garlic cloves, minced
2 tablespoons chili powder
2 tablespoons unsweetened cocoa powder
2 teaspoons ground cumin
1 teaspoon ground coriander
¼ teaspoon ground cinnamon
1 (14.5-ounce) can diced tomatoes, undrained

1¾ cups Chicken Stock (page 15) or purchased stock
3 tablespoons smooth peanut butter
1 chipotle chile in adobo sauce, finely chopped
2 teaspoons adobo sauce
1 tablespoon cornstarch
Salt and freshly ground black pepper to taste

GARNISH
½ cup coarsely chopped roasted peanuts
½ cup firmly packed cilantro leaves

Trim any visible fat off the turkey and cut it into 1½-inch cubes.

Heat the oil in a cooker over medium-high heat or use the browning function of an electric cooker. Add the onions and garlic, and cook, stirring frequently, for 3 minutes, or until the onions are translucent. Reduce the heat to low and stir in the chili powder, cocoa powder, cumin, coriander, and cinnamon. Cook for 1 minute, stirring constantly. Add the turkey, tomatoes, stock, peanut butter, chipotle chile, and adobo sauce to the cooker and stir well.

Close and lock the lid of the cooker.

STOVETOP: Place the cooker over high heat, and bring it to high pressure. Once high pressure is reached, reduce the heat as much as possible while retaining the high-pressure level. Cook for 5 minutes. Then take the pot off the heat and quick release the pressure according to the instructions provided by the manufacturer. Remove the lid, tilting it away from you, to allow the steam to escape.

OR

ELECTRIC: Set the machine to cook at high pressure for 5 minutes. After 5 minutes, unplug the pot so that it does not go into warming mode. Quick release the pressure according to the instructions provided by the manufacturer. Remove the lid, tilting it away from you, to allow the steam to escape.

Combine the cornstarch with 2 tablespoons of cold water in a small cup, stirring well to dissolve the cornstarch. Stir the mixture into the cooker, and bring to a boil over high heat or use the browning function of an electric cooker. Cook for 1 minute, or until the sauce thickens.

Season to taste with salt and pepper. Serve immediately, sprinkling the dish with the peanuts and the cilantro leaves.

NOTE Mole, a thick and rich sauce made with unsweetened chocolate, dates back to the Aztec empire in Mexico. Legend has it that King Montezuma, thinking that Cortez was a god, served mole at a banquet to receive him. The word *mole* comes from the Nahuatl word *milli*, which means "sauce" or "concoction."

VARIATION

★ **Pork Mole:** Substitute 1½ pounds boneless pork loin, cut into 1-inch cubes, for the turkey. Cook the pork for 8 minutes at high pressure in a stovetop cooker and 9 minutes in an electric cooker, and allow the pressure to release naturally.

Turkey Tamale Pie

This is one of my favorite dishes for a buffet, because the cornbread topping is stunning when the casserole is put on the table. The filling is similar to a chili con carne, and all you need to complete the meal is a tossed salad and some Refried Beans (page 222).

SERVES **4 to 6**

SIZE **6-quart or larger pressure cooker**

TIME **5 to 7 minutes at high pressure with quick pressure release**

The filling can be prepared up to 2 days in advance and refrigerated, tightly covered. Reheat it over low heat until hot before baking.

FILLING

- 2 tablespoons olive oil
- 1 large onion, diced
- 1 large carrot, diced
- 2 celery ribs, diced
- 1 red bell pepper, seeds and ribs removed, chopped
- 1 jalapeño or serrano chile, seeds and ribs removed, finely chopped
- 3 garlic cloves, minced
- 2 tablespoons chili powder
- 1 tablespoon ground cumin
- 1 tablespoon sweet smoked Spanish paprika (pimetón de la vera dulce)
- 1½ pounds ground turkey, preferably dark meat
- 1 (4-ounce) can chopped mild green chiles, drained
- 1 (14.5-ounce) can diced tomatoes, undrained
- 1 (8-ounce) can tomato sauce
- 1 cup fresh corn kernels
- ¼ cup chopped fresh cilantro
  Salt and cayenne to taste

TOPPING

- 2 large eggs, lightly beaten
- 1 cup well-stirred buttermilk
- 4 tablespoons unsalted butter, melted
- 1½ cups yellow cornmeal
- ½ cup all-purpose flour
- 2½ teaspoons baking powder
- ½ teaspoon salt

For the filling, heat the oil in the cooker over medium-high heat or use the browning function of an electric cooker. Add the onion, carrot, celery, red bell pepper, chile, and garlic. Cook, stirring frequently, for 3 minutes, or until the onion is translucent. Stir in chili powder, cumin, and smoked paprika, and cook for 1 minute, stirring constantly. Add the turkey, breaking up lumps with a fork. Stir in the green chiles, tomatoes, and tomato sauce.

Preheat the oven to 400°F and grease a 9 × 13-inch baking dish.

Close and lock the lid of the cooker.

STOVETOP: Place the cooker over high heat, and bring it to high pressure. Once high pressure is reached, reduce the heat as much as possible while retaining the high-pressure level. Cook for 5 minutes. Then take the pot off the heat and quick release the pressure according to the instructions provided by the manufacturer. Remove the lid, tilting it away from you, to allow the steam to escape.

OR

ELECTRIC: Set the machine to cook at high pressure for 7 minutes. After 7 minutes, unplug the pot so that it does not go into warming mode. Quick release the pressure according to the instructions provided by the manufacturer. Remove the lid, tilting it away from you, to allow the steam to escape.

Stir the corn and the cilantro into the filling. Season to taste with salt and cayenne, and spread the mixture into the prepared pan.

While the filling cooks, prepare the topping. Combine the eggs, buttermilk, melted butter, cornmeal, flour, baking powder, and salt in a mixing bowl and whisk well. Spoon the batter over the filling, leaving a ½-inch margin around the edges.

Bake the topping for 15 to 20 minutes, or until it is golden and an inserted toothpick comes out clean. Allow the dish to sit for 5 minutes; then serve.

NOTE Chili powder is actually a spice blend and can be made as follows: Combine 2 tablespoons ground red chile, 2 tablespoons paprika, 1 tablespoon ground coriander, 1 tablespoon garlic powder, 1 tablespoon onion powder, 2 teaspoons ground cumin, 2 teaspoons ground red pepper or cayenne, 1 teaspoon ground black pepper, and 1 teaspoon dried oregano.

Turkey Chili

I've often said that ground turkey meat is the hamburger of the twenty-first century, and one of its most popular forms is in a steaming bowl of chili. This version can be on the table in minutes, and the flavor of the spices really permeates the dish because of the pressure. Serve it over rice with traditional chili garnishes.

SERVES **4 to 6**

SIZE **6-quart or larger pressure cooker**

TIME **5 to 7 minutes at high pressure with quick pressure release**

The chili can be prepared up to 2 days in advance and refrigerated, tightly covered. Reheat it over low heat, stirring occasionally.

2 tablespoons olive oil
1 medium onion, diced
2 medium carrots, diced
3 celery ribs, diced
1 medium red bell pepper, seeds and ribs removed, diced
5 cloves garlic, minced
1 pound ground turkey, preferably dark meat
1½ tablespoons chili powder
1½ teaspoons dried oregano
1½ teaspoons ground cumin
½ teaspoon dried thyme
½ teaspoon crushed red pepper flakes
2 bay leaves
2 dashes hot red pepper sauce

1 tablespoon tomato paste
1 chipotle pepper in adobo sauce, drained and finely chopped
2 cups crushed tomatoes
1 cup Chicken Stock (page 15) or purchased stock
1 (15-ounce) can red kidney beans, drained and rinsed
Salt and freshly ground black pepper to taste
3 to 4 cups hot cooked brown or white rice for serving

GARNISH
Shredded sharp cheddar cheese, guacamole, crushed tortilla chips, sour cream

Heat the oil in the cooker over medium-high heat or use the browning function of an electric cooker. Add the onion, carrot, celery, red bell pepper, and garlic. Cook, stirring frequently, for 3 minutes, or until the onion is translucent. Add the turkey and break up any lumps with a spoon. Cook the turkey for 2 minutes, or until it lightens in color. Add the chili powder, oregano, cumin, thyme, crushed red pepper flakes, bay leaves, tomato paste, and chipotle pepper. Cook for 1 minute, stirring constantly. Stir in the tomatoes and stock.

Close and lock the lid of the cooker.

STOVETOP: Place the cooker over high heat, and bring it to high pressure. Once high pressure is reached, reduce the heat as much as possible while retaining the high-pressure level. Cook for 5 minutes. Then take the pot off the heat and quick release the pressure according to the instructions provided by the manufacturer. Remove the lid, tilting it away from you, to allow the steam to escape.

OR

ELECTRIC: Set the machine to cook at high pressure for 7 minutes. After 7 minutes, unplug the pot so that it does not go into warming mode. Quick release the pressure according to the instructions provided by the manufacturer. Remove the lid, tilting it away from you, to allow the steam to escape.

NOTE Cooking dried herbs and spices before liquid is added to a recipe helps bring out their flavors and aromas and takes away any "raw" taste. This process is especially important for mixtures such as chili powder and curry powder.

Stir in the kidney beans, and cook for 2 minutes over medium heat or use the browning function of an electric cooker. Remove and discard the bay leaves and season to taste with salt and pepper. Serve immediately over rice. To top off the chili, pass around bowls of shredded cheddar, guacamole, crushed tortilla chips, and sour cream.

Duck Legs in Red Wine Sauce

Back in the era of "Continental Cuisine," roasted Duck à l'Orange was deemed the height of culinary sophistication. But that was before we realized that ducks are really two different animals; the lean breasts are best quickly seared but the legs should be braised. The pressure cooker is an excellent way to cook the legs because the fat virtually melts away from under the skin, and the delicious red wine sauce pairs magically with a classic Bordeaux or Rioja. Serve the duck with Fluffy Mashed Potatoes (page 245) or Creamy Polenta (page 214).

SERVES **4 to 6**

SIZE **6-quart pressure cooker or larger**

TIME **30 to 35 minutes at high pressure; then allow the pressure to release naturally**

The dish can be prepared up to 2 days in advance and refrigerated, tightly covered. Reheat it, covered, in a 350°F oven for 20 to 25 minutes, or until hot. Do not broil the duck legs until just before serving.

4 to 6 (⅔-pound) duck leg quarters
2 tablespoons olive oil
1 small onion, diced
3 garlic cloves, minced
1 carrot, thickly sliced
2 celery ribs, thickly sliced
1½ cups dry red wine

1 cup Chicken Stock (page 15) or purchased stock
⅓ cup chopped fresh parsley
1 tablespoon fresh thyme leaves
1 bay leaf
1 tablespoon cornstarch
Salt and freshly ground black pepper to taste

Using a metal skewer held parallel to the surface of the duck leg, prick the skin so that the skin, but not the meat, is pierced.

Heat the oil in the cooker over medium-high heat or use the browning function of an electric cooker. Add the onion, garlic, carrot, and celery. Cook, stirring frequently, for 3 minutes, or until the onion is translucent. Add the wine to the cooker, raise the heat to high, and boil the wine until it is reduced by one-third. Add the stock, parsley, thyme, and bay leaf to the slow cooker and stir well. Add the duck legs, skin side down.

Close and lock the lid of the cooker.

STOVETOP: Place the cooker over high heat, and bring it to high pressure. Once high pressure is reached, reduce the heat as much as possible while retaining the high-pressure level. Cook for 30 minutes. Then take the pot off the heat and allow it to return to normal pressure naturally. Remove the lid, tilting it away from you, to allow the steam to escape.

OR

ELECTRIC: Set the machine to cook at high pressure for 35 minutes. After 35 minutes, unplug the pot so that it does not go into warming mode. Allow the pressure to return to normal naturally. Remove the lid, tilting it away from you, to allow the steam to escape.

Line a broiler pan with heavy-duty aluminum foil. Remove the duck from the cooker with a slotted spatula and arrange the legs on the foil, skin side up.

Allow the liquid to sit undisturbed for 10 minutes. Spoon the fat off the surface of the sauce with a soup ladle. Bring the sauce to a boil over high heat or use the browning function of an electric cooker and reduce the sauce by one-third. Remove and discard the bay leaf.

Combine the cornstarch with 2 tablespoons of cold water in a small cup, stirring well to dissolve the cornstarch. Stir the cornstarch mixture into the cooker, and bring to a boil over high heat or use the browning function with an electric cooker. Cook for 1 minute, or until the sauce thickens. Season to taste with salt and pepper.

Preheat the oven broiler. Broil the duck legs 8 inches away from the broiler element for 2 to 3 minutes, or until the skin is crisp. Serve the duck hot and pass around the sauce separately.

> **NOTE** You'll probably ladle more than a half cup of fat off the surface of the duck sauce, and duck fat is like gold in the kitchen because it adds such incredible flavor to foods cooked in it. Allow the liquid to sit at room temperature until the fat has risen to the top, and then refrigerate it. Once it's chilled, remove the fat and discard the liquid at the bottom of the cup.

Duck Legs in Red Wine Sauce, page 114

Crispy Chinese Duck Legs

A crispy duck dish is always my favorite part of a Chinese meal, and there are two great advantages to making it in a pressure cooker: speed and intensity of flavor—the braising liquid really infuses the meat. Serve this dish with rice and stir-fried bok choy.

SERVES **4 to 6**

SIZE **6-quart pressure cooker or larger**

TIME **30 to 35 minutes at high pressure; then allow the pressure to release naturally**

The dish can be prepared up to 2 days in advance and refrigerated, tightly covered. Reheat it, covered, in a 350°F oven for 20 to 25 minutes, or until hot. Do not broil the duck legs until just before serving.

- 4 to 6 (10- to 12-ounce) duck leg quarters
- 2 tablespoons sesame oil
- 1 bunch scallions, white parts and 4 inches of green tops, cut into 2-inch lengths
- 3 garlic cloves, peeled
- ¼ cup sliced fresh ginger
- 1 cup Chicken Stock (page 15), Chinese Chicken Stock (page 15), or purchased stock
- ½ cup cream sherry
- ½ cup hoisin sauce
- ¼ cup reduced-sodium soy sauce
- 2 (3-inch) cinnamon sticks
- 4 star anise pods
- 1 small dried Chinese chile pepper (optional)
- 1 tablespoon cornstarch
- Freshly ground black pepper to taste

Using a metal skewer held parallel to the surface of the duck leg, prick the skin so that the skin but not the meat is pierced.

Heat the oil in the cooker over medium-high heat or use the browning function of an electric cooker. Add the scallions, garlic, and ginger, and cook, stirring constantly, for 30 seconds, or until fragrant. Add the stock, sherry, hoisin sauce, soy sauce, cinnamon sticks, star anise, and chile pepper, if using. Add the duck legs, skin side down.

Close and lock the lid of the cooker.

STOVETOP: Place the cooker over high heat, and bring it to high pressure. Once high pressure is reached, reduce the heat as much as possible while retaining the high-pressure level. Cook for 30 minutes. Then take the pot off the heat and allow it to return to normal pressure naturally. Remove the lid, tilting it away from you, to allow the steam to escape.

OR

ELECTRIC: Set the machine to cook at high pressure for 35 minutes. After 35 minutes, unplug the pot so that it does not go into warming mode. Allow the pressure to return to normal naturally. Remove the lid, tilting it away from you, to allow the steam to escape.

Line a broiler pan with heavy-duty aluminum foil. Remove the duck from the cooker with a slotted spatula and arrange the legs on the foil, skin side up.

Strain the liquid, pressing with the back of a spoon to extract all the liquid, and discard the solids. Return the sauce to the cooker.

Allow the liquid to sit undisturbed for 10 minutes. Spoon the fat off the surface of the sauce with a soup ladle. Bring the sauce to a boil over high heat or use the browning function of an electric cooker and reduce it by one-third.

Combine the cornstarch with 2 tablespoons of cold water in a small cup, stirring well to dissolve the cornstarch. Stir the cornstarch mixture into the cooker, and bring to a boil over high heat or use the browning function with an electric cooker. Cook for 1 minute, or until the sauce thickens. Season to taste with pepper.

Preheat the oven broiler. Broil the duck legs 8 inches away from the broiler element for 2 to 3 minutes, or until the skin is crisp. Serve hot and pass around the sauce separately.

NOTE When preparing this recipe, I usually make two additional duck legs and transform them into an easy stir-fry the next day. Dice the cooked meat, along with its skin, into ¾-inch pieces. Heat a few tablespoons of oil in a wok or heavy skillet over medium-high heat. Add the duck pieces and stir-fry until they are hot and crisp. Add 2 cups of your favorite raw vegetables (or a combination of bok choy, carrots, celery, onion, scallions, etc.) and stir-fry for 1 minute. Add ¾ cup of the reserved sauce to the work and cook for 2 minutes.

Daube Niçoise, page 124

CHAPTER 5

Beef and Lamb

No cuisine or culture can claim braising as its own, although we've borrowed our English word from the French. Every culture has dishes made from less tender (and often less expensive) cuts of meat: they may be called sand pots in China, ragouts in France, and stews in North America. The meats are usually simmered in aromatic liquid for many hours until they're tender; with a pressure cooker, however, the hours turn into mere minutes.

That's what braising is all about—tenderness. And the amount of time it takes to reach the state of "fork tender" depends on each individual piece of meat; there are no hard-and-fast rules.

Picking Your Parts

The best beef in terms of both flavor and texture comes from 18- to 24-month-old cows. Beef is graded in the United States by the Department of Agriculture as Prime, Choice, or Select. Prime usually is reserved for restaurants, and the other two grades are sold in supermarkets.

When you're looking at beef in the store, seek deep red, moist meat that is generously marbled with white fat. Yellow fat is a tip-off to old age. Beef is purple after cutting, but the meat quickly "blooms" to bright red on exposure to the air.

For braising, the beef you want is chuck or round. Chuck is the beef taken from the area between the cow's neck and shoulder blades. Some chuck roasts also contain a piece of the blade bone. Round is the general name for the large quantity of beef taken from the hind leg extending from the rump to the ankle. The eye of the round and the bottom round are the two least tender cuts, and the top round should be reserved for roasting.

For lamb, the shoulder—both as chops and as a roast—and the shanks are the two best cuts for braising. Although you can braise a leg of lamb, it will be stringier than the shoulder.

COOKING TIMES (IN MINUTES)
FOR BEEF AND LAMB IN THE PRESSURE COOKER

	STOVETOP	ELECTRIC	RELEASE METHOD
BEEF CUT			
BRISKET, 3 LB.	50	55	NATURAL
BRISKET, 4 LB.	60	65	NATURAL
CHUCK ROAST, 2 LB.	40	45	NATURAL
CHUCK ROAST, 3 LB.	50	55	NATURAL
GROUND	6	7	NATURAL
SHORT RIBS, BONE-IN	40	45	NATURAL
STEW, 1-INCH CUBES	10	12	NATURAL
STEW, 1½-INCH CUBES	15	18	NATURAL
STEW, 2-INCH CUBES	25	30	NATURAL
TONGUE	45	50	NATURAL
LAMB CUT			
CHOPS, SHOULDER	8	10	NATURAL
GROUND	6	7	NATURAL
LEG, 1½-INCH CUBES	15	18	NATURAL
SHANKS, ¾ POUND	30	25	NATURAL
SHOULDER, BONELESS	45	50	NATURAL

Daube Niçoise
(Provençal Beef Stew)

We tend to associate the foods of Provence with warmth, sun, and seafood, but the region does have a few harsh months in the winter. That's when this vibrant dish of braised beef flavored with the region's prized olives, tomato, and orange zest is popular. Serve it with Creamy Polenta (page 214) and Kale with Pancetta (page 251).

SERVES **6 to 8**

SIZE **6-quart or larger pressure cooker**

TIME **25 to 30 minutes at high pressure; then allow the pressure to release naturally**

The dish can be prepared up to 2 days in advance and refrigerated, tightly covered. Reheat it, covered, in a 350°F oven for 20 to 25 minutes, or until hot.

- 2 cups Beef Stock (page 16) or purchased stock, divided
- ½ cup dried chanterelle mushrooms
- 2½ pounds boneless beef chuck roast, cut into 2-inch cubes
- Freshly ground black pepper to taste
- 1 tablespoon olive oil
- ¼ pound salt pork or slab bacon in one piece
- 3 carrots, cut into 2-inch lengths
- 2 large onions, quartered
- 4 garlic cloves, minced
- 3 tablespoons tomato paste
- 1 (750 ml) bottle dry red wine
- 2 teaspoons anchovy paste
- ¼ cup chopped fresh parsley
- 2 tablespoons fresh thyme leaves
- 2 bay leaves
- ½ cup pitted oil-cured Niçoise olives, halved
- 2 tablespoons cornstarch
- 2 tablespoons julienne orange zest
- 2 large tomatoes, seeded and diced

Bring 1 cup of the stock to a boil in a small saucepan or a microwave-safe bowl. Soak the mushrooms in the boiling stock, pushing them down into the liquid with the back of a spoon, for 10 minutes. Drain the mushrooms, reserving the stock. Discard the mushroom stems and slice the caps thickly. Strain the stock through a sieve lined with a paper coffee filter or a paper towel. Set it aside.

Preheat the oven broiler and line a broiler pan with heavy-duty aluminum foil. Pat the beef dry with paper towels and sprinkle the cubes with pepper. Arrange the beef in a single layer on the foil and broil for 3 minutes on each side, or until beef is lightly browned. Remove the beef from the broiler and set it aside.

Heat the oil in the cooker over medium-high heat or use the browning function of an electric cooker. Add the salt pork, carrots, onions, and garlic. Cook, stirring frequently, for 3 minutes, or until the onion is translucent. Stir in the tomato paste and cook for 1 minute, stirring constantly. Stir in the wine, mushroom stock, remaining stock, mushrooms, anchovy paste, parsley, thyme, bay leaves, and olives. Add the meat to the cooker along with any juices that have accumulated.

Close and lock the lid of the cooker.

STOVETOP: Place the cooker over high heat, and bring it to high pressure. Once high pressure is reached, reduce the heat as much as possible while retaining the high-pressure level. Cook for 25 minutes. Then take the pot off the heat and allow it to return to normal pressure naturally. Remove the lid, tilting it away from you, to allow the steam to escape.

OR

ELECTRIC: Set the machine to cook at high pressure for 30 minutes. After 30 minutes, unplug the pot so that it does not go into warming mode. Allow the pressure to return to normal naturally. Remove the lid, tilting it away from you, to allow the steam to escape.

NOTE You'll notice that salt is not listed in the ingredients—that's because there are a few ingredients in the dish that contain large amounts of it. All the salt you'll need comes from the anchovy paste, salt pork (which is discarded), and olives. These salty foods add complexity rather than mere saltiness to the flavor of the finished dish

Remove and discard the salt pork and bay leaves. Allow the liquid to rest for 10 minutes and then tilt the cooker and spoon off as much fat as possible.

Combine the cornstarch with 2 tablespoons of cold water in a small cup, stirring well to dissolve the cornstarch. Stir the mixture, orange zest, and tomato into the cooker, and bring to a boil over high heat or use the browning function of an electric cooker. Cook for 1 minute, or until the sauce thickens. Season to taste with pepper and serve immediately.

Asian Beef Stew with Star Anise

Aromatic star anise and cinnamon are the dominant flavors of this hearty winter stew,
which can either remain savory or take on a spicy note with the inclusion of crushed
red pepper flakes. Serve it with Asian Eggplant with Garlic Sauce (page 242).

SERVES **6 to 8**

SIZE **6-quart or larger pressure cooker**

TIME **25 to 30 minutes at high pressure; then allow the pressure to release naturally**

The dish can be prepared up to 2 days in advance and refrigerated, tightly covered. Reheat it, covered, in a 350°F oven for 20 to 25 minutes, or until hot.

3 pounds boneless beef chuck roast, cut into 2-inch cubes
Salt and freshly ground black pepper to taste
2 tablespoons fermented black beans
¼ cup dry sherry
1 juice orange
2 tablespoons toasted sesame oil
¼ cup diced ginger
4 garlic cloves, minced
3 scallions, white parts and 4 inches of green tops, sliced
½ teaspoon crushed red pepper flakes (optional)

1½ teaspoons Chinese five-spice powder
4 star anise pods
1 (3-inch) cinnamon stick
2 cups Beef Stock (page 16) or purchased stock
¼ cup reduced-sodium soy sauce
2 tablespoons cornstarch
3 to 4 cups hot cooked rice for serving

GARNISH
½ cup chopped fresh cilantro

Preheat the oven broiler and line a broiler pan with heavy-duty aluminum foil. Pat the beef dry with paper towels and sprinkle it with salt and pepper. Arrange the beef in a single layer on the foil and broil for 3 minutes on each side, or until beef is lightly browned. Remove the beef from the broiler and set it aside.

Place the black beans on a cutting board, and hit them with the bottom of a small skillet or the flat side of a meat mallet to crush them. Stir the black beans into the sherry to plump them up. Cut thick strips of zest from the orange with a vegetable peeler and then squeeze the orange.

Heat the oil in the cooker over medium-high heat or use the browning function of an electric cooker. Add the ginger, garlic, scallions, and crushed red pepper flakes, if using. Cook the mixture for 30 seconds, or until fragrant, stirring constantly. Add the beef, orange zest, orange juice, five-spice powder, star anise pods, cinnamon stick, stock, and soy sauce to the cooker. Stir well.

Close and lock the lid of the cooker.

STOVETOP: Place the cooker over high heat, and bring it to high pressure. Once high pressure is reached, reduce the heat as much as possible while retaining the high-pressure level. Cook for 25 minutes. Then take the pot off the heat and allow it to return to normal pressure naturally. Remove the lid, tilting it away from you, to allow the steam to escape.

OR

ELECTRIC: Set the machine to cook at high pressure for 30 minutes. After 30 minutes, unplug the pot so that it does not go into warming mode. Allow the pressure to return to normal naturally. Remove the lid, tilting it away from you, to allow the steam to escape.

NOTE Star anise, which looks like an eight-pointed star, is the fruit of a tree in the magnolia family that is native to China and Vietnam. The rust-colored fruits are picked and dried before ripening, and their flavor is far more aromatic, pungent, and "licorice-like" than European anise. It's one of the traditional ingredients in five-spice powder, as well as a component of *garam masala*.

Remove and discard the cinnamon stick, anise pods, and orange peel from the cooker. Allow the liquid to rest for 10 minutes; then tilt the cooker and spoon off as much fat as possible.

Combine the cornstarch with 2 tablespoons of cold water in a small cup, stirring well to dissolve the cornstarch. Stir the cornstarch mixture into the cooker, and bring it to a boil over high heat or use the browning function of an electric cooker. Cook for 1 minute, or until the sauce thickens. Serve the stew over rice right away and sprinkle each dish with chopped cilantro leaves.

Guinness Beef Stew

This stew is a heartier version of the classic Belgian dish Carbonnade Flemande,
which is beef cooked in a light beer. It's traditionally served with steamed potatoes,
but I like roasted potatoes to provide some textural contrast.

SERVES **4 to 6**

SIZE **6-quart or larger pressure cooker**

TIME **25 to 30 minutes at high pressure; then allow the pressure to release naturally**

The dish can be prepared up to 2 days in advance and refrigerated, tightly covered. Reheat it, covered, in a 350°F oven for 20 to 25 minutes, or until hot.

1 (2-pound) chuck roast, trimmed and cut into 2-inch cubes
Salt and freshly ground black pepper to taste
2 tablespoons vegetable oil
4 large onions, thinly sliced
2 teaspoons granulated sugar
¼ teaspoon baking soda
2 garlic cloves, minced
1½ cups Beef Stock (page 16) or purchased stock

1 (12-ounce) bottle Guinness Stout beer
2 tablespoons firmly packed dark brown sugar
2 tablespoons chopped fresh parsley
2 teaspoons fresh thyme leaves
1 bay leaf
2 tablespoons cornstarch

Preheat the oven broiler and line a broiler pan with heavy-duty aluminum foil. Pat the beef dry with paper towels and sprinkle the cubes with salt and pepper. Arrange the beef in a single layer on the foil and broil for 3 minutes on each side, or until the beef is lightly browned.

Heat the oil in the cooker over medium heat or use the browning function of an electric cooker. Add the onions, toss to coat them well, and cook with the cover on but not locked for 10 minutes. Uncover the cooker, raise the heat to medium-high, and sprinkle onions with the sugar, baking soda, and salt. Cook the mixture, stirring occasionally, for 10 to 12 minutes, or until onions are lightly browned. Stir in the garlic and cook for 1 minute. Add the beef to the cooker and stir in the stock, beer, brown sugar, parsley, thyme, and bay leaf.

Close and lock the lid of the cooker.

STOVETOP: Place the cooker over high heat, and bring it to high pressure. Once high pressure is reached, reduce the heat as much as possible while retaining the high-pressure level. Cook for 25 minutes. Then take the pot off the heat and allow it to return to normal pressure naturally. Remove the lid, tilting it away from you, to allow the steam to escape.

OR

ELECTRIC: Set the machine to cook at high pressure for 30 minutes. After 30 minutes, unplug the pot so that it does not go into warming mode. Allow the pressure to return to normal naturally. Remove the lid, tilting it away from you, to allow the steam to escape.

Remove and discard the bay leaf. Let the stew sit for 10 minutes; then tilt the cooker and spoon off as much fat as possible from the surface.

Combine the cornstarch with 2 tablespoons of cold water in a small cup, stirring well to dissolve the cornstarch. Stir the cornstarch mixture into the cooker, and bring it to a boil over high heat or use the browning function of an electric cooker. Cook tor 1 minute, or until the sauce thickens. Season to taste with salt and pepper, and serve immediately.

VARIATION

★ **Guinness Shepherd's Pie** Prepare the stew as instructed above. After the pressure is released, add ½ cup diced carrots and ½ cup diced parsnips to the stew, and cook over medium heat or use the browning function of an electric cooker for 5 minutes. Prepare Fluffy Mashed Potatoes (page 245) or Gruyère Mashed Potatoes (page 144) as directed.

Preheat the oven to 400°F and grease a 12-inch ovenproof skillet. Stir 1 cup of green peas into the stew and transfer the stew to the prepared skillet. Layer the potatoes on top of the stew and bake for 20 minutes, or until the top is lightly browned and the filling is bubbling. Allow the pie to sit for 5 minutes and then serve.

Texas-Style Chili con Carne

I am offering my apologies in advance to Texans, because I put kidney beans in this chili recipe; that's why it's "Texas-Style." I happen to like beans in chili, and when the dish is cooked in a pressure cooker, they absorb so much flavor from the sauce. With that exception, this chili has the flavor of real Texas Chili con Carne, and thickening it with a bit of masa harina *adds yet another dimension of authenticity.*

SERVES **4 to 6**

SIZE **6-quart or larger pressure cooker**

TIME **30 to 35 minutes at high pressure; then allow the pressure to release naturally**

The chili is really better if it is made up to 2 days in advance and refrigerated, to allow the flavors to blend. Reheat it over low heat, covered, until hot.

2 pounds boneless chuck roast, cut into 2½-inch pieces

2 tablespoons olive oil

1 large sweet onion such as Bermuda or Vidalia, diced

1 red bell pepper, seeds and ribs removed, diced

6 garlic cloves, minced

3 tablespoons chili powder

2 tablespoons ground cumin

1 tablespoon dried oregano

¾ teaspoon Chinese five-spice powder

3 cups Beef Stock (page 16) or purchased stock

1 tablespoon unsweetened cocoa powder

1 chipotle pepper in adobo sauce, finely chopped, or more to taste

2 bay leaves

½ pound dried red kidney beans, rinsed

1 (28-ounce) can crushed tomatoes

3 tablespoons masa harina

Salt and freshly ground black pepper to taste

Hot red pepper sauce to taste

2 to 3 cups hot cooked brown or white rice for serving

GARNISH
Chopped cilantro, chopped onion or scallions, shredded cheddar cheese, sour cream, and diced avocado

Preheat the oven broiler and line a broiler pan with heavy-duty aluminum foil. Pat the beef dry with paper towels. Arrange the beef in a single layer on the foil and broil for 3 minutes on each side, or until the beef is lightly browned. Remove the beef from the broiler and set it aside.

Heat the oil in the cooker over medium-high heat or use the browning function of an electric cooker. Add the onion, red bell pepper, and garlic, and cook, stirring frequently, for 3 minutes, or until the onion is translucent. Stir in the chili powder, cumin, oregano, and five-spice powder. Cook for 1 minute, stirring constantly. Stir in the stock, cocoa powder, chipotle chile, bay leaves, beans, and browned meat. Add the tomatoes to the cooker, but do not stir them in.

Close and lock the lid of the cooker.

STOVETOP: Place the cooker over high heat, and bring it to high pressure. Once high pressure is reached, reduce the heat as much as possible while retaining the high-pressure level. Cook for 30 minutes. Then take the pot off the heat and allow it to return to normal pressure naturally. Remove the lid, tilting it away from you, to allow the steam to escape.

OR

ELECTRIC: Set the machine to cook at high pressure for 35 minutes. After 35 minutes, unplug the pot so that it does not go into warming mode. Allow the pressure to return to normal naturally. Remove the lid, tilting it away from you, to allow the steam to escape.

Remove and discard the bay leaves. Stir the *masa harina* into the cooker, and cook over medium heat or use the browning function of an electric cooker for 2 minutes. Season to taste with salt, pepper, and hot red pepper sauce. Serve the chili over rice, and pass around bowls of the garnishes separately.

NOTE Tomatoes tend to scorch in the pressure cooker because of their high sugar content, but that pitfall can be avoided if they're added to the cooker right before the lid is locked and the pressure is allowed to mount. The tomatoes will stay at the top of the pot as the pressure builds and will not scorch.

Boeuf Bourguignon

This famous stew from Burgundy is one of the region's most famous dishes, and it holds a place in the heart of every red wine lover. Although it's easy enough to serve the stew as a family meal, it's also elegant enough for company. Serve it with Fluffy Mashed Potatoes (page 245) or White Vegetable Puree (page 253).

SERVES **4 to 6**

SIZE **6-quart or larger pressure cooker**

TIME **25 to 30 minutes at high pressure; then allow the pressure to release naturally**

The dish can be prepared up to 2 days in advance and refrigerated, tightly covered. Reheat it, covered, in a 350°F oven for 20 to 25 minutes, or until hot.

2½ pounds boneless beef chuck roast, cut into 2-inch cubes

Salt and freshly ground black pepper to taste

3 slices bacon, cut into 1-inch pieces

¾ pound button mushrooms, trimmed and halved (quartered if large)

1 large onion, diced

3 garlic cloves, minced

2 tablespoons tomato paste

¼ cup all-purpose flour

2¼ cups dry red wine, preferably Burgundy

¾ cup Beef Stock (page 16) or purchased stock

3 tablespoons chopped fresh parsley

1 tablespoon fresh thyme leaves

1 bay leaf

1 (1-pound) bag frozen pearl onions

1 tablespoon unsalted butter

Preheat the oven broiler and line a broiler pan with heavy-duty aluminum foil. Pat the beef dry with paper towels and sprinkle the cubes with salt and pepper. Arrange the beef in a single layer on the foil and broil for 3 minutes on each side, or until it is lightly browned. Remove the beef from the broiler and set it aside.

Cook the bacon in the cooker over medium-high heat or use the browning function of an electric cooker for 5 to 7 minutes, or until crisp. Remove the bacon from the cooker with a slotted spoon and drain on paper towels. Set it aside.

Add the mushrooms, onion, and garlic to the cooker and cook, stirring frequently, for 3 minutes, or until the onion is translucent. Stir in the tomato paste and flour, and cook for 1 minute, stirring constantly. Whisk in the wine and bring to a boil. Boil for 5 minutes. Add the beef to the cooker, along with the stock, parsley, thyme, and bay leaf.

Close and lock the lid of the cooker.

STOVETOP: Place the cooker over high heat, and bring it to high pressure. Once high pressure is reached, reduce the heat as much as possible while retaining the high-pressure level. Cook for 25 minutes. Then take the pot off the heat and allow it to return to normal pressure naturally. Remove the lid, tilting it away from you, to allow the steam to escape.

OR

ELECTRIC: Set the machine to cook at high pressure for 30 minutes. After 30 minutes, unplug the pot so that it does not go into warming mode. Allow the pressure to return to normal naturally. Remove the lid, tilting it away from you, to allow the steam to escape.

NOTE When making a dish that contains more than a cup of wine in the pressure cooker, boil the wine for a few minutes before bringing the pot up to pressure. Evaporation, which rounds out the flavor of wine when it is cooked conventionally, doesn't happen in the pressure cooker's closed environment.

While the beef cooks, prepare the onions. Place the onions in a skillet with the butter, salt, pepper, and ⅓ cup water. Cook over medium heat, covered, for 2 minutes. Uncover the pan and cook for an additional 3 minutes.

Remove and discard the bay leaf. Allow the liquid to rest for 10 minutes and then tilt the cooker and spoon off as much fat as possible. Add the onions to the cooker with a slotted spoon and serve immediately, sprinkling the bacon bits on top of each serving.

Corned Beef and Cabbage

The pressure cooker makes short work of cooking corned beef, but the vegetables served alongside it must be cooked separately. Although it's a two-step process, the vegetables cook in a matter of minutes; you won't even have to reheat the meat. Another option is to serve Colcannon (page 239)—an authentic Irish mix of potatoes and cabbage—rather than have corned beef and cabbage as a one-pot meal.

SERVES 6 to 10, depending on the size of the corned beef

SIZE 8-quart or larger pressure cooker

TIME 55 minutes to 80 minutes at high pressure, depending on the weight of the corned beef; then allow the pressure to release naturally

> Both the corned beef and the vegetables can be cooked up to 2 days in advance and refrigerated. If you are preparing it in advance, save 1 quart of the braising liquid to reheat the food.

1 (3- to 5-pound) corned beef brisket, preferably flat cut

2 (12-ounce) cans or bottles of lager beer

1 large onion, halved

1 celery rib, broken into 2-inch pieces

3 sprigs fresh thyme

4 sprigs fresh parsley

3 bay leaves

2 dried red chiles (optional)

6 garlic cloves, peeled (optional)

3 large carrots, cut into 2-inch chunks

1 (2- to 3-pound) head green cabbage, cored and cut into 2-inch wedges

1 to 1½ pounds baby potatoes, scrubbed

Remove the corned beef from its wrapper and rinse it well under cold running water. Soak it in cold water for a minimum of 2 hours, or, preferably, refrigerate it for 12 hours and change the water every 2 hours. (This will rid the corned beef of much of its salinity.)

Rinse the corned beef again and place it in the pressure cooker. Add the beer, onion, celery, thyme, parsley, and bay leaves. Add the chiles and garlic, if using. Fill the cooker with water up to the fill line.

Close and lock the lid of the cooker.

STOVETOP: Place the cooker over high heat, and bring it to high pressure. Once high pressure is reached, reduce the heat as much as possible while retaining the high-pressure level. Cook a 3-pound corned beef for 55 minutes, a 4-pound corned beef for 60 minutes, and a 5-pound corned beef for 70 minutes. Then take the pot off the heat and allow it to return to normal pressure naturally. Remove the lid, tilting it away from you, to allow the steam to escape.

OR

ELECTRIC: Set the machine to cook at high pressure for 60 minutes for a 3-pound corned beef, 70 minutes for a 4-pound corned beef, and 80 minutes for a 5-pound corned beef. After cooking, unplug the pot so that it does not go into warming mode. Allow the pressure to return to normal naturally. Remove the lid, tilting it away from you, to allow the steam to escape.

Remove the corned beef from the cooker and transfer it to a platter. Cover it with foil to keep it hot. Use a slotted spoon to remove and discard the seasoning solids from the cooker. Add the carrots, cabbage, and potatoes to the cooker.

Place a heavy skillet on top of the corned beef to weigh it down while the vegetables are cooking. (This will compact the meat and ease carving.)

Close and lock the lid of the cooker.

STOVETOP: Place the cooker over high heat, and bring it to high pressure. Once high pressure is reached, reduce the heat as much as possible while retaining the high-pressure level. Cook for 4 minutes. Then take the pot off the heat and quick release the pressure according to the instructions provided by the manufacturer. Remove the lid, tilting it away from you, to allow the steam to escape.

OR

ELECTRIC: Set the machine to cook at high pressure for 5 minutes. After 5 minutes, unplug the pot so that it does not go into warming mode. Quick release the pressure according to the instructions provided by the manufacturer. Remove the lid, tilting it away from you, to allow the steam to escape.

> **NOTE** All corned beef comes from the brisket of the cow, which is in its front section, above the legs. The whole brisket is then divided into the point cut, an irregular shape that contains a lot of fat, and the flat cut, a neat, rectangular cap of meat only with a thin layer of fat on the top. Although the point cut is less expensive, the edible portion makes it about the same price as the flat cut when the fat is trimmed off. When you are cooking a corned beef conventionally, the flat cut can become tough, but that's not a problem when it's cooked in a pressure cooker.

To serve, carve the corned beef, across the grain, into thin slices. Arrange the slices on a platter with the vegetables around them.

Corned Beef and Cabbage,
page 134

Corned Beef Hash

Real corned beef hash is a delight. I recommend making more corned beef than you need so that you can make hash.

SERVES **4 to 6**

SIZE **4-quart or larger pressure cooker**

TIME **5 minutes at high pressure with quick pressure release**

The hash can be prepared, up to baking, 2 days in advance and refrigerated, tightly covered. Bake it for 15 to 20 minutes if it has been chilled.

VARIATION

* Before baking the hash, make 4 to 6 evenly spaced indentations in it with the back of a spoon. Break an egg into each indentation and sprinkle the egg with salt and pepper.

1½ pounds redskin potatoes, scrubbed and cut into 1-inch dice
1 teaspoon salt
2 tablespoons vegetable oil
1 large sweet onion, diced
1 small red bell pepper, seeds and ribs removed, diced
2 garlic cloves, minced
1 pound cooked corned beef, coarsely chopped
¼ teaspoon dried thyme
Salt and freshly ground black pepper to taste

Preheat the oven to 400°F and grease a 9 × 13-inch baking pan.

Place the potato cubes in the cooker and add 1 cup of water and the salt. Then close and lock the lid.

STOVETOP: Place the cooker over high heat, and bring it to high pressure. Once high pressure is reached, reduce the heat as much as possible while retaining the high-pressure level. Cook for 5 minutes. Then take the pot off the heat and quick release the pressure according to the instructions provided by the manufacturer. Remove the lid, tilting it away from you, to allow the steam to escape.

OR

ELECTRIC: Set the machine to cook at high pressure for 7 minutes. After 7 minutes, unplug the pot so that it does not go into warming mode. Quick release the pressure according to the instructions provided by the manufacturer. Remove the lid, tilting it away from you, to allow the steam to escape.

Drain the potatoes, shaking them well in a colander. Return the potatoes to the cooker and mash them roughly.

While the potatoes cook, heat the oil in a large skillet over medium heat. Add the onion, bell pepper, and garlic. Cook, stirring frequently, for 10 to 12 minutes, or until the vegetables soften. Add the corned beef, mashed potatoes, and thyme, and mix well. Season to taste with salt and pepper.

Spread the hash evenly and bake for 12 to 15 minutes, or until slightly browned on top. Serve immediately.

Picadillo

Although this traditional Cuban dish resembles Tex-Mex chili con carne,
it also includes some surprising flavor accents from olives, raisins, and cinnamon.
Serve it over brown or white rice with a tossed salad on the side.

SERVES **4 to 6**

SIZE **6-quart or larger pressure cooker**

TIME **5 to 7 minutes at high pressure with quick pressure release**

The dish can be prepared up to 2 days in advance and refrigerated, tightly covered. Reheat it, covered, over low heat until hot, stirring occasionally.

3 tablespoons olive oil, divided
1½ pounds (85 percent lean) ground beef
1 large onion, diced
3 garlic cloves, minced
½ red bell pepper, seeds and ribs removed, diced
1 or 2 jalapeño or serrano chiles, seeds and ribs removed, finely chopped
2 tablespoons chili powder
1 tablespoon ground cumin
1 tablespoon unsweetened cocoa powder

1 teaspoon dried oregano
½ teaspoon ground cinnamon
1 (14.5-ounce) can diced tomatoes, undrained
¼ cup firmly packed dark brown sugar
2 tablespoons cider vinegar
½ cup raisins
½ cup diced green olives
1 cup cooked garbanzo beans or red kidney beans (optional)
Salt and hot red pepper sauce to taste

Heat 1 tablespoon of the oil in the cooker over medium-high heat or use the browning function of an electric cooker. Crumble the ground beef into the cooker and cook for 3 to 5 minutes, or until no pink remains. Remove the beef from the cooker with a slotted spoon and set it aside. Discard the grease from the cooker.

Heat the remaining oil in the cooker over medium-high heat or use the browning function of an electric cooker. Add the onion, garlic, bell pepper, and chiles. Cook, stirring frequently, for 3 minutes, or until the onion is translucent. Reduce the heat to low or turn an electric cooker to the "keep warm" setting and stir in the chili powder, cumin, cocoa powder, oregano, and cinnamon. Cook for 1 minute, stirring constantly. Return the beef to the cooker and add the tomatoes, brown sugar, vinegar, raisins, olives, and ¼ cup water.

Close and lock the lid of the cooker.

STOVETOP: Place the cooker over high heat, and bring it to high pressure. Once high pressure is reached, reduce the heat as much as possible while retaining the high-pressure level. Cook for 5 minutes. Then take the pot off the heat and quick release the pressure according to the instructions provided by the manufacturer. Remove the lid, tilting it away from you, to allow the steam to escape.

OR

ELECTRIC: Set the machine to cook at high pressure for 7 minutes. After 7 minutes, unplug the pot so that it does not go into warming mode. Quick release the pressure according to the instructions provided by the manufacturer. Remove the lid, tilting it away from you, to allow the steam to escape.

Stir in the beans, if using, and then cook over medium-high heat or use the browning function of an electric cooker for 5 minutes, or until the liquid is reduced and has thickened. Season to taste with salt and hot red pepper sauce, and serve hot.

NOTE Any chili can become a finger food by turning it into nachos. Pile the chili on large nacho corn chips, top with some grated Monterey Jack cheese, and pop them under the broiler until the cheese is melted. Then sprinkle the top with some sliced radishes, diced cherry tomatoes, dabs of sour cream, and fresh cilantro leaves.

VARIATIONS

★ Substitute ground turkey for the ground beef.

★ Substitute chopped dried apricots or dried cranberries for the raisins.

Sweet and Sour Stuffed Cabbage

Sweet and sour foods, most of which are made with tomato as well as cabbage, are part of Eastern European Jewish heritage. It's a profile seen in soups as well as this one-pot meal. This dish is great for cold winter nights.

SERVES **4 to 6**

SIZE **6-quart or larger pressure cooker**

TIME **20 to 25 minutes at high pressure with quick pressure release**

The rolls can be cooked up to 2 days in advance and refrigerated, tightly covered. Reheat them in a 350°F oven for 20 to 30 minutes, or until hot.

1 small (1½-pound) head Savoy cabbage
2 tablespoons vegetable oil
1 medium onion, diced
1½ pounds (85 percent lean) ground beef
⅓ cup short-grain white sushi rice
2 tablespoons chopped fresh parsley
2 teaspoons fresh thyme leaves

Salt and freshly ground black pepper to taste
2 Granny Smith or Golden Delicious apples, peeled, cored, and cut into 1-inch wedges
½ cup raisins
1 (15-ounce) can tomato sauce
½ cup cider vinegar
½ cup firmly packed dark brown sugar

Core the cabbage and wrap the head in plastic wrap. Microwave on high (100 percent power) for 30 seconds. Pull off the pliable outer leaves and set aside. Rewrap the remaining head and microwave again. Repeat this process until you have 12 leaves separated. Then shred the remaining cabbage.

Heat the oil in a small skillet over medium-high heat. Add the onion and cook, stirring frequently, for 3 minutes, or until the onion is translucent. Scrape the mixture into a mixing bowl and add the ground beef, rice, parsley, thyme, salt, and pepper. Mix well.

Place half of the shredded cabbage leaves on the bottom of the cooker. Top with half of the apple slices and half of the raisins. Place ½ cup of the beef mixture at the stem end of a cabbage leaf. Tuck in the sides, and roll up the leaf into a cylinder. Repeat with the remaining cabbage leaves and beef filling. Place the rolls seam side down in the cooker. Top with the remaining cabbage shreds, apple, and raisins and a new layer of cabbage rolls if necessary.

Mix the tomato sauce, vinegar, and brown sugar in a mixing bowl, stirring well to dissolve the sugar. Pour the sauce over the cabbage rolls.

Close and lock the lid of the cooker.

STOVETOP: Place the cooker over high heat, and bring it to high pressure. Once high pressure is reached, reduce the heat as much as possible while retaining the high-pressure level. Cook for 20 minutes. Then take the pot off the heat and quick release the pressure according to the instructions provided by the manufacturer. Remove the lid, tilting it away from you, to allow the steam to escape.

OR

ELECTRIC: Set the machine to cook at high pressure for 25 minutes. After 25 minutes, unplug the pot so that it does not go into warming mode. Quick release the pressure according to the instructions provided by the manufacturer. Remove the lid, tilting it away from you, to allow the steam to escape.

Tilt the cooker and ladle off as much fat as possible from the surface. Serve immediately.

NOTE When you're selecting a head of cabbage, look for one that still has the dark green outer leaves attached. Supermarkets pull off those leaves as the head ages, and so if they're still attached it's a sign that the head is fresh.

VARIATION

★ Substitute ground turkey, ground pork, or ground veal for the ground beef.

Meatballs in Marinara Sauce

This creation of the Italian-American kitchen takes mere minutes to prepare. Start the water for cooking your pasta before you even start making the meatballs. Serve the dish with a loaf of crusty garlic bread and a tossed salad.

SERVES **4 to 6**

SIZE **6-quart or larger pressure cooker**

TIME **5 to 7 minutes at high pressure with quick pressure release**

The meatballs can be prepared for cooking up to 1 day in advance and refrigerated, tightly covered.

NOTE Meatballs made in the pressure cooker have a different proportion of breadcrumbs to liquid than meatballs that are prepared for conventional cooking. Although they come out extremely fluffy, they still need some breadcrumbs to serve as binder as they cook. If you want to make some of your favorite meatball recipes in the pressure cooker, use this recipe as a guide.

½ cup panko breadcrumbs
¼ cup whole milk
1 large egg, lightly beaten
½ pound (85 percent lean) ground beef
½ pound ground pork
¼ pound bulk Italian sausage (mild or hot)
3 garlic cloves, minced
⅓ cup freshly grated Parmesan cheese

2 tablespoons chopped fresh parsley
Salt and freshly ground black pepper to taste
1 batch Marinara Sauce (page 263) or 1 quart purchased marinara sauce
¾ to 1 pound cooked hot spaghetti for serving
Additional freshly grated Parmesan cheese for serving

Combine the breadcrumbs, milk, and egg in a mixing bowl and mix well. Add the ground beef, ground pork, sausage, garlic, Parmesan, and parsley. Season to taste with salt and pepper. Mix together well with your hands and then form the mixture into 12 meatballs. Pour the sauce into the cooker and place the meatballs gently into the sauce.

Close and lock the lid of the cooker.

STOVETOP: Place the cooker over high heat, and bring it to high pressure. Once high pressure is reached, reduce the heat as much as possible while retaining the high-pressure level. Cook for 5 minutes. Then take the pot off the heat and quick release the pressure according to the instructions provided by the manufacturer. Remove the lid, tilting it away from you, to allow the steam to escape.

OR

ELECTRIC: Set the machine to cook at high pressure for 7 minutes. After 7 minutes, unplug the pot so that it does not go into warming mode. Quick release the pressure according to the instructions provided by the manufacturer. Remove the lid, tilting it away from you, to allow the steam to escape.

Serve the meatballs and sauce over hot spaghetti and pass around some additional Parmesan cheese.

Herbed Mushroom Meatloaf
with Gruyère Mashed Potatoes, page 144

Herbed Mushroom Meatloaf
with Gruyère Mashed Potatoes

In the annals of comfort food, meatloaf and mashed potatoes rank high on the list. In this recipe, the meatloaf and potatoes cook in the same amount of time, so you can make the whole meal in mere minutes. The meatloaf is studded with vegetables and flavored with herbs, and the addition of cheese elevates the spuds to elegance.

SERVES **6 to 8**

SIZE **6-quart or larger pressure cooker**

TIME **10 to 12 minutes at high pressure with quick pressure release**

The meatloaf and potatoes can be cooked up to 2 days in advance and refrigerated separately, tightly covered. Reheat the meatloaf in a 350°F oven for 10 to 12 minutes, or until hot. Reheat the potatoes in a microwave oven.

MEATLOAF
- ½ cup whole milk
- 1 large egg
- 2 tablespoons Worcestershire sauce
- 1 tablespoon tomato paste
- 2 slices white sandwich bread, torn into small pieces
- 2 tablespoons chopped fresh parsley
- 2 teaspoons fresh thyme leaves
- 2 tablespoons unsalted butter
- 3 tablespoons olive oil, divided
- ¼ pound crimini mushrooms, diced
- Salt and freshly ground black pepper to taste
- 1 large onion, diced
- 1 large carrot, diced
- 1 celery rib, diced
- 3 garlic cloves, minced
- 1¼ pounds ground (85 percent lean) beef
- ¼ pound bulk Italian sausage (mild or hot)
- ¾ cup ketchup

POTATOES
- 2½ pounds russet potatoes, peeled and cut into 1-inch slices
- ¼ pound Gruyère, grated
- 2 tablespoons unsalted butter
- ¼ to ½ cup whole milk
- Salt and freshly ground black pepper to taste

For the meatloaf, combine the milk, egg, Worcestershire sauce, tomato paste, bread, parsley, and thyme in a large mixing bowl and whisk well.

Heat the butter and 1 tablespoon of the oil in the cooker over medium-high heat or use the browning function of an electric cooker. Add the mushrooms and sprinkle them with salt and pepper. Cook the mushrooms, stirring frequently, for 4 to 5 minutes, or until brown. Scrape the mushrooms into the bowl with the bread mixture.

Heat the remaining oil in the cooker over medium-high heat or use the browning function of an electric cooker. Add the onion, carrot, celery, and garlic. Cook, stirring frequently, for 3 minutes, or until the onion is translucent. Scrape the vegetables into the bowl with the mushrooms. Add the ground beef and sausage, and mix well.

Create an aluminum foil sling as described on page 11 and fit it into the steamer basket of the cooker. Form the meatloaf into a circle of an even thickness in the basket, leaving at least 1½ inches empty around the periphery.

Place the potatoes in the bottom of the cooker and pour 1½ cups of water over them. Season to taste with salt and pepper.

Place the steamer basket with the meatloaf on top of the potatoes. Close and lock the lid of the cooker.

STOVETOP: Place the cooker over high heat, and bring it to high pressure. Once high pressure is reached, reduce the heat as much as possible while retaining the high-pressure level. Cook for 10 minutes. Then take the pot off the heat and quick release the pressure according to the instructions provided by the manufacturer. Remove the lid, tilting it away from you, to allow the steam to escape.

OR

ELECTRIC: Set the machine to cook at high pressure for 12 minutes. After 12 minutes, unplug the pot so that it does not go into warming mode. Quick release the pressure according to the instructions provided by the manufacturer. Remove the lid, tilting it away from you, to allow the steam to escape.

Once high pressure is reached, preheat the oven to 450°F and line a baking sheet with heavy-duty aluminum foil.

Remove the steamer from the cooker and transfer the meatloaf to the baking sheet, using the sling. Coat the top and sides of the meatloaf with the ketchup and bake it for 10 minutes, or until it browns.

While the meatloaf is baking, drain the potatoes and return them to the cooker. Place the cooker over medium heat or use the browning function of an electric cooker. Cook the potatoes for 2 minutes, or until they appear dry. Add the cheese, butter, and milk, and mash with a potato masher to the desired consistency. Season to taste with salt and pepper, and serve hot alongside slices of the meatloaf.

NOTE Foods that are cooked in a pressure cooker don't achieve the appealing color of foods that are cooked, uncovered, in a conventional oven. To remedy this problem, simply coat the meatloaf with ketchup and bake it in a far hotter oven than you usually would use to bake a conventional meatloaf. The ketchup browns, but the meat does not dry out.

VARIATIONS

⋆ Substitute Swiss cheese or cheddar cheese for the Gruyère.

⋆ Substitute ground turkey for the ground beef and sausage.

Creole Bison Meatloaf

Certain ingredient combinations distinguish one American regional cuisine from another. In this case, the flavors of onion, green bell pepper, and celery, combined with thyme and oregano, evoke Creole cooking. Serve this meatloaf with Colcannon (page 239) and Collard Greens with Bacon (page 248).

SERVES **4 to 6**

SIZE **6-quart or larger pressure cooker**

TIME **10 to 12 minutes at high pressure with quick pressure release**

The bison mixture can be prepared up to 1 day in advance and refrigerated, tightly covered. Also, the meatloaf can be baked up to 2 days in advance and refrigerated, tightly covered. Reheat it in a 350°F oven, covered, for 20 to 25 minutes, or until hot.

3 tablespoons olive oil
1 medium onion, diced
1 small green bell pepper, seeds and ribs removed, chopped
2 celery ribs, chopped
3 garlic cloves, minced
1 large egg
¼ cup whole milk
2 tablespoons tomato paste
½ cup panko breadcrumbs
¼ cup chopped fresh parsley
1 tablespoon fresh thyme leaves
1 teaspoon dried oregano
1½ pounds ground bison
½ cup grated Monterey Jack cheese
Salt and freshly ground black pepper to taste
¾ cup bottled chili sauce

Heat the oil in a medium skillet over medium-high heat. Add the onion, green bell pepper, celery, and garlic, and cook, stirring frequently, for 5 to 7 minutes, or until the vegetables soften.

Combine the egg, milk, and tomato paste in a mixing bowl and whisk well to dissolve tomato paste. Add the breadcrumbs, parsley, thyme, and oregano, and mix well. Add the vegetable mixture, bison, and cheese to the mixing bowl and mix well again. Season to taste with salt and pepper.

Create an aluminum foil sling as described on page 11 and fit it into the steamer basket of the cooker. Form the meatloaf into a circle of an even thickness in the basket, leaving at least 1½ inches empty around the periphery.

Pour 1 cup of water into the cooker and place the steamer basket with the meatloaf on top of a trivet.

Close and lock the lid of the cooker.

STOVETOP: Place the cooker over high heat, and bring it to high pressure. Once high pressure is reached, reduce the heat as much as possible while retaining the high-pressure level. Cook for 10 minutes. Then take the pot off the heat and quick release the pressure according to the instructions provided by the manufacturer. Remove the lid, tilting it away from you, to allow the steam to escape.

OR

ELECTRIC: Set the machine to cook at high pressure for 12 minutes. After 12 minutes, unplug the pot so that it does not go into warming mode. Quick release the pressure according to the instructions provided by the manufacturer. Remove the lid, tilting it away from you, to allow the steam to escape.

NOTE Contrary to its name, chili sauce is closer to a chunky ketchup than to a fiery sauce. It's a tomato-based condiment that contains onions, green peppers, vinegar, sugar, and spices. It serves as the basis for traditional cocktail sauce, too, so it's worthwhile to keep a bottle in the house.

Once high pressure is reached, preheat the oven to 450°F and line a baking sheet with heavy-duty aluminum foil.

Remove the steamer from the cooker and transfer the meatloaf to the baking sheet, using the sling. Coat the top and sides of the meatloaf with the chili sauce and bake it for 10 minutes, or until it browns.

Lamb Shanks with White Beans

Lamb and white beans, braised together in an herbed broth, is a classic combination that takes a lot of advance planning and time. But now you can prepare this dish on the spur of the moment with a pressure cooker, which cooks the beans, in their dry state, as quickly as it takes the lamb to become meltingly tender. Serve it with Caponata (page 240) or Kale with Pancetta (page 251).

SERVES **4 to 6**

SIZE **6-quart or larger pressure cooker**

TIME **30 to 35 minutes at high pressure; then allow the pressure to release naturally**

The shanks can be prepared up to 2 days in advance and refrigerated, tightly covered. Reheat them, covered, in a 350°F oven for 20 to 25 minutes, or until hot.

4 to 6 (3/4-pound) lamb shanks
Salt and freshly ground black
   pepper to taste
2 tablespoons olive oil
1 large onion, diced
4 garlic cloves, minced
4 cups Beef Stock (page 16)
   or purchased stock
2 carrots, diced
2 celery ribs, diced

3 ripe plum tomatoes, cored,
   seeded, and diced
3 sprigs fresh rosemary
2 sprigs fresh thyme
1 bay leaf
1½ cups dried navy beans,
   picked over and rinsed

GARNISH
Fresh rosemary sprigs

Preheat the oven broiler and line a broiler pan with heavy-duty aluminum foil. Sprinkle the lamb with salt and pepper, and broil the lamb for 3 minutes on each side, or until browned.

Heat the oil in the pressure cooker over medium-high heat or use the browning function of an electric cooker. Add the onion and garlic and cook, stirring frequently, for 3 minutes, or until the onion is translucent. Stir in the stock, carrots, celery, tomatoes, rosemary sprigs, thyme, bay leaf, and beans. Arrange the lamb shanks in the cooker.

Close and lock the lid of the cooker.

STOVETOP: Place the cooker over high heat, and bring it to high pressure. Once high pressure is reached, reduce the heat as much as possible while retaining the high-pressure level. Cook for 30 minutes. Then take the pot off the heat and allow it to return to normal pressure naturally. Remove the lid, tilting it away from you, to allow the steam to escape.

OR

ELECTRIC: Set the machine to cook at high pressure for 35 minutes. After 35 minutes, unplug the pot so that it does not go into warming mode. Allow the pressure to return to normal naturally. Remove the lid, tilting it away from you, to allow the steam to escape.

Remove the shanks from the cooker and set them aside. Allow the liquid to rest for 10 minutes; then tilt the cooker and spoon off as much fat as possible. Remove and discard the bay leaf, rosemary sprigs, and thyme sprigs. Return the shanks to the sauce to reheat, season to taste with salt and pepper, and serve.

NOTE Lamb shanks range in size from ½ pound to almost 2 pounds. The size specified for this recipe will fit into a 6-quart cooker; however if the shanks are larger, they will require an 8-quart cooker. Three-quarter-pound shanks are intended to be served individually but you can cut the meat off the bones once the shanks are cooked and divide the meat among the diners.

Lamb Shanks
with White Beans, page 148

Braised Lamb Shanks

Here, the addition of a bit of citrus and smoked paprika, contrasted with woodsy dried mushrooms, fresh herbs, and caramelized onions, brings out all the luscious fruit in a rich red wine. Serve the lamb shanks with Creamy Polenta (page 214) or Gruyère Mashed Potatoes (page 144).

SERVES **4 to 6**

SIZE **6-quart or larger pressure cooker**

TIME **30 to 35 minutes at high pressure; then allow the pressure to release naturally**

> The shanks can be prepared up to 2 days in advance and refrigerated, tightly covered. Reheat them, covered, in a 350°F oven for 20 to 25 minutes, or until hot.

1¼ cups Beef Stock (page 16) or purchased stock
½ cup dried porcini mushrooms
4 to 6 (¾-pound) lamb shanks
Salt and freshly ground black pepper to taste
2 juice oranges
2 tablespoons olive oil
1 large sweet onion, diced
3 garlic cloves, minced

2 tablespoons sweet smoked Spanish paprika (*pimentón de la vera dulce*)
3 tablespoons all-purpose flour
1½ cups dry red wine
3 tablespoons tomato paste
3 tablespoons chopped fresh rosemary
2 tablespoons chopped fresh parsley
2 bay leaves

Bring the stock to a boil in a small saucepan or a microwave-safe bowl. Soak the mushrooms in the boiling stock, pushing them down into the liquid with the back of a spoon, for 10 minutes. Drain the mushrooms, reserving the stock. Discard the mushroom stems and slice the caps thickly. Strain the stock through a sieve lined with a paper coffee filter or paper towel. Set aside.

Preheat the oven broiler and line a broiler pan with heavy-duty aluminum foil. Sprinkle the lamb with salt and pepper, and broil the lamb for 3 minutes on each side, or until browned. While the shanks brown, grate the zest from one of the oranges and squeeze the juice from both oranges.

Heat the oil in the pressure cooker over medium-high heat or use the browning function of an electric cooker. Add the onion and garlic and cook, stirring frequently, for 3 minutes, or until the onion is translucent. Stir in the paprika and flour, and cook for 1 minute, stirring constantly. Add the soaked mushrooms, strained stock, orange zest, orange juice, wine, tomato paste, rosemary, parsley, and bay leaves. Stir well to dissolve the tomato paste. Arrange the lamb shanks in the cooker.

Close and lock the lid of the cooker.

STOVETOP: Place the cooker over high heat, and bring it to high pressure. Once high pressure is reached, reduce the heat as much as possible while retaining the high-pressure level. Cook for 30 minutes. Then take the pot off the heat and allow it to return to normal pressure naturally. Remove the lid, tilting it away from you, to allow the steam to escape.

OR

ELECTRIC: Set the machine to cook at high pressure for 35 minutes. After 35 minutes, unplug the pot so that it does not go into warming mode. Allow the pressure to return to normal naturally. Remove the lid, tilting it away from you, to allow the steam to escape.

VARIATIONS

★ Add ¼ pound of soaked dried garbanzo beans to the cooker and increase the amount of stock to 2 cups.

★ Substitute boneless beef chuck, cut into 3-inch cubes, for the lamb shanks.

Remove the shanks from the cooker and set them aside. Allow the liquid to rest for 10 minutes; then tilt the cooker and spoon off as much fat as possible. Place the cooker over medium-high heat or use the browning function of an electric cooker. Boil the sauce until it is reduced by half. Remove and discard the bay leaves. Return the shanks to the sauce to reheat, season to taste with salt and pepper, and serve.

Greek Braised Lamb

The combination of lemon and egg—one of the cornerstones of Greek cooking and perhaps best known in Avgolemono, the famous soup with that combination—enriches this robust lamb stew. Serve it with Creamy Polenta (page 214) or Farro Pilaf (page 207).

SERVES **4 to 6**

SIZE **6-quart or larger pressure cooker**

TIME **20 to 25 minutes; then allow the pressure to release naturally**

> Up to adding the lemon-egg mixture, the dish can be made up to 3 days in advance and refrigerated, tightly covered. Reheat it over low heat to a simmer and add the enrichment just before serving.

3 pounds boneless lamb shoulder, cut into 2-inch pieces
Salt and freshly ground black pepper to taste
3 tablespoons olive oil
1 large onion, diced
4 garlic cloves, minced
1 tablespoon tomato paste
3 tablespoons all-purpose flour
½ cup dry white wine
2 cups Chicken Stock (page 15) or purchased stock
3 sprigs fresh thyme

3 sprigs fresh rosemary
2 bay leaves
2 large eggs
2 large egg yolks
½ cup freshly squeezed lemon juice
1 teaspoon grated lemon zest

GARNISH
¼ cup chopped fresh dill
3 scallions, white parts and 3 inches of green tops, sliced on the diagonal

Preheat the oven broiler and line a broiler pan with heavy-duty aluminum foil. Pat the lamb dry with paper towels and sprinkle it with salt and pepper. Arrange the lamb in a single layer on the foil and broil for 3 minutes on each side, or until the lamb is browned. Remove the lamb from the broiler and set it aside.

Heat the oil in the cooker over medium-high heat or use the browning function of an electric cooker. Add the onion and garlic and cook, stirring occasionally, for 3 minutes, or until the onion is translucent. Stir in the tomato paste and cook for 1 minute, stirring constantly. Reduce the heat to low, stir in the flour, and cook for 1 minute, stirring constantly.

Whisk in the wine and cook for 2 minutes. Add the stock, thyme, rosemary, bay leaves, and lamb to the cooker and stir well.

Close and lock the lid of the cooker.

STOVETOP: Place the cooker over high heat, and bring it to high pressure. Once high pressure is reached, reduce the heat as much as possible while retaining the high-pressure level. Cook for 20 minutes. Then take the pot off the heat and allow it to return to normal pressure naturally. Remove the lid, tilting it away from you, to allow the steam to escape.

OR

ELECTRIC: Set the machine to cook at high pressure for 25 minutes. After 25 minutes, unplug the pot so that it does not go into warming mode. Allow the pressure to return to normal naturally. Remove the lid, tilting it away from you, to allow the steam to escape.

Remove the lamb from the cooker with a slotted spoon and set aside. Remove and discard the thyme sprigs, rosemary sprigs, and bay leaves. Allow the liquid to rest for 10 minutes; then tilt the cooker and spoon off as much fat as possible. Return the lamb to the cooker and bring the sauce back to a simmer.

Whisk the eggs, egg yolks, lemon juice, and lemon zest together in a mixing bowl until light and frothy. Slowly whisk in 1 cup of the lamb sauce into the eggs and then return the mixture to the pot. Stir it in, turn off the heat, cover the pot, and allow the sauce to sit for 3 minutes to thicken.

Season to taste with salt and pepper, and add additional lemon juice if desired. Serve immediately, garnishing each portion with chopped dill and scallions.

NOTE It's easier to remove the zest from citrus fruits before the juice is extracted, because the skin is taut. Remove all the zest, not just the amount specified in a recipe, and store it in a small plastic bag in the refrigerator

VARIATION

⋆ **Greek Chicken Stew**: Substitute 4 to 6 bone-in, skin-on chicken pieces of your choice (breasts cut in half, thighs, legs) for the lamb and reduce the cooking time to 12 minutes for a stovetop cooker and 14 minutes for an electric cooker.

Middle Eastern Lamb Chili
with Beans and Zucchini

This recipe, based on the classic seasonings of Morocco, combines aromatic cumin and coriander, tomato, beans, and healthful zucchini. Serve it alongside a bowl of Quinoa Tabbouleh (page 212).

SERVES **4 to 6**

SIZE **6-quart or larger pressure cooker**

TIME **6 to 8 minutes at high pressure; then allow the pressure to release naturally**

The chili can be made up to 2 days in advance and refrigerated, tightly covered. Reheat it over low heat, covered, or in a microwave oven.

- 1 cup dried cannellini beans
- 2 to 3 medium zucchini
- 2 tablespoons kosher salt
- 3 tablespoons olive oil, divided
- 1¼ pounds ground lamb
- 1 medium onion, diced
- 3 garlic cloves, minced
- 1 red bell pepper, seeds and ribs removed, diced
- 2 tablespoons ground cumin
- 1 tablespoon ground coriander
- 1 (14.5-ounce) can diced tomatoes, undrained
- 2 tablespoons tomato paste
- 1 tablespoon chopped fresh parsley
- Hot red pepper sauce to taste
- 2 to 3 cups hot cooked couscous for serving

Rinse the beans in a colander and place them in a mixing bowl covered with cold salted water. Allow the beans to soak for a minimum of 6 hours, or overnight. Or place the beans into a saucepan of salted water and bring to a boil over high heat. Boil 1 minute. Turn off the heat, cover the pan, and soak the beans for 1 hour. After using either of these soaking methods, drain the beans, discard the soaking water, and cook or refrigerate the beans as soon as possible.

Cut the zucchini in half lengthwise and then cut them into ½-inch slices. Place 4 cups of cold water in a mixing bowl and stir in the kosher salt. Add the zucchini slices and soak them for 15 minutes. Drain and rinse well.

Heat 1 tablespoon of the oil in the cooker over medium-high heat or use the browning function of an electric cooker. Crumble the lamb into the cooker, breaking up lumps with a fork. Cook for 3 minutes, stirring frequently, or until the lamb is browned. Remove the lamb from the cooker with a slotted spoon and discard the grease from the cooker.

Heat the remaining oil in the cooker. Add the onion, garlic, and red bell pepper, and cook, stirring frequently, for 3 minutes, or until the onion is translucent. Add the cumin and coriander, and cook for 1 minute, stirring constantly.

Return the lamb to the cooker and add the tomatoes, tomato paste, and drained beans. Stir well to dissolve the tomato paste.

Close and lock the lid of the cooker.

STOVETOP: Place the cooker over high heat and bring it to high pressure. Once high pressure is reached, reduce the heat as much as possible while retaining the high-pressure level. Cook for 6 minutes. Then take the pot off the heat and allow it to return to normal pressure naturally. Remove the lid, tilting it away from you, to allow the steam to escape.

OR

ELECTRIC: Set the machine to cook at high pressure for 8 minutes. After 8 minutes, unplug the pot so that it does not go into warming mode. Allow the pressure to return to normal naturally. Remove the lid, tilting it away from you, to allow the steam to escape.

Add the drained zucchini to the cooker, and place it over medium heat or use the browning function of an electric cooker. Cook the zucchini, uncovered, for 7 to 10 minutes, or until the zucchini is crisp-tender. Stir in the parsley and season to taste with salt and hot red pepper sauce. Serve immediately.

NOTE If you soak the zucchini in the salt water, it retains its shape and texture when cooked rather than falling apart. The same technique can be used for yellow crookneck squash.

Moussaka

Although this dish was once an integral part of cuisines all over the Ottoman Empire, we now associate it with Greece, where every taverna has its own version—although almost all of them contain the same mélange of eggplant and lamb topped with a cheesy béchamel custard and an aromatic seasoning such as cinnamon. I've added some zesty dried currants to this version as well as some fresh-tasting dill to the sauce. The pressure cooker makes quick work of the meat filling, but you do have to allow some time for baking the custard.

SERVES **4 to 6**

SIZE **6-quart or larger pressure cooker**

TIME **6 to 8 minutes at high pressure with quick pressure release**

The dish can be prepared up to 2 days in advance and refrigerated, tightly covered. Reheat it, covered with foil, for 20 minutes at 325°F.

LAMB

- 1 (1-pound) eggplant, cut into 1-inch cubes
- ¼ cup kosher salt
- ⅓ cup olive oil, divided
- 1 pound ground lamb
- 1 large onion, diced
- 2 garlic cloves, minced
- ¼ cup dried currants
- ¾ cup dry red wine
- 1 (8-ounce) can tomato sauce
- 2 tablespoons tomato paste
- 1 tablespoons chopped fresh rosemary
- 1 teaspoon dried oregano
- ¼ teaspoon ground cinnamon
- ¼ teaspoon ground ginger
- 2 tablespoons chopped fresh parsley
- Salt and freshly ground black pepper to taste
- Vegetable oil spray

TOPPING

- 3 tablespoons unsalted butter
- ¼ cup all-purpose flour
- 1¼ cups whole milk
- 3 large eggs, lightly beaten
- ⅓ cup freshly grated Parmesan cheese
- ¼ cup chopped fresh dill
- Salt and freshly ground black pepper to taste

Place the eggplant cubes in a mixing bowl with 4 cups of cold water. Add the salt and stir well. Place a plate on top of the cubes to keep them submerged and soak them for 20 minutes. Drain the eggplant in a colander and run cold water over the cubes. Squeeze handfuls of the cubes in your hands and then place them on a cloth dishtowel. Wring them in the towel and set aside.

While the eggplant soaks, heat 1 tablespoon of the oil in a cooker over medium-high heat or use the browning function of an electric cooker. Crumble the lamb into the cooker and cook, stirring frequently, for 3 to 4 minutes, or until the lamb is browned. Remove the lamb from the cooker with a slotted spoon and set it aside. Discard the fat from the cooker.

Heat ¼ cup of the remaining oil over medium heat. Add the eggplant cubes and cook, stirring frequently, for 5 minutes, or until the eggplant begins to soften. Remove the eggplant and set it aside.

Heat the remaining oil in the cooker and add the onion and garlic. Cook, stirring frequently, for 3 minutes, or until onion is translucent. Return the lamb and eggplant to the cooker and stir in the dried currants, wine, tomato sauce, tomato paste, rosemary, oregano, cinnamon, and ginger.

Close and lock the lid of the cooker.

STOVETOP: Place the cooker over high heat, and bring it to high pressure. Once high pressure is reached, reduce the heat as much as possible while retaining the high-pressure level. Cook for 6 minutes. Then take the pot off the heat and quick release the pressure according to the instructions provided by the manufacturer. Remove the lid, tilting it away from you, to allow the steam to escape.

OR

ELECTRIC: Set the machine to cook at high pressure for 8 minutes. After 8 minutes, unplug the pot so that it does not go into warming mode. Quick release the pressure according to the instructions provided by the manufacturer. Remove the lid, tilting it away from you, to allow the steam to escape.

NOTE It's important that dishes such as this one or lasagna be allowed to cool for at least 10 minutes before you cut and serve them. The sitting time allows the custard to set so that it will not fall apart when you remove a portion from the pan.

Stir the parsley into the lamb mixture and season it to taste with salt and pepper.

Preheat the oven to 350°F and grease a 2½-quart casserole with vegetable oil spray.

While the lamb mixture cooks, prepare the topping. Heat the butter in a medium saucepan over low heat. Stir in the flour and cook for 2 minutes, stirring constantly. Gradually add the milk, whisking constantly. Bring the mixture to a boil and remove the pan from the heat. Stir 1 cup of the hot liquid into the eggs and then stir that mixture along with the cheese and dill back into the pan. Stir well and season to taste with salt and pepper.

Transfer the lamb mixture to the casserole, spreading it evenly, and top it with the custard. Bake the custard for 35 to 45 minutes, or until it is set and brown. Cool for 10 minutes before serving.

Southern Pulled Pork Barbecue, page 164

CHAPTER 6

Pork and Veal

The recipes in Chapter 5 all unabashedly glorify the heartiness of rich red meats, the sort of food that begs for a good bottle of Bordeaux or Barolo. In this chapter the stars are "the other white meats"—pork and veal. You'll find that these recipes cook in a shorter amount of time, and some of them pair quite nicely with a white wine or even a glass of beer.

Pork has very little internal connective tissue and is inherently tender, because pigs don't wander and run around the prairies the way cows and lambs do. It is one of the few meats that can be equally good roasted or braised in aromatic liquid in the pressure cooker. With the exception of pork shoulder, which is more muscular and fatty and should be cooked with liquid, almost all loin cuts can be prepared either way.

Pork has layers of fat that encircle the meat rather than marbling it. Some fat should be left on so that the meat does not dry out when cooking. With the exception of the tenderloin, which will become stringy if subjected to braising, almost all cuts of pork are up for grabs. That's why you don't find precut pork for stews the way other animals' trimmings are packaged. Just choose pork that looks lean and is the least expensive.

The two best cuts of pork for dishes made in the pressure cooker are boneless country ribs and boneless butt. Boneless country ribs are the pork equivalent of a chuck roast; they have great flavor and become meltingly tender. In this chapter you'll also find a pair of recipes for my favorite way to enjoy pork, as meaty baby back ribs. The pressure cooker adds so much flavor as it tenderizes the ribs, and then you pop them under the broiler to add a crispy veneer.

There is some confusion about veal because it's referred to by different names, depending on the age and weight of the animal. Most of what we get is veal from calves, which are of either sex, about 9 months old and weighing about 750 pounds. What is prized are the younger animals, about 2 months old and weighing about 150 pounds. They are called "vealers" or "Bob" veal and have been fed only the milk of their mothers.

Because the meat is so tender, there are few cuts of veal that are appropriate for a trip to the pressure cooker. Perhaps the most popular are the crosscut sections of the hind shanks, called *osso buco* in Italian, a term that has been adopted around the world.

COOKING TIMES (IN MINUTES)
FOR PORK AND VEAL IN THE PRESSURE COOKER

	STOVETOP	ELECTRIC	RELEASE METHOD
PORK CUT			
BABY BACK RIBS	12	14	NATURAL
BELLY	25	30	NATURAL
BUTT, 2-INCH CUBES	12	14	NATURAL
BUTT, 3-LB. ROAST	25	30	NATURAL
CHOPS, 1 INCH THICK	14	16	NATURAL
GROUND	5	6	NATURAL
SAUSAGES	5	6	NATURAL
SHANKS	20	22	NATURAL
VEAL CUT			
BREAST	30	35	NATURAL
CHOP, BLADE	12	14	NATURAL
GROUND	5	6	NATURAL
OSSO BUCO	25	30	NATURAL
SHOULDER, 3-LB. ROAST	40	45	NATURAL
STEW MEAT, 1-INCH CUBES	18	20	NATURAL

Southern Pulled Pork Barbecue

Anyone who eats this meltingly tender, flavorful meat will assume that you tended a low-temperature smoker or grill for many hours, because the rich and flavorful barbecued flavor belies how quickly it was made. Serve it with New England "Baked" Beans (page 216) and German Potato Salad (page 254).

SERVES **6 to 8**

SIZE **6-quart pressure cooker or larger**

TIME **35 to 40 minutes at high pressure; then allow the pressure to release naturally**

> The pork can be prepared up to 3 days in advance and refrigerated, tightly covered. Reheat it over low heat, stirring occasionally.

- 1 (3-pound) boneless pork butt roast
- 1 cup ketchup, divided
- ½ cup cider vinegar
- ¼ cup firmly packed dark brown sugar
- 3 tablespoons Worcestershire sauce
- ¼ teaspoon liquid smoke
- 1 tablespoon dry mustard powder
- 2 garlic cloves, minced
- 1 tablespoon grated fresh ginger
- ½ lemon, thinly sliced with seeds discarded
- ½ to 1 teaspoon hot red pepper sauce or to taste
- 6 to 8 large sandwich buns, toasted, for serving
- 1 batch Celery Seed Slaw (page 167) for serving

Cut the pork into quarters and trim off large areas of visible fat.

Combine ½ cup of the ketchup, the vinegar, brown sugar, Worcestershire sauce, liquid smoke, mustard, garlic, ginger, lemon, red pepper sauce, and 1 cup of water in the cooker and stir well. Nestle the pork pieces into the liquid.

Close and lock the lid of the cooker.

STOVETOP: Place the cooker over high heat, and bring it to high pressure. Once high pressure is reached, reduce the heat as much as possible while retaining the high-pressure level. Cook for 35 minutes. Then take the pot off the heat and allow it to return to normal pressure naturally. Remove the lid, tilting it away from you, to allow the steam to escape.

OR

ELECTRIC: Set the machine to cook at high pressure for 40 minutes. Afer 40 minutes, unplug the pot so that it does not go into warming mode. Allow the pressure to return to normal naturally. Remove the lid, tilting it away from you, to allow the steam to escape.

Remove the pork from the cooker with a slotted spatula and transfer it to a mixing bowl. Remove and discard the lemon slices. Allow the liquid to rest for 10 minutes and then tilt the cooker and spoon off as much fat as possible.

Stir the remaining ketchup into the sauce, and bring it to a boil over medium-high heat or use the browning function of an electric cooker. Reduce the sauce by half.

When the pork is cool enough to handle, shred it with two forks or your fingers. Stir 1 cup of the sauce into the pork and adjust the seasoning, adding more salt, pepper, or hot red pepper sauce as desired.

To serve, mound some of the pork on a toasted bun and top with a spoonful of the slaw. Pass around the remaining sauce.

NOTE Liquid smoke, produced by a few manufacturers, is not some chemical created in a test tube by a mad scientist. It's a natural product that is produced by a safe, water-based process: When wood chips, such as hickory and mesquite, are burned, the condensed smoke forms into a liquid that is filtered to remove impurities before bottling. Use it sparingly; a little goes a long way. But it does add a tantalizing flavor to foods such as barbecue sauces and marinades.

Celery Seed Slaw, page 167

Celery Seed Slaw

This is my signature coleslaw, and it's very low in calories, because it contains no mayonnaise. It's a crunchy sweet-and-sour slaw that's flavored with sharp mustard and tasty celery seed, and it's perfect to top a luscious sandwich of pulled pork.

SERVES **6 to 8**

The slaw can be made 1 day in advance and refrigerated, tightly covered with plastic wrap.

⅓ cup vegetable oil
½ cup granulated sugar
½ cup cider vinegar
1 tablespoon celery seeds
1 tablespoon dry mustard powder
Salt and freshly ground black pepper to taste
1 (1½-pound) head green cabbage, cored and shredded

1 small red onion, halved and thinly sliced
1 green pepper, seeds and ribs removed, thinly sliced
1 red bell pepper, seeds and ribs removed, thinly sliced

Combine the oil, sugar, and vinegar in a small saucepan and bring to a boil over medium heat, stirring occasionally. Reduce the heat to low and stir in the celery seed, mustard, and salt and pepper. Simmer for 2 minutes.

Combine the cabbage, onion, green pepper, and red pepper in a large mixing bowl. Toss the dressing with the salad. Allow the slaw to sit at room temperature for 2 hours, tossing it occasionally. Refrigerate the slaw for 4 to 6 hours. Drain it well before serving.

Asian Pulled Pork Tacos

Flour tortillas are a great stand-in for the Mandarin pancakes served with traditional Chinese dishes. The inspiration for this dish is Hawaiian kalua pig, made by cooking pork wrapped in banana leaves in a sunken pit on the beach. In this case, green tea adds a vegetal note, and a few drops of liquid smoke add the aroma of the barbecue. Serve it with Jasmine Rice Salad (page 208).

SERVES **6 to 8**

SIZE **6-quart pressure cooker or larger**

TIME **35 to 40 minutes at high pressure; then allow the pressure to release naturally**

> The pork can be prepared up to 3 days in advance and refrigerated, tightly covered. Reheat it over low heat, stirring occasionally.

- 3 pounds pork butt
- 2 green tea bags
- 6 garlic cloves, peeled
- 1 (2-inch) piece fresh ginger, thickly sliced
- ⅔ cup hoisin sauce, divided
- 3 tablespoons fish sauce
- 2 teaspoons sriracha sauce or to taste
- 1 tablespoon sesame oil
- ¼ teaspoon liquid smoke
- 1 tablespoon cornstarch
- 12 to 16 (6-inch) flour tortillas, warmed
- 4 scallions, white parts and 4 inches of green tops, julienned
- ½ Kirby cucumber, julienned

Cut the pork into quarters and trim off large areas of visible fat.

Cut the tea bags open and empty the contents into the cooker. Add the garlic, ginger, ¼ cup of the hoisin sauce, fish sauce, sriracha sauce, sesame oil, liquid smoke, and 1 cup of water to the cooker and stir well. Nestle the pork pieces into the liquid.

Close and lock the lid of the cooker.

STOVETOP: Place the cooker over high heat, and bring it to high pressure. Once high pressure is reached, reduce the heat as much as possible while retaining the high-pressure level. Cook for 35 minutes. Then take the pot off the heat and allow it to return to normal pressure naturally. Remove the lid, tilting it away from you, to allow the steam to escape.

OR

ELECTRIC: Set the machine to cook at high pressure for 40 minutes. After 40 minutes, unplug the pot so that it does not go into warming mode. Allow the pressure to return to normal naturally. Remove the lid, tilting it away from you, to allow the steam to

---

Remove the pork from the cooker with a slotted spatula and transfer it to a mixing bowl. Remove and discard the garlic cloves and ginger slices. Allow the liquid to rest for 10 minutes; then tilt the cooker and spoon off as much fat as possible.

Bring the sauce to a boil over medium-high heat or use the browning function of an electric cooker. Reduce the sauce by half. Combine the cornstarch with 2 tablespoons of cold water in a small cup, stirring well to dissolve the cornstarch. Stir the cornstarch mixture into the cooker. Bring to a boil over high heat or use the browning function of an electric cooker. Cook for 1 minute, or until the sauce thickens.

When the pork is cool enough to handle, shred it with two forks or your fingers. Stir ½ to ⅔ cup of the sauce into the pork and adjust the seasoning.

To serve, spread some of the remaining hoisin sauce on the center of a tortilla. Top it with some pork and the julienned scallions and cucumbers. Fold the bottom and sides over the filling to enclose it, and repeat with the remaining tortillas. Pass around the remaining sauce separately.

NOTE There are many ways to warm flour tortillas to make them pliable, including placing them in a dry skillet or holding them over an open flame. For a dish such as this one, the easiest way to warm the tortillas is to wrap them in plastic wrap and microwave them on high (100 percent) power for 30 seconds.

Pork in Black Bean Sauce
with Bok Choy

Because so many Chinese immigrants came from Canton and other parts of southern China early on, many Americans tend to think that quickly stir-fried dishes are typical of Chinese regional cooking, when in fact there is also a long history in China of making braised dishes—vividly flavored comfort foods that are appropriate to winter weather anywhere in the world.

SERVES **4 to 6**

SIZE **6-quart or larger pressure cooker**

TIME **12 to 14 minutes at high pressure; then allow the pressure to release naturally**

The pork can be cooked up to 3 days in advance and refrigerated, tightly covered. Reheat it over low heat, covered. Do not cook the bok choy until just before serving.

- 1½ pounds boneless country spare ribs
- 2 tablespoons vegetable oil
- 1 (2-inch) piece ginger, peeled and cut into julienne slices
- 4 garlic cloves, peeled
- 5 scallions, white parts and 4 inches of green tops, divided
- ½ teaspoon crushed red pepper flakes
- ½ cup Chicken Stock (page 15), Chinese Chicken Stock (page 15), or purchased stock
- ½ cup black bean sauce with garlic
- ¼ cup hoisin sauce
- ¼ cup dry sherry
- 3 tablespoons oyster sauce
- 3 tablespoons reduced-sodium soy sauce
- 1 star anise pod
- 1 tablespoon cornstarch
- 2 teaspoons sesame oil
- ½ pound bok choy, cut into 1-inch slices
- 2 to 3 cups hot cooked white rice for serving

Cut the pork into 2-inch cubes and pat them dry with paper towels.

Heat the oil in the cooker over medium-high heat or use the browning function of an electric cooker. Add the pork pieces and brown well on all sides. Remove the pork from the cooker and set it aside. Add the ginger, garlic, half of the scallions, and the crushed red pepper flakes to the cooker and cook for 30 seconds, stirring constantly.

Return the pork to the cooker and add the chicken stock, black bean sauce, hoisin sauce, sherry, oyster sauce, soy sauce, and star anise pod. Stir well.

Close and lock the lid of the cooker.

STOVETOP: Place the cooker over high heat, and bring it to high pressure. Once high pressure is reached, reduce the heat as much as possible while retaining the high-pressure level. Cook for 12 minutes. Then take the pot off the heat and allow it to return to normal pressure naturally. Remove the lid, tilting it away from you, to allow the steam to escape.

OR

ELECTRIC: Set the machine to cook at high pressure for 14 minutes. After 14 minutes, unplug the pot so that it does not go into warming mode. Allow the pressure to return to normal naturally. Remove the lid, tilting it away from you, to allow the steam to escape.

Remove and discard the star anise pod. Combine the cornstarch with 2 tablespoons of cold water and stir well to dissolve the powder. Bring to a boil over high heat or use the browning function of an electric cooker. Cook for 1 minute, or until the sauce thickens.

A few minutes before the pork is done, heat the sesame oil in a large skillet over high heat. Add the bok choy and turn it with tongs to coat. Add ¼ cup water to the skillet and cover it. Steam the bok choy for 1 minute.

To serve, top cooked rice with pork and bok choy, and sprinkle each serving with the remaining scallions.

NOTE The skin on fresh ginger is so thin that you really don't need a knife to peel it; you can use the tip of a soupspoon. That way the skin comes off the irregularly shaped knobs easily, with no fear of cutting yourself.

VARIATION

★ Substitute boneless, skinless chicken thighs for the cubes of pork. The cooking time will be the same.

Posole
(Mexican Pork and Hominy Stew)

Posole, *sometimes spelled* pozole, *is a wonderful earthy and hearty Mexican stew based on dried hominy (a food made from kernels of corn), and like dishes that use dried—instead of canned—beans, the finished product is so much better than the canned alternative. A pressure cooker makes it possible to turn hours of simmering into mere minutes, making it a breeze to use dried products such as hominy. Here, the pork and chiles meld beautifully with the corn kernels. Serve this stew with corn tortillas and Refried Beans (page 222).*

SERVES **6 to 8**

SIZE **6-quart or larger pressure cooker**

TIME **10 to 12 minutes at high pressure for the hominy with quick pressure release and then 10 to 12 minutes at high pressure for the stew; then allow the pressure to release naturally**

The dish can be prepared up to 2 days in advance and refrigerated, tightly covered. Reheat it over low heat, covered.

2 cups dried hominy
Salt
1 head garlic, papery coating removed and top ½ inch discarded
1 small onion, halved
2½ pounds boneless pork butt, cut into 1½-inch cubes
2 dried ancho chiles, stemmed with seeds discarded
3 guajillo chiles, stemmed with seeds discarded
1 tablespoon ground cumin
1 teaspoon dried oregano, preferably Mexican

Pinch of ground cloves
1 red bell pepper, seeds and ribs removed, chopped
3 garlic cloves, minced
2 tablespoons olive oil

GARNISH
3 limes, cut into wedges
6 radishes, halved and thinly sliced
¾ cup chopped onion
½ cup chopped fresh cilantro
1½ cups firmly packed shredded green cabbage
1 avocado, peeled and diced

Rinse the hominy in a colander and place it in a mixing bowl covered with cold salted water. Allow the hominy to soak for a minimum of 12 hours or up to 24 hours. Change the water at least once during the soaking time. Drain the hominy, rinse it well, and cook or refrigerate it as soon as possible.

Combine the hominy, head of garlic, onion, and 4 cups of water in the pressure cooker.

Close and lock the lid of the cooker.

STOVETOP: Place the cooker over high heat, and bring it to high pressure. Once high pressure is reached, reduce the heat as much as possible while retaining the high-pressure level. Cook for 10 minutes. Then take the pot off the heat and quick release the pressure according to the instructions provided by the manufacturer. Remove the lid, tilting it away from you, to allow the steam to escape.

OR

ELECTRIC: Set the machine to cook at high pressure for 12 minutes. After 12 minutes unplug the pot so that it does not go into warming mode. Quick release the pressure according to the instructions provided by the manufacturer. Remove the lid, tilting it away from you, to allow the steam to escape.

Remove and discard the garlic head and onion halves. Add the pork, ancho chiles, guajillo chiles, cumin, oregano, and ground cloves to the pressure cooker.

Close and lock the lid of the cooker.

STOVETOP: Place the cooker over high heat, and bring it to high pressure. Once high pressure is reached, reduce the heat as much as possible while retaining the high-pressure level. Cook for 10 minutes. Then take the pot off the heat and allow it to return to normal pressure naturally. Remove the lid, tilting it away from you, to allow the steam to escape.

OR

ELECTRIC: Set the machine to cook at high pressure for 12 minutes. After 12 minutes, unplug the pot so that it does not go into warming mode. Allow the pressure to return to normal naturally. Remove the lid, tilting it away from you, to allow the steam to escape.

Transfer ¾ cup of the cooking liquid, ½ cup of the hominy, the ancho chiles, and the guajillo chiles to a food processor fitted with a steel blade or to a blender. Add the red bell pepper and garlic cloves, and puree until smooth. Press the mixture through a strainer, pushing with the back of a spoon, to extract as much liquid as possible.

Heat the oil in a saucepan over medium-high heat. Add the puree, reduce the heat to medium, and cook the puree for 5 minutes, or until it begins to thicken. Stir the puree into the cooker, and simmer the dish for 15 minutes over medium heat or use the browning function of an electric cooker. Season to taste with salt and serve immediately. Pass around the garnishes separately.

NOTE If you think it's confusing to figure out how fresh chiles are, it's even trickier with dried chiles, because most of the time they don't use the same name as their fresh counterparts. For example, ancho (pronounced *AHN-choh*) chiles are fairly mild because they are dried poblano peppers. The word *ancho* means "wide" in Spanish, and they're easy to spot at the market. Guajillo (pronounced *gwa-HEE-yoh*) is a sweet chile with thick flesh and is used extensively in Mexican cooking.

Asian Baby Back Ribs
with Peanuts

Meaty back ribs that are so meltingly tender that they fall off the bone but also have a crisp exterior are one of my great passions, especially when they're flavored with Asian seasonings. These ribs have all of that, plus they're encrusted with crispy peanuts. Serve them with Jasmine Rice Salad (page 208) and Stewed Asian Black Beans (page 220).

SERVES **3 to 4 as an entrée or 6 to 8 as an appetizer**

SIZE **6-quart or larger pressure cooker**

TIME **15 to 18 minutes at high pressure; then allow the pressure to release naturally**

The ribs can be cooked and the sauce can be finished up to 2 days in advance and refrigerated, tightly covered. They are best glazed and baked just before serving.

- 1 (2½-pound) rack baby back ribs
- ½ cup freshly squeezed orange juice
- ¼ cup reduced-sodium soy sauce
- ¼ cup Chicken Stock (page 15), Chinese Chicken Stock (page 15), or purchased stock
- ¼ cup sliced fresh ginger
- 4 garlic cloves, smashed
- 1 cup hoisin sauce, divided
- 1 tablespoon toasted sesame oil

GARNISH

- 4 ounces salted, roasted peanuts, coarsely chopped
- 2 scallions, white parts and 4 inches of green tops, thinly sliced

Cut the rack into individual ribs. Combine the orange juice, soy sauce, stock, ginger, garlic, and ½ cup of the hoisin sauce in the pressure cooker and stir well. Place the ribs into the pot with the meaty side down.

Close and lock the lid of the cooker.

STOVETOP: Place the cooker over high heat, and bring it to high pressure. Once high pressure is reached, reduce the heat as much as possible while retaining the high-pressure level. Cook for 15 minutes. Then take the pot off the heat and allow it to return to normal pressure naturally. Remove the lid, tilting it away from you, to allow the steam to escape.

OR

ELECTRIC: Set the machine to cook at high pressure for 18 minutes. After 18 minutes, unplug the pot so that it does not go into warming mode. Allow the pressure to return to normal naturally. Remove the lid, tilting it away from you, to allow the steam to escape.

Preheat the oven to 400°F. Line a rimmed baking sheet with heavy-duty aluminum foil and place a wire rack on top of the foil.

Remove the ribs from the cooker with tongs, and remove and discard the ginger and garlic with a slotted spoon. Allow the liquid to sit for 10 minutes. Tilt the pan to spoon off as much fat as possible; then stir in the remaining hoisin sauce and the sesame oil. Bring to a boil over high heat or use the browning function of an electric cooker and cook until the sauce is reduced by half.

Return the ribs to the cooker to coat them well with the sauce. Arrange the ribs on the wire rack with the meaty side up. Bake them for 10 minutes in the preheated oven; then remove the pan from the oven and baste the ribs again with the sauce. Sprinkle the peanuts over the ribs, patting gently so that they adhere. Bake for an additional 7 to 10 minutes, or until glossy and dark. Sprinkle the ribs with the scallions and serve immediately.

NOTE Hoisin sauce (pronounced *hoy-ZAHN*), the equivalent of American barbecue sauce, is used in traditional Chinese cooking. It has a sweet and salty profile from soybeans and is flavored with Chinese five-spice powder. *Hoisin* means "seafood" in Mandarin Chinese, although there's no fish or seafood in the sauce. It also contains no plums, although it's frequently misidentified as plum sauce. Hoisin sauce is widely available in supermarkets, but if you're out of it, combine ¼ cup ketchup with 1 teaspoon five-spice powder, 2 tablespoons soy sauce, 2 tablespoons molasses, and 1 tablespoon unseasoned rice wine vinegar to make ½ cup of the sauce.

Asian Baby Back Ribs
with Peanuts, page 174

Bourbon Baby Back Ribs

One of the many advantages to preparing foods in the pressure cooker is that the flavor of the braising ingredients really penetrates the meats, which makes them very succulent and flavorful. Serve these down-home ribs with New England "Baked" Beans (page 216) and your favorite coleslaw.

SERVES **3 to 4**

SIZE **6-quart or larger pressure cooker**

TIME **20 to 22 minutes at high pressure; then allow the pressure to release naturally**

> The ribs can be cooked and the sauce can be finished up to 2 days in advance and refrigerated, tightly covered. The ribs are best glazed and broiled just before serving.

1 (2½-pound) rack baby back ribs
¾ cup ketchup
½ cup bourbon
½ cup freshly squeezed orange juice
½ cup cider vinegar
½ cup firmly packed dark brown sugar

2 tablespoons Worcestershire sauce
1 tablespoon grainy mustard
2 sprigs fresh rosemary
3 garlic cloves, minced
Salt and freshly ground black pepper to taste
2 teaspoons grated orange zest
Hot red pepper sauce to taste

Cut the rack of ribs into 3 or 4 pieces.

Combine the ketchup, bourbon, orange juice, brown sugar, Worcestershire sauce, mustard, rosemary, and garlic in the pressure cooker. Sprinkle the ribs with salt and pepper, and arrange them in the cooker.

Close and lock the lid of the cooker.

STOVETOP: Place the cooker over high heat, and bring it to high pressure. Once high pressure is reached, reduce the heat as much as possible while retaining the high-pressure level. Cook for 20 minutes. Then take the pot off the heat and allow it to return to normal pressure naturally. Remove the lid, tilting it away from you, to allow the steam to escape.

— OR —

ELECTRIC: Set the machine to cook at high pressure for 22 minutes. After 22 minutes, unplug the pot so that it does not go into warming mode. Allow the pressure to return to normal naturally. Remove the lid, tilting it away from you, to allow the steam to escape.

> NOTE The aromatic oil found in the colored zest of citrus fruit is very delicate, and it really doesn't hold up to the battering of the pressure cooker. While large strips of zest can be added at the onset of cooking, grated zest should be stirred into a sauce after the pressure is released.

Preheat the oven broiler, line a baking pan with heavy-duty aluminum foil, and place a wire rack on the foil. Remove the ribs from the cooker with tongs and arrange them with the meaty side down on the rack.

Tilt the pan and spoon off as much fat as possible. Remove and discard the rosemary, and stir in the orange zest and hot red pepper sauce. Bring to a boil over high heat or use the browning function of an electric cooker. Cook until the sauce is reduced by half.

Brush the sauce over the ribs and broil 8 inches from the element until browned. Turn the ribs so the meaty side is up, brush it with sauce, and broil until browned. Serve immediately.

Choucroute Garnie
(Alsatian Braised Sauerkraut with Sausages and Ham)

The cuisine of Alsace-Lorraine contains both French and German elements as a result of that region's geographic location at the border of France and Germany, both of which ruled over Alsace-Lorraine at different times in the nineteenth and twentieth centuries. The region's most famous dish, which goes beautifully with either a glass of lush Alsatian wine or a mug of chilled beer, is Choucroute Garnie. Soaking the sauerkraut and braising it in wine makes it silky and mellow. Serve this dish with a few choices of mustard and German Potato Salad (page 254) or steamed baby potatoes.

SERVES **4 to 6**

SIZE **6-quart or larger pressure cooker**

TIME **10 to 12 minutes at high pressure with quick pressure relief**

The dish can be prepared up to 2 days in advance and refrigerated, tightly covered. Reheat it over low heat, covered, until hot.

2 pounds sauerkraut

¾ pound kielbasa or other smoked sausage, cut into 1½-inch chunks

¾ pound smoked pork shoulder butt, cut into 1-inch slices

½ pound cooked bratwurst or other sausage, cut into 1½-inch chunks

2 ounces salt pork or slab bacon, cut into small dice

1 large onion, thickly sliced

3 garlic cloves, minced

1 large carrot, thickly sliced

1 Granny Smith apple, peeled, cored, and thickly sliced

¾ cup Chicken Stock (page 15) or purchased stock

½ cup dry white wine

3 tablespoons gin

3 tablespoons chopped fresh parsley

2 teaspoons fresh thyme leaves

¾ teaspoon caraway seeds

1 bay leaf

Freshly ground black pepper to taste

Variety of mustards for serving

Drain the sauerkraut in a colander and run it under cold water for 2 minutes. Squeeze it dry, transfer it to a large mixing bowl, and soak it in cold water for 10 minutes. Drain and repeat the soaking process.

Preheat the oven broiler and line a broiler pan with heavy-duty aluminum foil. Arrange the kielbasa, smoked pork, and bratwurst in the pan and brown it well under the broiler, turning the pieces with tongs. Cut the smoked pork slices into bite-sized pieces and set them aside.

Heat the cooker over medium-high heat or use the browning function of an electric cooker. Add the salt pork and cook, stirring occasionally, for 4 minutes, or until the salt pork renders some of its fat and browns. Add the onion, garlic, and carrot, and cook, stirring frequently, for 3 minutes, or until the onion is translucent.

Add the apple, stock, wine, gin, parsley, thyme, caraway seeds, and bay leaf to the cooker. Wring out the sauerkraut with your hands, add it to the cooker, and stir well. Add the meats to the cooker.

Close and lock the lid of the cooker.

STOVETOP: Place the cooker over high heat, and bring it to high pressure. Once high pressure is reached, reduce the heat as much as possible while retaining the high-pressure level. Cook for 10 minutes. Then take the pot off the heat and quick release the pressure according to the instructions provided by the manufacturer. Remove the lid, tilting it away from you, to allow the steam to escape.

—OR—

ELECTRIC: Set the machine to cook at high pressure for 12 minutes. After 12 minutes, unplug the pot so that it does not go into warming mode. Quick release the pressure according to the instructions provided by the manufacturer. Remove the lid, tilting it away from you, to allow the steam to escape.

NOTE Traditional recipes for *Choucroute* include juniper berries in the ingredient list, but few of us keep them around at all times. In fact, it can be a challenge to find them in many supermarkets. The good news is that juniper berries are the most prominent flavor in gin, and a few tablespoons of it impart the same flavor.

Remove and discard the bay leaf, and season to taste with pepper. With the residual salt in the sauerkraut and the salt in the sausages, you will not need to adjust it. Serve immediately, passing around dishes of the mustards.

Hoppin' John with Ham

No self-respecting Southerner would start the New Year without eating a bowl of this flavorful stew of black-eyed peas and vegetables studded with cubes of tender ham; it's the region's good luck charm. The dish probably came from Africa, and it is mentioned in literature long before the Civil War. Some food authorities say the name comes from children hopping around the table on New Year's Day as a prelude to eating the dish.

SERVES **4 to 6**

SIZE **6-quart or larger pressure cooker**

TIME **4 to 5 minutes at high pressure; then allow the pressure to release naturally**

> The stew can be prepared up to 2 days in advance and refrigerated, tightly covered. Reheat it over low heat, covered, stirring occasionally.

- 1 **pound black-eyed peas**
- 2 **tablespoons olive oil**
- 1 **large onion, diced**
- 4 **garlic cloves, minced**
- 1 **celery rib, diced**
- 1 **red bell pepper, seeds and ribs removed, diced**
- 4 **cups Ham Stock (page 15), Chicken Stock (page 15), or purchased stock**
- 1½ **pounds boneless ham, cut into ¾-inch cubes**
- 2 **tablespoons chopped fresh parsley**
- 1 **tablespoon fresh thyme leaves**
- 2 **bay leaves**
- 3 **scallions, white parts and 3 inches of green tops, sliced**
- **Salt and freshly ground black pepper to taste**
- **Hot red pepper sauce to taste**
- 2 **to 3 cups hot cooked brown or white rice for serving**

Rinse the beans in a colander and place them in a mixing bowl covered with cold salted water. Allow the beans to soak for a minimum of 6 hours, or overnight. Or place the beans into a saucepan of salted water and bring to a boil over high heat. Boil 1 minute. Turn off the heat, cover the pan, and soak the beans for 1 hour. After using either of these soaking methods, drain the beans, discard the soaking water, and cook or refrigerate the beans as soon as possible.

Heat the oil in the cooker over medium-high heat or use the browning function of an electric cooker. Add the onion, garlic, celery, and red bell pepper. Cook, stirring frequently, for 3 minutes, or until the onion is translucent. Stir in the stock, ham, parsley, thyme, bay leaves, and drained beans.

Close and lock the lid of the cooker.

STOVETOP: Place the cooker over high heat, and bring it to high pressure. Once high pressure is reached, reduce the heat as much as possible while retaining the high-pressure level. Cook for 4 minutes. Then take the pot off the heat and allow it to return to normal pressure naturally. Remove the lid, tilting it away from you, to allow the steam to escape.

OR

ELECTRIC: Set the machine to cook at high pressure for 5 minutes. After 5 minutes, unplug the pot so that it does not go into warming mode. Allow the pressure to return to normal naturally. Remove the lid, tilting it away from you, to allow the steam to escape.

Remove and discard the bay leaves. Stir in the scallions and season to taste with salt, pepper, and hot red pepper sauce; then serve immediately over a portion of rice.

NOTE When you are cutting up vegetables for the pressure cooker, dainty is not the rule. In a dish such as this one, the beans are what require the longest time under pressure, so to preserve the texture of vegetables such as celery and red bell pepper, the size of the dice should be about ½ inch rather than the ¼ inch of a traditional dice.

Ragù Bolognese

Just as the pressure cooker has revolutionized making stocks, you're not going to believe that the same depth of flavor can be achieved in a sauce that's cooked for less than a half hour. The flavors in this sauce marry perfectly, and the consistency is thick and rich after a bit of postpressure simmering. Serve the pasta with Garbanzo Bean Salad Parmesan (page 227) or Kale with Pancetta (page 251).

SERVES **6 to 8**

SIZE **6-quart or larger pressure cooker**

TIME **20 to 23 minutes at high pressure; then allow the pressure to release naturally**

> The sauce can be refrigerated for up to 5 days, tightly covered, or frozen for up to 3 months.

2 tablespoons olive oil
¼ pound pancetta, diced
1 large onion, diced
4 garlic cloves, minced
1 pound ground pork
¾ pound (85 percent lean) ground beef
½ pound bulk Italian sausage (mild or hot)
2 carrots, diced
1 celery rib, diced
¼ cup tomato paste
1 tablespoon anchovy paste
½ cup dry white wine
1 (28-ounce) can crushed tomatoes in tomato puree, preferably San Marzano

1 tablespoon chopped fresh rosemary
1 tablespoon chopped fresh oregano
2 bay leaves
1 (3-inch) Parmesan rind (optional)
½ cup heavy cream
¼ cup chopped fresh parsley
¼ cup chopped fresh basil
Salt and freshly ground black pepper to taste
Hot cooked pasta for serving
Freshly grated Parmesan cheese for serving

Heat the oil in the cooker over medium-high heat or use the browning function of an electric cooker. Add the pancetta and cook, stirring occasionally, for 5 to 7 minutes or until browned. Add the onion, garlic, pork, beef, and sausage. Cook, stirring occasionally, for 5 to 7 minutes, or until the onion is translucent and the meats have lost their raw color.

Stir in the carrots, celery, tomato paste, anchovy paste, and wine. Cook for 3 minutes, stirring to incorporate the tomato paste. Stir in the tomatoes, rosemary, oregano, bay leaves, and Parmesan rind, if using.

Close and lock the lid of the cooker.

STOVETOP: Place the cooker over high heat, and bring it to high pressure. Once high pressure is reached, reduce the heat as much as possible while retaining the high-pressure level. Cook for 20 minutes. Then take the pot off the heat and allow it to return to normal pressure naturally. Remove the lid, tilting it away from you, to allow the steam to escape.

OR

ELECTRIC: Set the machine to cook at high pressure for 23 minutes. After 23 minutes, unplug the pot so that it does not go into warming mode. Allow the pressure to return to normal naturally. Remove the lid, tilting it away from you, to allow the steam to escape.

Remove and discard the bay leaves and Parmesan rind, if used. Bring the sauce to a boil over medium heat or use the browning function of an electric cooker. Stir in the cream and cook the sauce, stirring frequently, for 10 to 15 minutes, or until thick. Stir in the parsley and basil and season to taste with salt and pepper. Serve over pasta and pass around the Parmesan cheese.

NOTE San Marzano tomatoes are touted as the best in the world. Promoters of these tomatoes claim that the climate and fertile soil in the eponymous region of southern Italy where they grow create the fruit's meaty texture, juiciness, and extraordinary flavor. As with many foods these days, only tomatoes grown in the region from seeds of the original cultivar can be awarded the Denominazione d'Origine Protetta (DOP) label. And that's the label you should look for on a can of tomatoes, because San Marzano seeds have traveled around the world, but only tomatoes from that small part of Italy have the official designation.

Dilled Swedish Meatballs

The pressure cooker makes world-class meatballs. Not only are they fast, they're also light and fluffy, and you don't have to brown them to keep them together. This version of Swedish meatballs, scented with nutmeg and flecked with aromatic fresh dill, is one of my favorite comfort foods. Serve it with Fluffy Mashed Potatoes (page 245) and Braised Red Cabbage (page 234).

SERVES **4 to 6**

SIZE **6-quart or larger pressure cooker**

TIME **5 to 6 minutes at high pressure with quick pressure release**

The meatballs can be made up to 2 days in advance and refrigerated, tightly covered. Reheat them over low heat or in a microwave oven.

- 4 tablespoons (½ stick) unsalted butter, divided
- 1 large shallot, minced
- 2 garlic cloves, minced (optional)
- ½ cup panko breadcrumbs
- ¼ cup whole milk
- 1 large egg, lightly beaten
- ¼ teaspoon freshly grated nutmeg
- ¾ pound ground pork
- ¾ pound ground veal
- ⅓ cup chopped fresh dill
- Salt and freshly ground black pepper to taste
- 3 tablespoons all-purpose flour
- 1 cup Chicken Stock (page 15) or purchased stock
- ½ cup heavy cream

Melt 2 tablespoons of the butter in a small skillet over medium heat. Add the shallot and garlic, if using, and cook, stirring frequently, for 5 minutes, or until the shallot softens. Scrape the mixture into a large mixing bowl and allow it to cool.

Add the breadcrumbs, milk, egg, and nutmeg to the mixing bowl and whisk until smooth. Add the pork, veal, and dill and mix well. Season to taste with salt and pepper, and form the mixture into meatballs about the size of walnuts.

Heat the remaining butter in the cooker over medium heat or use the browning function of an electric cooker. Stir in the flour and cook, stirring constantly, for 1 minute, or until the mixture turns slightly beige, is bubbly, and appears to have grown in volume. Slowly whisk in the stock. Bring to a boil, whisking frequently. Reduce the heat to low and simmer the sauce for 2 minutes. Turn off the heat and place the meatballs in the sauce.

Close and lock the lid of the cooker.

STOVETOP: Place the cooker over high heat, and bring it to high pressure. Once high pressure is reached, reduce the heat as much as possible while retaining the high-pressure level. Cook for 5 minutes. Then take the pot off the heat and quick-release the pressure according to the instructions provided by the manufacturer. Remove the lid, tilting it away from you, to allow the steam to escape.

OR

ELECTRIC: Set the machine to cook at high pressure for 6 minutes. After 6 minutes, unplug the pot so that it does not go into warming mode. Quick release the pressure according to the instructions provided by the manufacturer. Remove the lid, tilting it away from you, to allow the steam to escape.

Remove the meatballs from the cooker with a slotted spoon. Allow the liquid to rest for 10 minutes; then tilt the cooker and spoon off as much fat as possible.

Add the cream to the sauce in the cooker and simmer for 1 minute. Adjust the seasoning and serve immediately.

NOTE If you've noticed, none of the recipes that contain a dairy product such as milk or cream use that dairy product under pressure. That's the case because the high temperature created under pressure causes most dairy products to curdle. Dairy products are added at the end of the pressurized cooking time. One exception is using a piece of Parmesan rind. Not enough of the cheese melts into the dish to cause it to curdle.

Osso Buco alla Milanese

Tender veal shanks braised in an herbed red wine and tomato sauce are one of the most famous and popular dishes of northern Italy. The flavor of Osso Buco gets a bright note from fresh herbs added at the end of the cooking time and also from a sprinkling of gremolata, the traditional citrus zest, parsley, and garlic garnish. Serve Osso Buco with Risotto alla Milanese (page 200) and Kale with Pancetta (page 251).

SERVES **4 to 6**

SIZE **6-quart or larger pressure cooker**

TIME **25 to 30 minutes at high pressure; then allow the pressure to release naturally**

> The veal can be prepared up to 2 days in advance and refrigerated, tightly covered. Reheat it, covered, over low heat.

VEAL

- 4 to 6 (¾-pound) veal shanks
- Salt and freshly ground black pepper to taste
- 3 tablespoons olive oil
- 1 large onion, diced
- 4 garlic cloves, minced
- 2 carrots, diced
- 2 celery ribs, diced
- 3 tablespoons tomato paste
- 3 tablespoons all-purpose flour
- 1¼ cups dry red wine
- 2 cups Veal Stock (page 16), Chicken Stock (page 15), or purchased stock

- 1 tablespoon fresh thyme leaves, divided
- 1 tablespoon fresh rosemary, divided
- 2 bay leaves

GREMOLATA

- ⅓ cup chopped fresh parsley
- 3 garlic cloves, minced
- Grated zest of 1 lemon
- Grated zest of ½ orange
- Salt and freshly ground black pepper to taste

Preheat the oven broiler and line a broiler pan with heavy-duty aluminum foil. Pat the veal dry with paper towels, sprinkle it with salt and pepper, and tie the shanks tightly with kitchen twine around the circumference. Arrange the veal in a single layer on the foil and broil for 3 minutes on each side, or until the veal is lightly browned. Remove the veal from the broiler and set it aside.

Heat the oil in the cooker over medium-high heat or use the browning function of an electric cooker. Add the onion, garlic, carrots, and celery. Cook, stirring occasionally, for 3 minutes, or until the onion is translucent. Stir in the tomato paste and cook for 1 minute, stirring constantly. Stir in the flour and cook for 1 minute, stirring constantly. Stir the wine into the cooker and cook over medium-high heat for 3 minutes, or until the sauce thickens.

Stir the stock, 1½ teaspoons of the thyme, 1½ teaspoons of the rosemary, and the bay leaves into the cooker. Nestle the browned veal shanks in the liquid.

Close and lock the lid of the cooker.

STOVETOP: Place the cooker over high heat, and bring it to high pressure. Once high pressure is reached, reduce the heat as much as possible while retaining the high-pressure level. Cook for 25 minutes. Then take the pot off the heat and quick release the pressure according to the instructions provided by the manufacturer. Remove the lid, tilting it away from you, to allow the steam to escape.

OR

ELECTRIC: Set the machine to cook at high pressure for 30 minutes. After 30 minutes, unplug the pot so that it does not go into warming mode. Quick release the pressure according to the instructions provided by the manufacturer. Remove the lid, tilting it away from you, to allow the steam to escape.

While the veal cooks, make the gremolata. Combine the parsley, garlic, lemon zest, orange zest, salt, and pepper in a small dish and stir well. Refrigerate until ready to serve, tightly covered with plastic wrap.

Remove and discard the bay leaves from the cooker and stir in the remaining thyme and rosemary. Season the dish to taste with salt and pepper, and serve immediately, sprinkling some of the gremolata on each serving.

NOTE It's really important to tie the shanks firmly with kitchen twine to preserve their shape while they cook. Reusable silicone rubber bands are a new product on the market, and if you have some of them, they can be used in the pressure cooker.

Veal Marsala Stew

Traditional Veal Marsala is made with quickly sautéed veal scallops; that makes it both a last-minute and an expensive dish. This stew delivers all the same flavors and aromas. Serve it with Creamy Polenta (page 214) or Wild Mushroom Risotto (page 201) and a tossed green salad.

SERVES **6 to 8**

SIZE **6-quart or larger pressure cooker**

TIME **20 to 23 minutes at high pressure; then allow the pressure to release naturally**

The stew can be prepared up to 2 days in advance and refrigerated, tightly covered. Reheat it over low heat.

3 tablespoons olive oil

2½ pounds veal shoulder meat, cut into 1½-inch cubes

Salt and freshly ground black pepper to taste

2 large shallots, diced

6 garlic cloves, thinly sliced

½ pound crimini mushrooms, wiped with a damp paper towel, trimmed, and sliced

3 tablespoons all-purpose flour

¾ cup sweet Marsala wine

1½ cups Chicken Stock (page 15) or purchased stock

½ cup chopped fresh parsley

Heat the oil in the cooker over medium-high heat or use the browning function of an electric cooker. Pat the veal dry with paper towels and sprinkle it with salt and pepper. Add as much veal as will fit comfortably in the cooker and brown it well; this may have to be done in batches. Set the veal aside and add the shallots, garlic, and mushrooms to the cooker. Cook for 3 minutes, stirring often, or until the shallots are translucent.

Stir the flour into the cooker and cook over low heat for 1 minute, stirring constantly. Stir the Marsala into the cooker and cook over medium-high heat for 3 minutes, or until the sauce thickens. Return the veal to the cooker and add the stock and parsley.

Close and lock the lid of the cooker.

STOVETOP: Place the cooker over high heat, and bring it to high pressure. Once high pressure is reached, reduce the heat as much as possible while retaining the high-pressure level. Cook for 20 minutes. Then take the pot off the heat and quick release the pressure according to the instructions provided by the manufacturer. Remove the lid, tilting it away from you, to allow the steam to escape.

OR

ELECTRIC: Set the machine to cook at high pressure for 23 minutes. After 23 minutes, unplug the pot so that it does not go into warming mode. Quick release the pressure according to the instructions provided by the manufacturer. Remove the lid, tilting it away from you, to allow the steam to escape.

Season to taste with salt and pepper, and serve immediately.

NOTE Marsala is Italy's most famous fortified wine, and it comes from the town by that name on the sun-drenched coast of Sicily. Marsala is made from Grillo, Inzolia, and Catarratto white grapes native to the region, and the wine is fortified and stored in the same way as port, sherry, and Madeira. There are two styles of Marsala, depending on the amount of residual sugar in the wine. Dry Marsala is served as an aperitif, and sweet Marsala is used most often in cooking and can be served as a dessert wine.

VARIATION

★ **Chicken Marsala:** Substitute 2 pounds of boneless, skinless chicken thighs, cut into 1½-inch pieces, for the veal. Reduce the cooking time at high pressure to 10 minutes for a stovetop cooker and 12 minutes for an electric cooker; then allow the pressure to release naturally.

Veal Stew with Wild Mushrooms

Wild mushrooms add depth and richness to the flavor of delicate veal, and this dish is a meal in a bowl because it also contains potatoes and onions. Serve it with Fennel with Tomatoes and Orange (page 238) and Garbanzo Bean Salad Parmesan (page 227).

SERVES **6 to 8**

SIZE **6-quart or larger pressure cooker**

TIME **20 to 23 minutes at high pressure; then allow the pressure to release naturally**

> The stew can be prepared up to 2 days in advance and refrigerated, tightly covered. Reheat it over low heat.

½ cup dried porcini or chanterelle mushrooms

2 cups Veal Stock (page 16), Chicken Stock (page 15), or purchased stock, divided

¼ cup olive oil, divided

2½ pounds veal shoulder meat, cut into 1½-inch cubes

Salt and freshly ground black pepper to taste

1 large onion, diced

4 garlic cloves, minced

3 tablespoons all-purpose flour

½ cup dry white wine

3 tablespoons chopped fresh parsley

2 tablespoons chopped fresh sage

2 sprigs fresh thyme

1 bay leaf

2 tablespoons unsalted butter

⅔ pound crimini mushrooms, wiped with a damp paper towel, trimmed, and sliced

¼ pound fresh shiitake mushrooms, stemmed and sliced

1 pound cipollini onions, peeled

1½ pounds red potatoes, cut into 1-inch cubes

Combine the dried mushrooms and ¾ cup of the stock in a microwave-safe container. Microwave on high (100 percent power) for 1 to 1½ minutes, or until the stock boils. Soak the mushrooms in the stock, pushing them down into the liquid with the back of a spoon, for 10 minutes. Drain the mushrooms, reserving the stock. Strain the stock through a sieve lined with a paper coffee filter or paper towel. Chop the mushrooms. Set them aside.

Heat 2 tablespoons of the oil in the cooker over medium-high heat or use the browning function of an electric cooker. Add as much veal as will fit comfortably in the cooker and brown it well; this may have to be done in batches. Set the veal aside and add the onion and garlic to the cooker. Cook the onion for 3 minutes, stirring frequently, or until it is translucent.

Stir the flour into the cooker and cook over low heat for 1 minute, stirring constantly. Stir the wine into the cooker and cook over medium-high heat for 3 minutes, or until the sauce thickens. Return the veal to the cooker and add the dried mushrooms, mushroom stock, remaining stock, parsley, sage, thyme, and bay leaf.

Close and lock the lid of the cooker.

STOVETOP: Place the cooker over high heat, and bring it to high pressure. Once high pressure is reached, reduce the heat as much as possible while retaining the high-pressure level. Cook for 20 minutes. Then take the pot off the heat and quick release the pressure according to the instructions provided by the manufacturer. Remove the lid, tilting it away from you, to allow the steam to escape.

OR

ELECTRIC: Set the machine to cook at high pressure for 23 minutes. After 23 minutes, unplug the pot so that it does not go into warming mode. Quick release the pressure according to the instructions provided by the manufacturer. Remove the lid, tilting it away from you, to allow the steam to escape.

While the veal cooks, heat the remaining oil and the butter in a skillet over medium-high heat. Add the cremini mushrooms, shiitake mushrooms, and onions, and cook for 3 to 5 minutes, or until the onions begin to brown.

When the pressure releases on the cooker, remove and discard the thyme sprigs and bay leaf. Add the mushroom mixture and potato cubes to the cooker.

Close and lock the lid of the cooker.

STOVETOP: Place the cooker over high heat, and bring it to high pressure. Once high pressure is reached, reduce the heat as much as possible while retaining the high-pressure level. Cook for 3 minutes. Then take the pot off the heat and quick release the pressure according to the instructions provided by the manufacturer. Remove the lid, tilting it away from you, to allow the steam to escape.

OR

ELECTRIC: Set the machine to cook at high pressure for 4 minutes. After 4 minutes, unplug the pot so that it does not go into warming mode. Quick release the pressure according to the instructions provided by the manufacturer. Remove the lid, tilting it away from you, to allow the steam to escape.

Season to taste with salt and pepper, and serve immediately.

NOTE Cipollini (pronounced *chip-oh-LEE-knee*) onions range in size from a walnut to a golf ball, and they have a flattened appearance like a disk. What makes them so special is the high amount of residual sugar they contain and their sturdy constitution, which helps them retain their shape and texture during cooking. Cipollini are a pain to peel, however. Although you can pull off strips of the peel from the root end, I've found it's easier to drop them into a pot of boiling water for 15 seconds, at which time the peels will slip right off.

Risotto alla Milanese,
page 200

CHAPTER 7

Grains and Legumes

Grains, especially whole grains, and beans are leap-frogging ahead of more refined forms of carbohydrates as an important part of our diet, and you have no better friend than your pressure cooker when it comes to getting these high-fiber, low-fat foods onto the table quickly.

Beans are justly praised for their nutritional value as well as their availability and economy. Dried beans also play a role in almost all the world's cuisines, and this universality is reflected in the dishes in this chapter. Beans are high in fiber and protein, are low in fat, and contain no cholesterol. They are also a good source of B vitamins, especially vitamin B_6.

Although most people in the world look to one of the thousands of species of rice as the staple of their diet, far more view wheat as the foundation of theirs.

Other whole grains in the bulk food bins and on the shelves of grocery stores are joining brown rice in popularity because they share the level of nutrients and high fiber content found in its coating.

Cooking Legumes

Once you get into the habit of cooking your own dried beans, you'll never go back to eating beans from a can and you'll find many more ways to use them in your kitchen. I brought back some heirloom dried beans from Maine a few years ago, and it was so much fun to make dishes with calypso beans and Rio Zape. It was like taking a bite of an heirloom Brandywine tomato instead of an anemic-looking tomato from the supermarket. Canned beans are also very high in sodium, whereas dried beans contain almost none.

Here are some tips for preparing beans in the pressure cooker: soak the beans in salted water, using either the long or the quick soaking method (see page 216 for instructions). The salt in the soaking water penetrates the skin of the bean and allows it to soften more quickly when it is cooked under pressure. There are times when dry beans are added to the cooker, for example, in Lamb Shanks with Braised White Beans (page 148). The unsoaked beans take the same amount of time to cook as the shanks, so all elements reach the finish line simultaneously.

Each recipe in this chapter has exact timing that takes into account any ingredients that retard the legumes from softening. This chart, however, gives you general guidelines. Please note that both lentils and split peas have such a short cooking time that presoaking is not necessary.

After draining the beans, mix them with 2 tablespoons of vegetable oil in the cooker to prevent them from foaming as they cook. Do not fill the cooker more than halfway because the beans will expand as they cook. Then add 3 quarts of water to the cooker for a pound of beans. Allow the pressure to release naturally for 15 minutes after the cooking time and then quick release any remaining pressure.

When you remove the lid of the cooker, there probably will be some broken beans (sometimes called "floaters") on the surface of the water. Discard them. Then drain the beans and refrigerate them for up to 4 days.

COOKING TIMES (IN MINUTES)
FOR LEGUMES IN THE PRESSURE COOKER

LEGUME	SOAKED/STOVE	SOAKED/ELECTRIC	UNSOAKED	RELEASE METHOD
ADZUKI, RED/GREEN	5	7	15 TO 20	NATURAL
ANASAZI	5	7	20 TO 22	NATURAL
BLACK BEANS	4	6	20 TO 22	NATURAL
BLACK-EYED PEAS	3	5	22 TO 24	NATURAL
BORLOTTI	7	10	20 TO 25	NATURAL
CANNELLINI	6	8	25 TO 30	NATURAL
FAVA	10	12	25 TO 30	NATURAL
FLAGEOLET	6	8	18 TO 20	NATURAL
GARBANZO BEANS	10	12	25 TO 30	NATURAL
GREAT NORTHERN	6	8	25 TO 30	NATURAL
KIDNEY	6	8	25 TO 30	NATURAL
LENTILS	–	–	8 TO 10	NATURAL
LIMA, BABY	5	7	12 TO 15	NATURAL
NAVY	6	8	18 TO 20	NATURAL
PINTO	7	10	20 TO 25	NATURAL
SPLIT PEAS	–	–	5 TO 6	NATURAL

Cooking Rice

If you have a pressure cooker, there is no need to have a rice cooker. The pressure cooker does a wonderful job with all kinds of rice.

It's important to rinse rice under cold water in a sieve before placing it in the cooker, because rice is coated with a thin layer of starch that causes the grains to clump and become gummy when cooked. Rinsing also reduces the risk of the rice foaming up and blocking the cooker's steam vents. The potential for foaming is the reason for adding a bit of fat to the cooker, too. Do not fill the cooker more than halfway when cooking rice, because rice expands as it cooks, and remember to salt the water.

Except where indicated below, the pressure for rice should be released naturally for 10 minutes, and then you should quick release any remaining pressure. If you find that the rice is not done and there is still some liquid in the cooker when the pressure is released, cook the rice over low heat or use the browning function of an electric cooker with the cover on but not locked.

COOKING TIMES (IN MINUTES) FOR RICE IN THE PRESSURE COOKER

VARIETY	LIQUID PER 1 CUP OF RICE	STOVETOP	ELECTRIC	RELEASE METHOD
ARBORIO	2 CUPS	6	8	10 MIN. NATURAL
BASMATI	1½ CUPS	3	3	10 MIN. NATURAL
BLACK RICE	1¾ CUPS	15	18	NATURAL
BROWN RICE	1½ CUPS	18	0	NATURAL
CARNAROLI	2 CUPS	6	8	10 MIN. NATURAL
CONVERTED (UNCLE BEN'S)	1½ CUPS	5	5	NATURAL
JASMINE	1¼ CUPS	3	3	10 MIN. NATURAL
SUSHI RICE	1¼ CUPS	7	9	10. MIN. NATURAL
WHITE, COOKING GRAINS	1½ CUPS	6	8	NATURAL

Cooking Grains

Whole grains are another category of food that can benefit from presoaking, especially grains such as hominy and faro, which literally can take hours, even in a pressure cooker, if they are put in dry. Add a few tablespoons of oil to the cooker when preparing grains.

COOKING TIMES (IN MINUTES, UNLESS INDICATED OTHERWISE) FOR GRAINS IN THE PRESSURE COOKER

GRAIN	LIQUID PER 1 CUP OF GRAIN	STOVETOP	ELECTRIC	RELEASE METHOD
AMARANTH	2 CUPS	8	10	NATURAL
BARLEY, PEARLED	2 CUPS	18	20	10 MIN. NATURAL
BARLEY, WHOLE	2½ CUPS	35	40	NATURAL
WHOLE FARRO, NATURAL	2½ CUPS	18	20	10 MIN. NATURAL
SEMIPERLATO FARRO, WHOLE	3 CUPS	30	35	NATURAL
HOMINY, SOAKED	4 CUPS	22	25	NATURAL
HOMINY, UNSOAKED	6 CUPS	3 HOURS	4 HOURS	NATURAL
SOAKED KAMUT	2½ CUPS	18	20	NATURAL
UNSOAKED KAMUT	3¼ CUPS	30	35	NATURAL
UNSOAKED QUINOA	1¾ CUPS	1	2	NATURAL

Risotto alla Milanese

Bright yellow Risotto alla Milanese is always served as the accompaniment to Osso Buco (page 188) and is a wonderful side dish for almost all Italian specialties. I know I've touted the benefits of the pressure cooker many times, but making risotto without laboriously stirring it is enough reason to own one. And many Italian cooks are using the pressure cooker to make it today, too.

SERVES **4 to 6**

SIZE **4-quart or larger pressure cooker**

TIME **7 to 8 minutes at high pressure with quick pressure release**

Risotto should be cooked just before serving.

NOTE Although Arborio is the variety of rice that is used most often to make risotto, it's hardly the only one that can be used. All risotto rices have one thing in common: They have plump, short to medium grains. But the most important feature of any risotto rice is a high content of amylopectin, a type of sticky starch that gives risotto its creamy texture. Baldo, Carnaroli, and Vialone Nano are other types of rice than can be used to make risotto, along with a newly introduced domestic product, Calriso, a hybrid of Italian and Californian rice varieties.

3 tablespoons unsalted butter
1 small onion, chopped
2 garlic cloves, minced
1½ cups Arborio rice
½ cup dry white wine
4 cups Chicken Stock (page 15) or purchased stock
¼ teaspoon crushed saffron threads

½ cup freshly grated Parmesan cheese, plus additional for serving
Salt and freshly ground black pepper to taste

GARNISH
2 to 3 tablespoons chopped fresh parsley

Melt the butter in the cooker over medium heat or use the browning function of an electric cooker. Add the onion and garlic, and cook, stirring frequently, for 3 minutes, or until the onion is translucent. Stir in the rice and cook, stirring constantly, for 2 minutes. Stir in the wine and cook for 1 minute, or until the wine is almost evaporated. Stir in 3½ cups of the chicken stock and the saffron threads.

Close and lock the lid of the cooker.

STOVETOP: Place the cooker over high heat, and bring it to high pressure. Once high pressure is reached, reduce the heat as much as possible while retaining the high-pressure level. Cook for 7 minutes. Then take the pot off the heat and quick release the pressure according to the instructions provided by the manufacturer. Remove the lid, tilting it away from you, to allow the steam to escape.

OR

ELECTRIC: Set the machine to cook at high pressure for 8 minutes. After 8 minutes, unplug the pot so that it does not go into warming mode. Quick release the pressure according to the instructions provided by the manufacturer. Remove the lid, tilting it away from you, to allow the steam to escape.

Continue to cook the risotto over medium heat or use the browning function of an electric cooker for 4 to 5 minutes, stirring constantly, or until the liquid has thickened. Stir in the cheese and season to taste with salt and pepper. Add some of the remaining broth, if needed, to achieve the proper creamy consistency. Serve immediately.

VARIATIONS

★ **Butternut Squash Risotto with Prosciutto:** Omit the saffron from the master recipe. Cook 3 ounces of diced prosciutto with the onion and garlic. Cut 1 pound of peeled butternut or acorn squash into ¾-inch cubes and add it to the pressure cooker along with the stock.

★ **Wild Mushroom Risotto:** Omit the saffron from the master recipe. Cook ½ pound of cremini mushrooms, trimmed and thinly sliced, with the onion and garlic. Grind ½ ounce of dried porcini mushrooms in a spice grinder or with a mortar and pestle, and add it to the pressure cooker along with the stock.

Mexican Brown Rice

This vivid rice can be the star of the show if you're serving a simple entrée. It has so much flavor, color, and aroma that it elevates any meal. You also can use this rice as a base for poached eggs as a brunch dish, accompanied by fried chorizo, or with dishes such as Southwestern Shrimp and Pinto Beans (page 82).

SERVES **6 to 8**

SIZE **6-quart or larger pressure cooker**

TIME **14 to 16 minutes at high pressure; then allow the pressure to release naturally**

The rice can be prepared up to 2 days in advance and refrigerated, tightly covered. Reheat it over low heat or in a 300°F oven until hot.

- 1 (14.5-ounce) can peeled tomatoes, undrained
- 1 medium onion, diced
- 4 garlic cloves, minced, divided
- 3 jalapeño or serrano chiles, seeds and ribs removed, chopped, divided
- 2 cups brown rice
- ¼ cup olive oil
- 2 teaspoons ground cumin
- 1 teaspoon dried oregano, preferably Mexican
- 2 tablespoons tomato paste
- 2 cups Chicken Stock (page 15), Vegetable Stock (page 17), or purchased stock
- Salt and freshly ground black pepper to taste
- ⅔ cup green peas, thawed if frozen

GARNISH
- ¼ cup chopped fresh cilantro

Combine the tomatoes, onion, half the garlic, and 2 of the chiles in a food processor fitted with the steel blade or in a blender. Puree until smooth and pour the mixture into a measuring cup. You should have 2 cups. (Spoon off some of the mixture or add water to it to make that amount.)

Place the rice in a sieve and rinse it under cold running water for 1 to 2 minutes, or until the water runs clear. Shake the sieve to get off as much moisture from the rice as possible.

Heat the oil in the cooker over medium-high heat or use the browning function of an electric cooker. Add the rice and cook, stirring constantly, for 3 to 4 minutes, or until the rice is lightly browned. Add the remaining garlic, remaining chile, cumin, oregano, and tomato paste, and cook for 1 minute, stirring constantly. Add the tomato mixture and stock, season to taste with salt and pepper, and stir well.

Close and lock the lid of the cooker.

STOVETOP: Place the cooker over high heat, and bring it to high pressure. Once high pressure is reached, reduce the heat as much as possible while retaining the high-pressure level. Cook for 14 minutes. Then take the pot off the heat and allow it to return to normal pressure naturally. Remove the lid, tilting it away from you, to allow the steam to escape.

OR

ELECTRIC: Set the machine to cook at high pressure for 16 minutes. After 16 minutes, unplug the pot so that it does not go into warming mode. Allow the pressure to return to normal naturally. Remove the lid, tilting it away from you, to allow the steam to escape.

Stir the peas into the cooker and adjust the seasoning if necessary. Place the lid on the cooker and let the rice sit for 5 minutes. Serve immediately and sprinkle cilantro on each serving.

NOTE When you brown grains and pasta before adding liquid, it coats and cooks the exterior of these foods and prevents them from clumping and sticking together. Grains that have been browned take a little longer to soften; that is why this cooking time is a few minutes longer than it would have been if the rice had not been toasted.

Festive Basmati Rice Pilaf
with Dried Fruit

This dish—dotted with colorful vegetables and flavored with spices and succulent dried fruit —comes from traditional Persian cooking. It's wonderful served with any Middle Eastern or North African entrée such as Moroccan Chicken with Olives and Preserved Lemons (page 90) or Middle Eastern Lamb Chili with Beans and Zucchini (page 156).

SERVES **4 to 6**

SIZE **6-quart or larger pressure cooker**

TIME **3 to 4 minutes at high pressure; then allow the pressure to release naturally for 10 minutes**

The rice can be prepared up to 2 days in advance and refrigerated, tightly covered. Reheat it over low heat or in a 300°F oven until hot.

1½ cups basmati rice
2 tablespoons unsalted butter
2 tablespoons vegetable oil
1 small onion, diced
1 carrot, diced
¼ red bell pepper, seeds and ribs removed, diced
1 tablespoon garam masala
1 teaspoon ground cumin
1 teaspoon ground coriander
1 teaspoon fresh thyme leaves

1 bay leaf
2¼ cups Chicken Stock (page 15), Vegetable Stock (page 17), or purchased stock
⅓ cup chopped dried apricots
Salt and freshly ground black pepper to taste

GARNISH
½ cup chopped toasted cashew nuts

Place the rice in a sieve and rinse it under cold running water for 1 to 2 minutes, or until the water runs clear. Shake the rice in the sieve to get off as much moisture as possible.

Heat the butter and oil in the cooker over medium-high heat or use the browning function of an electric cooker. Add the onion, carrot, and bell pepper, and cook, stirring frequently, for 3 minutes, or until the onion is translucent. Add the garam masala, cumin, coriander, thyme, and bay leaf. Cook for 1 minute, stirring constantly. Add the rice, stock, and dried apricots, stir well, and season to taste with salt and pepper.

Close and lock the lid of the cooker.

STOVETOP: Place the cooker over high heat, and bring it to high pressure. Once high pressure is reached, reduce the heat as much as possible while retaining the high-pressure level. Cook for 3 minutes. Then take the pot off the heat and allow it to return to normal pressure naturally for 10 minutes. Quick release any remaining pressure. Remove the lid, tilting it away from you, to allow the steam to escape.

OR

ELECTRIC: Set the machine to cook at high pressure for 4 minutes. After 4 minutes, unplug the pot so that it does not go into warming mode. Allow the pressure to return to normal naturally for 10 minutes. Quick release any remaining pressure. Remove the lid, tilting it away from you, to allow the steam to escape.

NOTE Pilaf is a method more than a dish, and it's commonly eaten from the Balkans all the way to India and Pakistan. In a pilaf, the grains of rice—and occasionally other grains—are cooked in stock rather than water, with flavoring spices and, sometimes, vegetables.

Remove and discard the bay leaf. Season the mixture to taste with salt and pepper, and serve immediately, sprinkling each serving with the cashews.

Farro Pilaf, page 207

Farro Pilaf

Farro is an ancient grain that has been getting a lot of press these days for its cashewlike aroma and chewy bite. It also makes a wonderful pilaf braised in stock with some herbs. Serve this pilaf with Daube Niçoise *(page 124) or* Guinness Beef Stew *(page 128).*

SERVES **4 to 6**

SIZE **6-quart or larger pressure cooker**

TIME **6 to 8 minutes at high pressure; then allow the pressure to release naturally**

The farro can be made up to 1 day in advance, up to stirring in the parsley. Refrigerate it, tightly covered. Reheat the farro over low heat and then stir in the parsley.

NOTE Like rice and other grains, farro comes in a number of different forms, depending on how much of the grain has been processed. Whole-grain farro, like whole-grain barley and brown rice, is the most flavorful and nutritious, but it also takes the longest to cook. Although it will soften in the pressure cooker after 35 or 40 minutes—about the amount of time it takes to tenderize a pot roast—it really should be soaked overnight. This recipe calls for semiperlato, a grain that still has some, but not all, of its bran and germ. Although most people can tell the difference between white and brown rice, the two forms of farro look very similar. Make sure you read the label on the package to know what you're getting.

2 tablespoons olive oil
1 tablespoon unsalted butter
1 large shallot, minced
1 garlic clove, minced
¾ cup semiperlato farro
1½ cups Chicken Stock (page 15), Vegetable Stock (page 17), or purchased stock
2 teaspoons fresh thyme leaves
1 bay leaf
¼ cup chopped fresh parsley
Salt and freshly ground black pepper to taste

Heat the olive oil and butter in the cooker over medium heat or use the browning function of an electric cooker. Add the shallot and garlic, and cook, stirring frequently, for 3 minutes, or until the shallot is translucent. Stir in the farro and cook for 1 minute, stirring constantly. Add the stock, thyme, and bay leaf, and stir well.

Close and lock the lid of the cooker.

STOVETOP: Place the cooker over high heat, and bring it to high pressure. Once high pressure is reached, reduce the heat as much as possible while retaining the high-pressure level. Cook for 6 minutes. Then take the pot off the heat and allow it to return to normal pressure naturally. Remove the lid, tilting it away from you, to allow the steam to escape.

OR

ELECTRIC: Set the machine to cook at high pressure for 8 minutes. After 8 minutes, unplug the pot so that it does not go into warming mode. Allow the pressure to return to normal naturally. Remove the lid, tilting it away from you, to allow the steam to escape.

Remove and discard the bay leaf. Fluff the farro with a fork, add the parsley, and season to taste with salt and pepper. Serve immediately.

Jasmine Rice Salad

This colorful salad is the perfect summer side dish if you're serving a grilled entrée with an Asian marinade, or you can serve it with Chinese Red-Cooked Chicken with Plums (page 98) or Asian Baby Back Ribs with Peanuts (page 174). You also can add some leftover chicken or fish to the rice and serve it as an appetizer or a lunch dish.

SERVES **6 to 8**

SIZE **4-quart or larger pressure cooker**

TIME **2 to 3 minutes at high pressure; then allow the pressure to release naturally**

The salad can be made up to 2 days in advance and refrigerated, tightly covered.

SALAD

- 1½ cups jasmine rice
- 2 tablespoons vegetable oil
- 4 garlic cloves, minced
- 1 large shallot, minced
- 2 tablespoons finely chopped lemongrass
- ¾ teaspoon salt
- 1 large carrot, peeled and shredded
- 1 red bell pepper, seeds and ribs removed, cut into a fine julienne
- 6 scallions, white parts and 4 inches of green tops, cut into 1-inch sections and then cut into a fine julienne

GARNISH

- ¼ cup firmly packed cilantro leaves
- ¼ cup chopped roasted peanuts

DRESSING

- ½ cup unseasoned rice wine vinegar
- ¼ cup (firmly packed) dark brown sugar
- 2 tablespoons Thai or Vietnamese fish sauce
- 1 to 2 teaspoons sriracha sauce, or to taste
- ¼ cup vegetable oil

Place the rice in a sieve and rinse it under cold running water for 1 to 2 minutes, or until the water runs clear. Shake the sieve to get as much moisture off the rice as possible.

Heat the oil in the cooker over medium heat or use the browning function of an electric cooker. Add the garlic and shallot, and cook, stirring frequently, for 3 minutes, or until the shallot is translucent. Add the lemongrass, rice, salt, and 2½ cups of water.

Close and lock the lid of the cooker.

STOVETOP: Place the cooker over high heat, and bring it to high pressure. Once high pressure is reached, reduce the heat as much as possible while retaining the high-pressure level. Cook for 2 minutes. Then take the pot off the heat and allow it to return to normal pressure naturally. Remove the lid, tilting it away from you, to allow the steam to escape.

OR

ELECTRIC: Set the machine to cook at high pressure for 3 minutes. After 3 minutes, unplug the pot so that it does not go into warming mode. Allow the pressure to return to normal naturally. Remove the lid, tilting it away from you, to allow the steam to escape.

NOTE Salads like this one are a wonderful way to use up the odds and ends lurking in your refrigerator. Any cooked green vegetables—from asparagus and green beans, cut into bite-sized pieces, to a handful of leftover peas— make great additions.

While the rice cooks, prepare the dressing. Combine the vinegar, brown sugar, fish sauce, and sriracha sauce in a jar with a tight-fitting lid. Shake well until the sugar is dissolved. Add the oil and shake well again.

Pour the dressing over the hot rice and transfer it to a mixing bowl. Add the carrot, red pepper, and scallions. Mix well to combine. Refrigerate the salad until chilled, tightly covered with plastic wrap. To serve, plate the salad and sprinkle each portion with cilantro leaves and peanuts.

Wild Rice Pilaf
with Toasted Pine Nuts

Wild rice has a wonderful nutty flavor, and it pairs well with both poultry and meat. You also can use it as a stuffing for poultry, and it makes a wonderful cold salad, too. In this recipe, the dark grains of rice are enlivened by the colors of the vegetables, and the toasted nuts add textural interest. Serve the rice with Tarragon Chicken (page 100) or Creole Bison Meatloaf (page 146).

SERVES **4 to 6**

SIZE **4-quart or larger pressure cooker**

TIME **20 to 23 minutes at high pressure; then allow the pressure to release naturally**

The dish can be prepared up to 2 days in advance and refrigerated, tightly covered. Reheat it, covered, in a 350°F oven for 20 to 25 minutes, or until hot.

3 tablespoons unsalted butter, divided
1 large onion, diced
1 large carrot, diced
1 celery rib, diced
1 cup wild rice, rinsed
¼ cup dried currants

3 cups Vegetable Stock (page 17), Chicken Stock (page 15), or purchased stock
2 tablespoons chopped fresh parsley
1 teaspoon fresh thyme leaves
½ cup pine nuts
Salt and freshly ground black pepper to taste

Heat 2 tablespoons of the butter in the cooker over medium-high heat or use the browning function of an electric cooker. Add the onion, carrot, and celery, and cook, stirring frequently, for 3 minutes, or until the onion is translucent. Add the wild rice, currants, stock, parsley, and thyme, and stir well.

Close and lock the lid of the cooker.

STOVETOP: Place the cooker over high heat, and bring it to high pressure. Once high pressure is reached, reduce the heat as much as possible while retaining the high-pressure level. Cook for 20 minutes. Then take the pot off the heat and allow it to return to normal pressure naturally. Remove the lid, tilting it away from you, to allow the steam to escape.

OR

ELECTRIC: Set the machine to cook at high pressure for 23 minutes. After 23 minutes, unplug the pot so that it does not go into warming mode. Allow the pressure to return to normal naturally. Remove the lid, tilting it away from you, to allow the steam to escape.

While the rice cooks, melt the remaining butter in a small skillet over low heat. Add the pine nuts and cook them, stirring frequently, until browned. Season the rice to taste with salt and pepper, and serve immediately, garnishing each serving with some of the toasted pine nuts.

NOTE Wild rice (*Zizania palustris*) is a grain, not an official variety of rice. Wild rice is harvested primarily by Native Americans in Minnesota and some provinces of Canada. The Native Americans paddle canoes to the plants and then bend down the ripe grain heads with wooden sticks called *knockers* to extract the seeds. Some tribes, such as the Ojibwa, consider the grain sacred.

VARIATION

★ Substitute raisins or chopped dried apricots for the dried currants.

Quinoa Tabbouleh

Lip-puckering tabbouleh, with its lemony dressing and crunchy vegetables, is the potato salad of the Middle East and was one of the first dishes from that part of the world that was welcomed into the American kitchen. In this version the traditional bulgur is replaced with protein-rich quinoa.

SERVES **4 to 6**

SIZE **6-quart or larger pressure cooker**

TIME **1 minute at high pressure with quick pressure release after 5 minutes**

The quinoa and dressing can be made up to 1 day in advance. Do not cut up the other ingredients or toss the salad until just before serving.

1 cup quinoa
½ teaspoon salt
1 lemon
3 garlic cloves, divided
½ cup olive oil, divided
Salt and freshly ground black pepper to taste
3 Kirby cucumbers, cut into ½-inch dice

1½ cups cherry or grape tomatoes, halved
4 scallions, white parts and 4 inches of green tops, sliced
¾ cup chopped fresh parsley
⅓ cup chopped fresh mint

Rinse the quinoa in a sieve under cold running water for 2 minutes, or until the water runs clear. Place the quinoa in the pressure cooker, along with the salt and 1¼ cups water.

Cut 2 (3-inch) pieces of zest off the lemon and place them in the cooker; then juice the lemon and set it aside. Slice 1 of the garlic cloves and add it to the cooker. Mince the remaining cloves and set them aside. Add 1 tablespoon of the oil to the cooker.

Combine the lemon juice, remaining garlic, salt, and pepper in a jar with a tight-fitting lid and shake well. Add the remaining oil and shake well again.

Close and lock the lid of the cooker.

STOVETOP: Place the cooker over high heat, and bring it to high pressure. Once high pressure is reached, reduce the heat as much as possible while retaining the high-pressure level. Cook for 1 minute. Then take the pot off the heat and allow it to return to normal pressure naturally for 5 minutes. Quick release any remaining pressure. Remove the lid, tilting it away from you, to allow the steam to escape.

OR

ELECTRIC: Set the machine to cook at high pressure for 1 minute. After 1 minute, unplug the pot so that it does not go into warming mode. Allow the pressure to return to normal naturally for 5 minutes. Quick release any remaining pressure. Remove the lid, tilting it away from you, to allow the steam to escape.

NOTE Lemons give more juice when they're squeezed at room temperature, but to preserve their freshness we usually store them in the refrigerator. Microwave a cold lemon for 30 seconds and then roll it firmly on the counter before you squeeze it to get as much juice as possible.

Remove and discard the lemon zest. Transfer the quinoa to a mixing bowl and allow it to cool. Sprinkle it with ¼ cup of the dressing and refrigerate it, tightly covered, until chilled.

Add the cucumbers, tomatoes, scallions, parsley, and mint to the quinoa. Pour over the remaining dressing and toss to combine. Serve immediately.

Creamy Polenta

In 1992, when the legendary Marcella Hazan published Essentials of Classic Italian Cooking, *she released cooks from the drudgery of endlessly stirring polenta by revealing that it should be cooked covered and stirred only occasionally. But polenta still took an hour to cook, and the person in charge had to remember to give it the occasional stir. In the pressure cooker, however, you can make polenta in less time than it takes to bring a pot of water to a boil for pasta, and it has the same creamy, loose texture as polenta that has been stirred laboriously.*

SERVES **4 to 6**

SIZE **6-quart or larger pressure cooker**

TIME **7 to 8 minutes at high pressure; then allow the pressure to release naturally**

The polenta can be prepared up to a few hours in advance and kept warm. You may need to add some milk or water when reheating it.

NOTE Cornmeal ranges from coarse to very fine, and each type of granulation has its best uses. To make polenta or South American *arepas*, you want a coarse cornmeal because of the structure it lends to the finished dishes. But when you're making biscuits or corn bread, you want the cornmeal to be finely ground to avoid an unappealing gritty texture. All upscale supermarkets carry coarse polenta imported from Italy, but you can buy a coarse yellow cornmeal from Goya® Foods, a leading Hispanic food brand, for a fraction of the cost.

- 2 cups whole milk
- 1½ cups polenta
- 1 (4-inch) Parmesan rind (optional)
- 3 tablespoons unsalted butter
- Salt and freshly ground black pepper to taste

Combine the milk and 5 cups of water in the pressure cooker. Heat over medium-high heat or use the browning function of an electric cooker, and bring the liquid to a simmer, stirring occasionally. Whisk in the polenta in a thin stream, moving the whisk in only one direction. Add the Parmesan rind, if using.

Close and lock the lid of the cooker.

STOVETOP: Place the cooker over high heat, and bring it to high pressure. Once high pressure is reached, reduce the heat as much as possible while retaining the high-pressure level. Cook for 7 minutes. Then take the pot off the heat and allow it to return to normal pressure naturally. Remove the lid, tilting it away from you, to allow the steam to escape.

OR

ELECTRIC: Set the machine to cook at high pressure for 8 minutes. After 8 minutes, unplug the pot so that it does not go into warming mode. Allow the pressure to return to normal naturally. Remove the lid, tilting it away from you, to allow the steam to escape.

Remove and discard the Parmesan rind, if using. Beat the polenta with a heavy whisk until it is smooth and free of lumps. Beat in the butter and season to taste with salt and pepper. Spoon the polenta into warm serving bowls and add your choice of topping. Serve hot.

VARIATIONS

★ **Grilled Polenta:** To make grilled or fried polenta, reduce the amount of water by ½ cup. Scrape the cooked mixture into a greased 9 × 13-inch baking pan and chill. Cut the chilled polenta into squares or decorative shapes. Brush it on both sides with oil. Grill the polenta on the grill or fry it in a skillet over medium-high heat until crisp and brown.

★ **Polenta with Olives and Herbs:** Add 2/3 cup of chopped oil-cured olives and 1/3 cup of chopped mixed fresh herbs to the polenta after it finishes cooking.

★ **Polenta with Wild Mushrooms:** Combine ½ cup of dried porcini mushrooms and ¾ cup of the water to be used in a microwave-safe bowl, and microwave on high (100 percent power) for 2 minutes, or until boiling. Soak the mushrooms in the boiling water, pushing them down into the liquid with the back of a spoon, for 10 minutes. Drain the mushrooms, reserving the liquid. Dice the mushrooms and strain the soaking liquid through a sieve lined with a paper coffee filter or paper towel. Use the liquid as part of the recipe, and stir the mushrooms into the polenta before closing the lid of the pressure cooker.

New England "Baked" Beans

As we all know, this dish, dating back to the seventeenth century, isn't really baked; it's simmered in a warm oven for up to 12 hours, until the juices thicken and the beans soften. In this pressure cooker version, the same texture and depth of flavor is achieved in less than an hour. And during the summer there's no need to add heat to the kitchen by lighting the oven. Serve these beans with Bourbon Baby Back Ribs (page 178) or Southern Pulled Pork Barbecue (page 164).

SERVES **6 to 8**

SIZE **6-quart or larger pressure cooker**

TIME **40 to 45 minutes at high pressure; then allow the pressure to release naturally**

The beans can be refrigerated for up to 4 days, tightly covered, or frozen for up to 3 months. Reheat the beans over low heat or in a microwave oven. You can substitute any number of dried beans for the navy beans; however, the timing will need to be adjusted, up or down, by a few minutes; see the chart on page 197.

1 **pound dried navy beans**
Salt
¼ **pound thick-sliced bacon, cut into ½-inch pieces**
1 **large red onion, diced**
1 **(14.5-ounce) can petite diced tomatoes, undrained**
½ **cup barbecue sauce**

⅓ **cup molasses**
¼ **cup firmly packed dark brown sugar**
¼ **cup cider vinegar**
2 **tablespoons grainy mustard**
1 **tablespoon Worcestershire sauce**
Hot red pepper sauce to taste
Freshly ground black pepper to taste

Rinse the beans in a colander and place them in a mixing bowl covered with cold salted water. Allow the beans to soak for a minimum of 6 hours, or overnight. Or place the beans into a saucepan of salted water and bring to a boil over high heat. Boil 1 minute. Turn off the heat, cover the pan, and soak the beans for 1 hour. After using either of these soaking methods, drain the beans, discard the soaking water, and cook or refrigerate the beans as soon as possible.

Cook the bacon in the cooker over medium-high heat or use the browning function of an electric cooker for 5 to 7 minutes, or until crisp. Remove the bacon from the cooker with a slotted spoon and drain on paper towels. Set it aside.

Discard all but 2 tablespoons of bacon grease from the cooker. Add the onion and cook, stirring frequently, for 3 minutes, or until the onion is translucent. Add the tomatoes, barbecue sauce, molasses, brown sugar, vinegar, mustard, Worcestershire sauce, 1¾ cups of water, and the beans. Stir well.

Close and lock the lid of the cooker.

STOVETOP: Place the cooker over high heat, and bring it to high pressure. Once high pressure is reached, reduce the heat as much as possible while retaining the high-pressure level. Cook for 40 minutes. Then take the pot off the heat and allow it to return to normal pressure naturally. Remove the lid, tilting it away from you, to allow the steam to escape.

OR

ELECTRIC: Set the machine to cook at high pressure for 45 minutes. After 45 minutes, unplug the pot so that it does not go into warming mode. Allow the pressure to return to normal naturally. Remove the lid, tilting it away from you, to allow the steam to escape.

Stir the beans, and cook over medium heat or use the browning function of an electric cooker for 5 minutes, or until the juices thicken. Stir in the bacon and season to taste with salt, pepper, and hot red pepper sauce. Serve hot.

NOTE This dish cooks under pressure so much longer than other bean dishes because the acidic ingredients in which the beans are cooked—such as tomatoes, vinegar, and barbecue sauce—retard the softening process. The payoff for the longer cooking time is a dish in which each bean is vividly flavored.

New England
"Baked" Beans, page 216

Stewed Asian Black Beans

*The black beans used most frequently in Asian cooking are either
fermented with salt or ground up into a sauce. You'll find these flavors in this hearty
stew too, along with those from other Asian ingredients like hoisin sauce. Serve these
beans over rice with dishes such as Asian Beef Stew with Star Anise (page 126).*

SERVES **4 to 6**

SIZE **4-quart or larger pressure cooker**

TIME **6 to 8 minutes at high pressure; then allow the pressure to release naturally**

The dish can be prepared up to 2 days in advance and refrigerated, tightly covered. Reheat it, covered, over low heat until hot, stirring occasionally.

1½ cups dried black beans
2 tablespoons Asian sesame oil
8 scallions, white parts and 4 inches of green tops, cut into 1-inch pieces
3 garlic cloves, minced
2 tablespoons grated fresh ginger
4 cups Vegetable Stock (page 17) or purchased stock
½ cup dry sherry
¼ cup hoisin sauce

¼ cup tamari
2 tablespoons Chinese black bean sauce with garlic
2 tablespoons unseasoned rice wine vinegar
2 teaspoons sriracha sauce or to taste
2 teaspoons granulated sugar
½ cup chopped fresh cilantro
Freshly ground black pepper to taste

Rinse the beans in a colander and place them in a mixing bowl covered with cold salted water. Allow the beans to soak for a minimum of 6 hours, or overnight. Or place the beans into a saucepan of salted water and bring to a boil over high heat. Boil 1 minute. Turn off the heat, cover the pan, and soak the beans for 1 hour. After using either of these soaking methods, drain the beans, discard the soaking water, and cook or refrigerate the beans as soon as possible.

Heat the sesame oil in the cooker over medium-high heat or use the browning function of an electric cooker. Add the scallions, garlic, and ginger, and cook for 30 seconds, or until fragrant, stirring constantly. Place the drained beans in the cooker and add the stock, sherry, hoisin sauce, tamari, black bean sauce, vinegar, sriracha sauce, and sugar. Stir well.

Close and lock the lid of the cooker.

STOVETOP: Place the cooker over high heat, and bring it to high pressure. Once high pressure is reached, reduce the heat as much as possible while retaining the high-pressure level. Cook for 6 minutes. Then take the pot off the heat and allow it to return to normal pressure naturally. Remove the lid, tilting it away from you, to allow the steam to escape.

OR

ELECTRIC: Set the machine to cook at high pressure for 8 minutes. After 8 minutes, unplug the pot so that it does not go into warming mode. Allow the pressure to return to normal naturally. Remove the lid, tilting it away from you, to allow the steam to escape.

Stir in the cilantro and season to taste with freshly ground black pepper. Serve immediately.

NOTE You can prolong the life of leafy herbs such as cilantro, parsley, and dill with good storage. Treat a bunch of herbs like a bouquet of flowers; trim the stems when you get home from the market, put the herbs in a glass of water, and keep them fresh in the refrigerator.

Refried Beans

Refried beans, called frijoles refritos *south of the border, is an authentic Mexican dish. In this version, the beans gain a smoky nuance from the addition of both smoked paprika and chipotle chiles. This dish goes with any Mexican or Southwestern meal, and because the beans are mashed, there's no need to soak them in advance. The pressure cooker will make short work of them.*

SERVES **6 to 8**

SIZE **4-quart or larger pressure cooker**

TIME **30 to 35 minutes at high pressure; then allow the pressure to release naturally**

The dish can be prepared up to 2 days in advance and refrigerated, tightly covered. Reheat it, covered, in a 350°F oven for 20 to 25 minutes, or until hot. The bean mixture may need to be thinned slightly if it is reheated, so refrigerate the remaining ½ cup of the liquid in which the beans were cooked.

1 **pound dried red kidney beans**
½ **cup vegetable oil or strained bacon fat, divided**
2 **large red onions, diced**
6 **garlic cloves, minced**
2 **jalapeño or serrano chiles, seeds and ribs removed, finely chopped**
2 **tablespoons smoked Spanish paprika**
1 **tablespoon ground cumin**
1 **teaspoon dried oregano**
1 **chipotle chile in adobo sauce, finely chopped**
1 **tablespoon adobo sauce**
½ **cup refrigerated commercial tomato salsa**
Salt and freshly ground black pepper to taste

Rinse the beans and place them in the pressure cooker with 2 tablespoons of the oil and 7 cups of water.

Close and lock the lid of the cooker.

STOVETOP: Place the cooker over high heat, and bring it to high pressure. Once high pressure is reached, reduce the heat as much as possible while retaining the high-pressure level. Cook for 30 minutes. Then take the pot off the heat and allow it to return to normal pressure naturally. Remove the lid, tilting it away from you, to allow the steam to escape.

OR

ELECTRIC: Set the machine to cook at high pressure for 35 minutes. After 35 minutes, unplug the pot so that it does not go into warming mode. Allow the pressure to return to normal naturally. Remove the lid, tilting it away from you, to allow the steam to escape.

Remove the beans from the cooker with a slotted spoon, and reserve 1 cup of the cooking liquid.

Heat the remaining oil in a large skillet over medium-high heat. Add the onions, garlic, and fresh chiles, and cook, stirring frequently, for 4 to 5 minutes, or until the onions are soft. Reduce the heat to low and stir in the paprika, cumin, and oregano. Cook for 1 minute, stirring constantly.

Stir in the beans, ½ cup of the reserved bean cooking liquid, chipotle chile, adobo sauce, and salsa. Mash the beans with a potato masher or the back of a heavy spoon until the beans have the texture of lumpy mashed potatoes; the texture should be smooth but some whole beans should be visible. Season to taste with salt and pepper, and serve hot.

NOTE The reason you were given the direction to remove and discard the seeds of chile peppers is that they contain most of the heat. If you want to make a dish hotter, leave the seeds in at least one pepper. If you want to keep the level of heat in check, however, cut the stem end off the pepper. What you will see is the outline of the skeleton of ribs and seeds. Take a paring knife and cut out the flesh of the chile between the white lines of the ribs.

Black Bean and Papaya Salad

Two of the greatest advantages of cooking under pressure are short cooking times and intense flavors that lock into each ingredient. You'll find this is true of the beans, cinnamon, and garlic in this salad, which gets its crunch from jicama and its sweetness from fresh papaya. Serve it with Bourbon Baby Back Ribs (page 178) or Brazilian Fish Stew with Salsa (page 72).

SERVES **4 to 6**

SIZE **4-quart or larger pressure cooker**

TIME **6 to 8 minutes at high pressure; then allow the pressure to release naturally**

The beans can be cooked and the dressing can be made up to 2 days in advance and refrigerated, tightly covered. Do not assemble or dress the salad until just before serving.

½ pound dried black beans
1 (3-inch) cinnamon stick
4 garlic cloves, minced, divided
½ ripe papaya, peeled, seeded, cut into ½-inch dice
1 small jicama, peeled and cut into ½-inch dice
2 shallots, minced

1 teaspoon ground cumin
⅓ cup freshly squeezed orange juice
3 tablespoons balsamic vinegar
2 tablespoons freshly squeezed lime juice
Salt and cayenne to taste
⅓ cup olive oil

Rinse the beans in a colander and place them in a mixing bowl covered with cold salted water. Allow the beans to soak for a minimum of 6 hours, or overnight. Or place the beans into a saucepan of salted water and bring to a boil over high heat. Boil 1 minute. Turn off the heat, cover the pan, and soak the beans for 1 hour. After using either of these soaking methods, drain the beans, discard the soaking water, and cook or refrigerate the beans as soon as possible.

Place the beans in the pressure cooker and add the cinnamon stick, half of the garlic, and 2 cups of water.

Close and lock the lid of the cooker.

STOVETOP: Place the cooker over high heat, and bring it to high pressure. Once high pressure is reached, reduce the heat as much as possible while retaining the high-pressure level. Cook for 6 minutes. Then take the pot off the heat and allow it to return to normal pressure naturally. Remove the lid, tilting it away from you, to allow the steam to escape.

OR

ELECTRIC: Set the machine to cook at high pressure for 8 minutes. After 8 minutes, unplug the pot so that it does not go into warming mode. Allow the pressure to return to normal naturally. Remove the lid, tilting it away from you, to allow the steam to escape.

Remove and discard the cinnamon stick, drain the beans, and transfer them to the refrigerator to chill well. Combine the chilled beans with the papaya and jicama in a mixing bowl.

For the dressing, combine the shallots, remaining garlic, cumin, orange juice, vinegar, lime juice, salt, and cayenne in a jar with a tight-fitting lid. Shake well, add the oil, and shake well again. Pour the dressing over the salad and toss. Serve immediately.

NOTE Papaya contains papain, an enzyme that naturally tenderizes meats and poultry. When peeling the papaya, save the skin and add it to a marinade.

VARIATION

★ Substitute ripe mango for the papaya.

Garbanzo Bean
Salad Parmesan, page 227

Garbanzo Bean Salad Parmesan

This brightly colored salad combines nutty, meaty garbanzo beans with crunchy radicchio and a vivid dressing, punctuated with freshly grated Parmesan. It can be served as a light lunch or with dishes such as Ragù Bolognese (page 184) and Salmon en Papillote with Tomatoes, Capers, and Olives (page 58).

SERVES **4 to 6**

SIZE **4-quart or larger pressure cooker**

TIME **11 to 13 minutes at high pressure; then allow the pressure to release naturally**

The beans can be cooked up to 2 days in advance and refrigerated, tightly covered. The dressing can also be made up to 2 days in advance. Allow the dressing to sit at room temperature for 30 minutes before tossing it with the beans.

BEANS
1½ cups dried garbanzo beans
5 garlic cloves, peeled
1 tablespoon Italian seasoning
1 bay leaf

SALAD
¼ cup red wine vinegar
¼ cup freshly squeezed orange juice
3 tablespoons chopped fresh parsley
1 tablespoon chopped fresh rosemary
2 teaspoons fresh thyme leaves
2 teaspoons chopped fresh oregano
1 teaspoon grated orange zest
2 garlic cloves, minced
Salt and freshly ground black pepper to taste
½ cup olive oil
½ cup chopped pitted green or black brine-cured olives
5 scallions, white parts and 3 inches of green tops, chopped
2 ripe plum tomatoes, seeded and chopped
1 small head radicchio, cored and chopped
½ cup freshly grated Parmesan cheese

Rinse the beans in a colander and place them in a mixing bowl covered with cold salted water. Allow the beans to soak for a minimum of 6 hours, or overnight. Or place the beans into a saucepan of salted water and bring to a boil over high heat. Boil 1 minute. Turn off the heat, cover the pan, and soak the beans for 1 hour. After using either of these soaking methods, drain the beans, discard the soaking water, and cook or refrigerate the beans as soon as possible.

Place the beans in the cooker and add the peeled garlic cloves, Italian seasoning, bay leaf, and 6 cups of water.

(continued on the following page)

(continued from the previous page)

Close and lock the lid of the cooker.

STOVETOP: Place the cooker over high heat and bring it to high pressure. Once high pressure is reached, reduce the heat as much as possible while retaining the high-pressure level. Cook for 11 minutes. Then take the pot off the heat and allow it to return to normal pressure naturally. Remove the lid, tilting it away from you, to allow the steam to escape.

OR

ELECTRIC: Set the machine to cook at high pressure for 13 minutes. After 13 minutes, unplug the pot so that it does not go into warming mode. Allow the pressure to return to normal naturally. Remove the lid, tilting it away from you, to allow the steam to escape.

Drain the beans, discarding the bay leaf, and refrigerate them until cold.

Combine the vinegar, orange juice, parsley, rosemary, thyme, oregano, orange zest, garlic, salt, and pepper in a jar with a tight-fitting lid. Shake well. Add the olive oil and shake well again.

Add the olives, scallions, tomatoes, and radicchio to the bowl with the beans. Toss the salad with some of the dressing and the Parmesan. Serve immediately and pass around the extra dressing.

NOTE No matter what you call them—garbanzo beans, chickpeas, ceci, or chana—these beige nutty-flavored beans play a major role in many cuisines around the world, in both temperate and tropical climates, and take well to myriad seasonings. Garbanzo beans are high in protein and are a good source of dietary fiber. And, more than any other legume, they have been found to satisfy the appetite and deliver a sensation of fullness—perhaps because of their meaty texture.

Cannellini Beans with Tomatoes and Sage

Sage is a great herb that adds a woodsy flavor and aroma to food. In Italy it's used in many ways; it melds wonderfully with the beans and tomatoes in this Tuscan version of a classic bean dish. Serve it with Osso Buco alla Milanese (page 188) or Veal Stew with Wild Mushrooms (page 192).

SERVES **6 to 8**

SIZE **6-quart or larger pressure cooker**

TIME **6 to 8 minutes at high pressure; then allow the pressure to release naturally**

1 **pound dried cannellini beans**
¼ **cup olive oil**
1 **large shallot, minced**
3 **garlic cloves, minced**
¼ **cup chopped fresh sage**

1 **(14.5-ounce) can diced tomatoes, undrained**
3 **cups Vegetable Stock (page 17) or purchased stock**
Salt and freshly ground black pepper to taste

The dish can be prepared up to 2 days in advance and refrigerated, tightly covered. Reheat it, covered, in a 350°F oven for 20 to 25 minutes, or until hot.

NOTE The easiest way to chop leafy herbs such as sage or basil is to create a stack of leaves and roll them into a cylinder. Thinly slice the cylinder into shreds and turn the shreds at a right angle and cut them the other way.

VARIATION

★ **Tuscan Beans with Prosciutto and Olives:** Add ½ cup of diced prosciutto and ¼ cup of chopped oil-cured black olives to the cooker along with the beans. Taste the dish before adding any more salt.

Rinse the beans in a colander and place them in a mixing bowl covered with cold salted water. Allow the beans to soak for a minimum of 6 hours or overnight. Or place the beans into a saucepan of salted water and bring to a boil over high heat. Boil 1 minute. Turn off the heat, cover the pan, and soak the beans for 1 hour. After using either of these soaking methods, drain the beans, discard the soaking water, and cook or refrigerate the beans as soon as possible.

Heat the oil in a cooker over medium-high heat or use the browning function of an electric cooker. Add the shallot and garlic, and cook, stirring frequently, for 3 minutes, or until the shallot is translucent. Add the beans, sage, tomatoes, and stock to the cooker and stir well. Close and lock the lid of the cooker.

STOVETOP: Place the cooker over high heat, and bring it to high pressure. Once high pressure is reached, reduce the heat as much as possible while retaining the high-pressure level. Cook for 6 minutes. Then take the pot off the heat and allow it to return to normal pressure naturally. Remove the lid, tilting it away from you, to allow the steam to escape.

OR

ELECTRIC: Set the machine to cook at high pressure for 8 minutes. After 8 minutes, unplug the pot so that it does not go into warming mode. Allow the pressure to return to normal naturally. Remove the lid, tilting it away from you, to allow the steam to escape.

Season to taste with salt and pepper, and serve hot.

Braised Red Cabbage,
page 234

CHAPTER 8

Vegetables

Using the pressure cooker opens up many options for vegetable dishes because they can be cooked to perfection in minutes. I adore artichokes and now can have them whenever they look fresh in the produce department. Instead of taking almost an hour to cook with conventional methods, even jumbo artichokes are ready to put on the table in less than 15 minutes when they are prepared in a pressure cooker. Fresh beets are one of my favorite things to add to salads, and now I can cook them quickly under pressure without even peeling them.

Cooking Vegetables

You'll find that vegetables cooked under pressure retain far more of their natural color, as well as a higher percentage of their nutrients, than vegetables that are prepared conventionally. Nevertheless, I still shock green vegetables in ice water to cool them quickly after pressure-cooking.

COOKING TIMES (IN MINUTES) FOR VEGETABLES IN THE PRESSURE COOKER

VEGETABLE	STOVETOP	ELECTRIC	RELEASE METHOD
ARTICHOKE S, M, L	5, 9, 11	6, 10, 12	QUICK
BEETS S, M, L	10, 20, 25	12, 22, 29	QUICK
BEETS, SLICED	5	7	QUICK
BROCCOLI, FLORETS	2	3	QUICK
BROCCOLI, STEMS	4	6	QUICK
BRUSSELS SPROUTS	4	5	QUICK
CABBAGE, WEDGES	5	7	10 MIN. NATURAL
CABBAGE, SLICED	2	2	QUICK
CARROTS, 1-INCH CHUNKS	4	5	10 MIN. NATURAL
CARROTS, SLICED	1	2	QUICK
CAULIFLOWER, FLORETS	2	3	QUICK
CAULIFLOWER, WHOLE	8	10	QUICK
CELERY, SLICED	2	3	QUICK
COLLARD GREENS	5	7	10 MIN. NATURAL
EGGPLANT, SLICED	2	3	QUICK
FENNEL	2	3	QUICK
GREEN BEANS	2	3	QUICK
HARICOT VERTS	1	2	QUICK
LEEKS, SLICED	3	4	QUICK

MUSHROOMS	5	6	10 MIN. NATURAL
OKRA	2	3	QUICK
ONIONS, WHOLE	3 TO 4	4 TO 5	QUICK
PARSNIPS, SLICED	1	2	QUICK
PARSNIPS, 1-INCH CHUNKS	4	5	10 MIN. NATURAL
PEPPERS, BELL	3	4	QUICK
POTATOES, SLICED	4	5	NATURAL
POTATOES, WHOLE S, M, L	7, 10, 13	9, 12, 15	NATURAL
PUMPKIN, 2-INCH CUBES	5	6	QUICK
RUTABAGA	1	2	QUICK
ACORN OR BUTTERNUT SQUASH, 2-INCH CUBES	3	4	QUICK
ACORN OR BUTTERNUT SQUASH, HALVES	6	8	10 MIN. NATURAL
SPAGHETTI SQUASH, HALVES	5	6	10 MIN. NATURAL
SWEET POTATOES, SLICED	5	6	10 MIN. NATURAL
TURNIPS, WHOLE S, M, L	4, 6, 8	5, 8, 10	10 MIN. NATURAL

Making Baby Food in the Pressure Cooker

It's natural for parents to want to feed their children nutrient-dense, high-quality food, and that's where a pressure cooker comes in. Vegetables should be cut into ¾-inch pieces, and depending on preference, you can cook them in heatproof cups or ramekins on the steamer rack of the pressure cooker or arrange individual piles of vegetables on the rack itself.

Save the water used to cook the vegetables, because it contains nutrients, and use some of it to puree vegetable mixtures to achieve the desired consistency. The best appliances for pureeing baby food are an immersion blender, using the beaker it comes with; a blender; and a food processor.

You can freeze baby food puree in ice cube trays and then transfer the portions to heavy, resealable plastic bags.

Braised Red Cabbage

This spiced red cabbage is one of my favorite winter dishes. It pairs well with turkey for Thanksgiving and dishes such as Curried Chicken with Dried Currants and Toasted Almonds (page 96). The apple and jelly add a bit of sweetness to the mix and harmonize nicely with the aromatic cinnamon.

SERVES **6 to 8**

SIZE **6-quart or larger pressure cooker**

TIME **6 to 8 minutes at high pressure with quick pressure release**

> The cabbage can be prepared 2 days in advance and refrigerated, tightly covered. Reheat it over low heat, stirring occasionally.

- 1 (2-pound) head red cabbage, cored and sliced
- 2 tablespoons red wine vinegar
- 2 tablespoons granulated sugar
- 3 tablespoons unsalted butter, divided
- 1 onion, diced
- 1 Golden Delicious or Honeycrisp apple, peeled and chopped
- ¾ cup dry red wine
- ½ cup Chicken Stock (page 15), Vegetable Stock (page 17), or purchased stock
- 1 (3-inch) cinnamon stick
- 1 bay leaf
- Salt and freshly ground black pepper to taste
- ⅓ cup red currant jelly

Place the cabbage in a large bowl. Sprinkle it with the vinegar and sugar, and toss well. Allow the cabbage to sit at room temperature for 1 hour.

Heat 2 tablespoons of the butter in the cooker over medium heat or use the browning function of an electric cooker. Add the onion and apple, and cook for 3 minutes, stirring frequently, or until the onion is translucent. Add the wine, stock, cinnamon stick, and bay leaf. Bring to a boil and stir in the cabbage with any juices from the bowl.

Close and lock the lid of the cooker.

STOVETOP: Place the cooker over high heat, and bring it to high pressure. Once high pressure is reached, reduce the heat as much as possible while retaining the high-pressure level. Cook for 6 minutes. Then take the pot off the heat and quick release the pressure according to the instructions provided by the manufacturer. Remove the lid, tilting it away from you, to allow the steam to escape.

OR

ELECTRIC: Set the machine to cook at high pressure for 8 minutes. After 8 minutes, unplug the pot so that it does not go into warming mode. Quick release the pressure according to the instructions provided by the manufacturer. Remove the lid, tilting it away from you, to allow the steam to escape.

NOTE The purpose of tossing the cabbage with vinegar and sugar is to set the color so that the dish will retain its appealing red hue after it has been cooked. If you don't have time to let the cabbage sit for an hour, add the vinegar and sugar to the pressure cooker when you add the cabbage.

Remove and discard the cinnamon stick and bay leaf. Stir the jelly and the remaining butter into the cabbage. Cook, uncovered, over medium heat for 10 minutes or use the browning function of an electric cooker, or until the liquid reduces and becomes syrupy. Serve immediately.

Maple-Glazed Beets

Beets are innately sweet, and because they take so long to cook, they're obvious candidates for the pressure cooker. The addition of New England's prized maple syrup and heady balsamic vinegar makes this a memorable winter vegetable dish, and any leftovers will be a wonderful addition to green salads. Serve these beets with Dilled Swedish Meatballs (page 186) or Creole Bison Meatloaf (page 146).

SERVES **4 to 6**

SIZE **4-quart or larger pressure cooker**

TIME **10 to 28 minutes with quick pressure release**

The beets can be cooked up to 1 day in advance and refrigerated, tightly covered. Glaze them just before serving. The amount of time it takes beets to cook depends on their size:

Large beets
(7 to 10 ounces): 25 to 28 minutes

Medium beets
(5 to 7 ounces): 20 to 22 minutes

Baby beets
(less than 5 ounces): 10 to 12 minutes

2 pounds fresh beets
⅓ cup balsamic vinegar
¼ cup pure maple syrup
2 tablespoons unsalted butter

2 tablespoons chopped parsley
1 teaspoon fresh thyme leaves
Salt and freshly ground black pepper to taste

Remove the beet greens, leaving 1 inch attached to the beets. Scrub the beets and arrange them in the cooker. Add 2½ cups of water to the pressure cooker.

Close and lock the lid of the cooker.

STOVETOP: Place the cooker over high heat, and bring it to high pressure. Once high pressure is reached, reduce the heat as much as possible while retaining the high-pressure level. Cook the beets for the allotted number of minutes. Then take the pot off the heat and quick release the pressure according to the instructions provided by the manufacturer. Remove the lid, tilting it away from you, to allow the steam to escape.

OR

ELECTRIC: Set the machine to cook at high pressure for the allotted number of minutes. After cooking, unplug the pot so that it does not go into warming mode. Quick release the pressure according to the instructions provided by the manufacturer. Remove the lid, tilting it away from you, to allow the steam to escape.

Remove the beets from the pressure cooker with a slotted spoon and submerge them in a bowl of ice water. When the beets are cool enough to handle, slip off and discard the skins and cut the beets into ⅓-inch slices.

Discard the cooking liquid and rinse out the pressure cooker. Combine the vinegar, maple syrup, and butter in the pressure cooker. Bring to a boil over medium heat or use the browning function of an electric cooker. Stir until the butter is melted; then add the beets and cook for 2 minutes, or until they are heated through. Sprinkle the beets with the parsley and thyme, and season to taste with salt and pepper. Serve immediately.

NOTE You should always buy beets with the greens attached, because the look of the greens—they should be crisp and perky—indicates the freshness of the beets. The greens are also delicious cooked and served as a garnish. After rinsing the beets, cut them into ½-inch slices and sauté them in butter for 2 minutes, or until crisp-tender.

Fennel with Tomatoes and Orange

Only one element on a plate should be the star, and on an evening when you're serving a simple grilled or broiled entrée, that dish can be the vegetable. One of my favorite stars is this combination of silky braised fennel brightly flavored with fresh orange juice and tomatoes.

SERVES **4 to 6**

SIZE **6-quart or larger pressure cooker**

TIME **2 to 3 minutes at high pressure; then allow the pressure to release naturally**

The fennel can be made up to 2 days in advance and refrigerated, tightly covered. Reheat it in a skillet over low heat, covered, or in a microwave oven.

NOTE I'm addicted to the light licorice flavor of fresh fennel and use it in place of cabbage for almost all my coleslaw recipes. However, the flavor of fennel dissipates after it is cooked and has achieved its satiny texture. I've discovered that star anise pods, which often are used in Chinese cooking, restore the wonderful flavor of braised fennel.

2 tablespoons olive oil
1 large onion, thinly sliced
3 garlic cloves, minced
1 (28-ounce) can diced tomatoes, undrained
½ cup dry white wine
½ cup freshly squeezed orange juice
1 tablespoon grated orange zest
3 star anise pods
2 (¾-pound) fennel bulbs, stalks and core removed, cut into quarters
Salt and freshly ground black pepper to taste

Heat the oil in the cooker over medium-high heat or use the browning function of an electric cooker. Add the onion and garlic, and cook, stirring frequently, for 3 minutes, or until the onion is translucent.

Add the tomatoes, wine, orange juice, orange zest, and star anise pods to the cooker and stir well. Arrange the fennel sections in the liquid.

Close and lock the lid of the cooker.

STOVETOP: Place the cooker over high heat, and bring it to high pressure. Once high pressure is reached, reduce the heat as much as possible while retaining the high-pressure level. Cook for 2 minutes. Then take the pot off the heat and allow it to return to normal pressure naturally. Remove the lid, tilting it away from you, to allow the steam to escape.

OR

ELECTRIC: Set the machine to cook at high pressure for 3 minutes. After 3 minutes, unplug the pot so that it does not go into warming mode. Allow the pressure to return to normal naturally. Remove the lid, tilting it away from you, to allow the steam to escape.

Remove and discard the star anise pods. Season the fennel to taste with salt and pepper, and serve hot or at room temperature.

Colcannon

Serving corned beef and cabbage on St. Patrick's Day is as American as eating turkey on Thanksgiving. In Ireland, potatoes and cabbage are combined in Colcannon, a mélange of mashed potatoes and cabbage flavored with ham and scallions. It's delicious served with Guinness Beef Stew (page 128).

SERVES **4 to 6**

SIZE **6-quart or larger pressure cooker**

TIME **4 to 5 minutes at high pressure with quick pressure release**

The dish can be prepared up to 2 days in advance and refrigerated, tightly covered. However, do not stir the scallions into the dish if you are preparing it in advance.

NOTE There are more than 100 varieties of potatoes grown around the United States, with thousands more in other parts of the world. What divides them, more than shape or color, is starch content. Potatoes that are high in starch, such as the russet, are the best for baked and mashed potatoes, but they have a tendency to fall apart, which makes them unsuitable for potato salads. For salads, you want waxy potatoes such as fingerling or red potatoes.

- 3 large russet potatoes, peeled and cut into ¾-inch cubes
- 1 pound (½ of a small head) green cabbage, cored and cut into 2-inch chunks
- ¼ pound (1 stick) unsalted butter, divided
- ¼ to ½ cup whole milk
- 2 ounces baked him, diced
- 4 scallions, white parts and 3 inches of green tops, sliced
- Salt and freshly ground white pepper to taste

Combine the potatoes and cabbage in the cooker and add 2 tablespoons of the butter and 1 cup of water.

Close and lock the lid of the cooker.

STOVETOP: Place the cooker over high heat, and bring it to high pressure. Once high pressure is reached, reduce the heat as much as possible while retaining the high-pressure level. Cook for 4 minutes. Then take the pot off the heat and quick release the pressure according to the instructions provided by the manufacturer. Remove the lid, tilting it away from you, to allow the steam to escape.

OR

ELECTRIC: Set the machine to cook at high pressure for 5 minutes. After 5 minutes, unplug the pot so that it does not go into warming mode. Quick release the pressure according to the instructions provided by the manufacturer. Remove the lid, tilting it away from you, to allow the steam to escape.

Drain the vegetables in a colander, shaking them to remove excess water. Return the vegetables to the cooker. Add the remaining butter, ¼ cup milk, ham, and scallions. Place the cooker over low heat or use the "keep warm" function of an electric cooker. Mash the vegetables to the desired consistency; the more you mash, the smoother it will become. Add additional milk, if desired. Season to taste with salt and pepper, and serve hot.

Caponata

This classic Sicilian dish usually is served at room temperature as an antipasto, but I also enjoy it as a vegetable dish served at any temperature. The mixture of eggplant with other vegetables in a delicate sweet and sour sauce, garnished with crunchy toasted pine nuts, is downright seductive. Try it with Veal Marsala Stew (page 190) or Braised Lamb Shanks with White Beans (page 148).

SERVES **4 to 6**

SIZE **6-quart pressure cooker or larger**

TIME **2 to 3 minutes at high pressure with quick pressure release**

The dish can be prepared up to 2 days in advance and refrigerated, tightly covered. Serve it chilled or allow it to warm to room temperature but do not reheat it .

1 (1¼-pound) eggplant, cut into 1½-inch cubes
¼ cup kosher salt
½ cup pine nuts
2 tablespoons firmly packed light brown sugar
2 tablespoons red wine vinegar
2 tablespoons balsamic vinegar
¼ cup olive oil
1 small red onion, diced
4 garlic cloves, minced
1 celery rib, diced
½ red bell pepper, seeds and ribs removed, diced

1 (14.5-ounce) can diced tomatoes, undrained
1 tablespoon tomato paste
½ cup golden raisins
3 tablespoons chopped fresh parsley
1 tablespoon chopped fresh rosemary
¼ teaspoon ground cinnamon
2 tablespoons capers, drained and rinsed
Salt and freshly ground black pepper to taste

Place the eggplant cubes in a mixing bowl with 4 cups of cold water. Add the kosher salt and stir well. Place a plate on top of the cubes to keep them submerged, and soak them for 20 minutes. Drain the eggplant in a colander and run cold water over the cubes. Squeeze handfuls of the cubes in your hands and place them on a cloth dishtowel. Wring them in the towel and set them aside.

While the eggplant soaks, toast the pine nuts in a small dry skillet over low heat. Set them aside. Combine the sugar, red wine vinegar, and balsamic vinegar in a small cup and stir well.

Heat the oil in the cooker over medium-high heat or use the browning function of an electric cooker. Add the onion and garlic, and cook, stirring frequently, for 3 minutes, or until the onion is translucent. Add the eggplant cubes and cook for 1 minute, stirring constantly. Stir in the vinegar mixture and add the celery, red bell pepper, tomatoes, tomato paste, raisins, parsley, rosemary, and cinnamon. Stir well.

Close and lock the lid of the cooker.

STOVETOP: Place the cooker over high heat, and bring it to high pressure. Once high pressure is reached, reduce the heat as much as possible while retaining the high-pressure level. Cook for 2 minutes. Then take the pot off the heat and quick release the pressure according to the instructions provided by the manufacturer. Remove the lid, tilting it away from you, to allow the steam to escape.

OR

ELECTRIC: Set the machine to cook at high pressure for 3 minutes. After 3 minutes, unplug the pot so that it does not go into warming mode. Quick release the pressure according to the instructions provided by the manufacturer. Remove the lid, tilting it away from you, to allow the steam to escape.

NOTE All capers come from the same plant, *Capparis spinosa*, but they come in two different sizes because they're harvested at different times. Tiny capers really should be called *caper buds*, because they are the buds that the bushes produce in the spring. If the buds are left on the plant, they will become a beautiful purple and white flower that is replaced by a tiny fruit after the petals drop, and those are the large capers, which are actually *caper berries*.

Stir in the capers and season to taste with salt and pepper. Serve hot, at room temperature, or cold. Sprinkle each serving with some of the toasted pine nuts.

Asian Eggplant in Garlic Sauce

The flesh of an eggplant has a rich, earthy, almost nutlike flavor, and the skin retains its vibrant color even when cooked. Eggplant is part of many Chinese regional cuisines, especially those from the northern part of China. Although it is mellow, eggplant can be vividly flavored, making it the perfect partner for Crispy Chinese Duck Legs (page 118) or Asian Baby Back Ribs with Peanuts (page 174).

SERVES **4 to 6**

SIZE **4-quart or larger pressure cooker**

TIME **2 to 3 minutes at high pressure with quick pressure release**

> The dish also can be served at room temperature or chilled. Do not thicken it with the cornstarch unless you are serving it hot.

- 1 (1¼-pound) eggplant, trimmed and cut into 2-inch cubes
- ¼ cup kosher salt
- ¼ cup reduced-sodium soy sauce
- ¼ cup Chicken Stock (page 15), Chinese Chicken Stock (page 15), or purchased stock
- 2 tablespoons oyster sauce
- 3 tablespoons firmly packed dark brown sugar
- 1 tablespoon unseasoned rice wine vinegar
- 1 teaspoon toasted sesame oil
- 2 tablespoons vegetable oil
- 3 scallions, white parts and 4 inches of green tops, sliced
- 2 tablespoons grated fresh ginger
- 4 garlic cloves, minced
- ½ teaspoon crushed red pepper flakes or to taste
- 2 teaspoons cornstarch

GARNISH
- 2 tablespoons fresh cilantro leaves

Place the eggplant cubes in a mixing bowl with 4 cups of cold water. Add the kosher salt and stir well. Place a plate on top of the cubes to keep them submerged and soak them for 20 minutes. Drain the eggplant in a colander and run cold water over the cubes. Squeeze handfuls of the cubes in your hands and then place them on a cloth dishtowel. Wring them in the towel and set them aside.

Combine the soy sauce, stock, oyster sauce, brown sugar, vinegar, and sesame oil in a small bowl and stir well. Set it aside.

Heat the oil in the cooker over medium-high heat or use the browning function of an electric cooker. Add the eggplant, scallions, ginger, garlic, and crushed red pepper flakes. Cook for 2 minutes, stirring constantly. Add the liquid mixture to the cooker and stir well.

Close and lock the lid of the cooker.

STOVETOP: Place the cooker over high heat, and bring it to high pressure. Once high pressure is reached, reduce the heat as much as possible while retaining the high-pressure level. Cook for 2 minutes. Then take the pot off the heat and quick-release the pressure according to the instructions provided by the manufacturer. Remove the lid, tilting it away from you, to allow the steam to escape.

OR

ELECTRIC: Set the machine to cook at high pressure for 3 minutes. After 3 minutes, unplug the pot so that it does not go into warming mode. Quick release the pressure according to the instructions provided by the manufacturer. Remove the lid, tilting it away from you, to allow the steam to escape.

Combine the cornstarch with 2 tablespoons of cold water in a small cup, stirring well to dissolve the cornstarch. Stir the cornstarch mixture into the cooker and bring to a boil over high heat or use the browning function of an electric cooker. Cook the eggplant for 1 minute, or until the sauce thickens. Serve immediately, sprinkling the dish with cilantro leaves.

NOTE Although eggplants, like tomatoes, are thought of as vegetables, they are actually fruits. In the world of cooking, however, they are treated as a vegetable. An eggplant can be either male or female. Males are preferred because they have fewer seeds and taste less bitter than females. To tell a male from a female eggplant, look at the end away from the stem. The male is rounded at the bottom and has a more even hole, whereas the female hole is more indented.

Sardinian-Style Cabbage
with Pancetta and Herbs

This comfort food cabbage dish is subtly flavored with pancetta and herbs, and its short time in the pressure cooker makes it silky and tender. This is a great addition to any winter meal.

SERVES **6 to 8**

SIZE **6-quart or larger pressure cooker**

TIME **4 to 5 minutes at high pressure with quick pressure release**

The dish can be prepared up to 2 days in advance and refrigerated, tightly covered. Reheat it, covered, in a 350°F oven for 20 to 25 minutes, or until hot.

NOTE An advantage of cooking cruciferous vegetables such as cabbage, cauliflower, and broccoli in a pressure cooker is that it doesn't make your house smell like those vegetables for days, an odor that many people find offensive. Because very little liquid evaporates from a pressure cooker, there is almost no "fragrance" in any steam that may be released from the machine.

2 tablespoons olive oil
¼ pound pancetta, diced
1 large shallot, minced
2 garlic cloves, minced
1¼ cups Chicken Stock (page 15) or purchased stock
2 tablespoons fresh chopped parsley
1 tablespoon chopped fresh rosemary
2 teaspoons fresh thyme leaves
1 bay leaf
1 tablespoon anchovy paste (optional)
1 (2-pound) head green cabbage, cored and cut into 2-inch wedges
Salt and freshly ground black pepper to taste

Heat the oil in the cooker over medium-high heat or use the browning function of an electric cooker. Add the pancetta and cook, stirring frequently, for 3 to 4 minutes, or until the pancetta browns. Remove the pancetta from the cooker with a slotted spoon and set it aside. Add the shallot and garlic to the cooker and cook for 1 minute. Stir the stock, parsley, rosemary, thyme, bay leaf, and anchovy paste, if using, into the cooker. Arrange the cabbage wedges in the liquid. Close and lock the lid of the cooker.

STOVETOP: Place the cooker over high heat, and bring it to high pressure. Once high pressure is reached, reduce the heat as much as possible while retaining the high-pressure level. Cook for 4 minutes. Then take the pot off the heat and quick release the pressure according to the instructions provided by the manufacturer. Remove the lid, tilting it away from you, to allow the steam to escape.

OR

ELECTRIC: Set the machine to cook at high pressure for 5 minutes. After 5 minutes, unplug the pot so that it does not go into warming mode. Quick release the pressure according to the instructions provided by the manufacturer. Remove the lid, tilting it away from you, to allow the steam to escape.

Remove and discard the bay leaf, season to taste with salt and pepper, and serve hot.

Fluffy Mashed Potatoes

Mashed potatoes are the epitome of comfort food, and when made in the pressure cooker they become the epitome of convenience too. There are myriad ways to flavor potatoes or add additional vegetables to the pot.

SERVES **4 to 6**

SIZE **6-quart or larger pressure cooker**

TIME **6 to 7 minutes at high pressure with quick pressure release**

The potatoes are best made just before serving; however, they can be left in the pressure cooker for up to 4 hours and reheated over low heat, stirring occasionally, until hot.

NOTE If you add the butter to the potatoes first rather than along with the cream, it will keep the mashed potatoes from having a gluey texture.

VARIATIONS

⋆ **Garlic Mashed Potatoes:** Add 4 to 6 peeled garlic cloves to the cooker with the potatoes and mash them into the potatoes.

⋆ **Leek Mashed Potatoes:** Chop 1 large leek or 2 small leeks, white and light green parts only, and rinse them well under cold running water. Add the leeks to the cooker with the potatoes, and mash them into the potatoes.

2 pounds russet potatoes, peeled and cut into ½-inch slices
Salt and freshly ground black pepper to taste
6 tablespoons (¾ stick) unsalted butter

½ to ¾ cup heavy cream

GARNISH
2 tablespoons chopped fresh parsley

Place the potatoes, 1 teaspoon of salt, and 1 cup of water in the cooker.

Close and lock the lid of the cooker.

STOVETOP: Place the cooker over high heat, and bring it to high pressure. Once high pressure is reached, reduce the heat as much as possible while retaining the high-pressure level. Cook for 6 minutes. Then take the pot off the heat and quick release the pressure according to the instructions provided by the manufacturer. Remove the lid, tilting it away from you, to allow the steam to escape.

OR

ELECTRIC: Set the machine to cook at high pressure for 7 minutes. After 7 minutes, unplug the pot so that it does not go into warming mode. Quick release the pressure according to the instructions provided by the manufacturer. Remove the lid, tilting it away from you, to allow the steam to escape.

Drain the potatoes, shaking them in a colander to release extra moisture. Return the potatoes to the cooker and cook over medium heat or use the browning function of an electric cooker for 1 minute, or until the potatoes look dry. Add the butter and mash the potatoes with a potato masher. Then add ½ cup of the cream and continue to mash. Add additional cream, if necessary, to reach the desired consistency. Season to taste with salt and pepper, and serve immediately, sprinkling parsley over the top.

Brussels Sprouts with Lemon
and Parsley, page 247

Brussels Sprouts with Lemon and Parsley

I know the chic thing today is to roast every vegetable imaginable and serve them charred, half raw, and crunchy. But I'm really old-fashioned when it comes to Brussels sprouts; I like them soft and tender, and a little bit of sparkling lemon and aromatic parsley with a good amount of butter is all they need. Try them with Chicken Provençale (page 92) or Herbed Mushroom Meatloaf with Gruyère Mashed Potatoes (page 144).

SERVES **4 to 6**

SIZE **6-quart or larger pressure cooker**

TIME **4 to 5 minutes at high pressure with quick pressure release**

The sprouts can be cooked up to 1 day in advance and refrigerated, tightly covered. Do not add the lemon juice and butter until just before serving.

NOTE The reason I add some fat to the cooker with different forms of cabbage is that it helps tenderize the cabbage as it cooks. That's why traditional recipes are cooked with salt pork or bacon. The fat is poured off when the vegetable is drained.

1½ pounds Brussels sprouts
1 lemon
Salt and freshly ground black pepper to taste

5 tablespoons unsalted butter, divided
¼ cup chopped fresh parsley

Discard any yellow leaves from the outside of each Brussels sprout and cut them in half through the root end. Cut 2 (3-inch) pieces of zest off the lemon with a vegetable peeler and place them in the cooker; then juice the lemon and set it aside. Add 1 cup of water, some salt, and 2 tablespoons of the butter to the cooker.

Close and lock the lid of the cooker.

STOVETOP: Place the cooker over high heat, and bring it to high pressure. Once high pressure is reached, reduce the heat as much as possible while retaining the high-pressure level. Cook for 4 minutes. Then take the pot off the heat and quick release the pressure according to the instructions provided by the manufacturer. Remove the lid, tilting it away from you, to allow the steam to escape.

OR

ELECTRIC: Set the machine to cook at high pressure for 5 minutes. After 5 minutes, unplug the pot so that it does not go into warming mode. Quick release the pressure according to the instructions provided by the manufacturer. Remove the lid, tilting it away from you, to allow the steam to escape.

Drain the Brussels sprouts and discard the lemon zest. Shake the sprouts in a colander to remove excess water. Return the sprouts to the cooker and add the lemon juice, remaining butter, and parsley. Cook over low heat or use the browning function of an electric cooker until the butter melts and the mixture begins to steam. Season to taste with salt and pepper, and serve immediately.

Collard Greens with Bacon

Collard greens have been a pillar of nutrition since the first African slaves brought them to Jamestown in the early seventeenth century. Along with okra and black-eyed peas, collard greens are an integral part of soul food. The two-stage method of cooking them in this recipe, first under pressure and then simmered with flavoring elements, renders the greens tender and delicate. Serve them with Bourbon Baby Back Ribs (page 178).

SERVES **4 to 6**

SIZE **6-quart or larger pressure cooker**

TIME **8 to 10 minutes at high pressure with quick pressure release**

The dish can be prepared, up to sprinkling with the bacon, 2 days in advance and refrigerated, tightly covered. Reheat it over low heat, covered, until hot.

NOTE The reason I call for a skillet to finish the cooking is that the diameter of a skillet is larger than that of a pressure cooker, and so the liquid evaporates more successfully. If you have a stovetop pressure cooker and don't want to dirty a second pan, go ahead and use it. But if you're using an electric pressure cooker, you really can't control the amount of heat it generates enough to have it go from boiling to simmering.

2 pounds collard greens, stems and ribs discarded, rinsed well and thinly sliced
1 large carrot, diced
Salt and freshly ground black pepper to taste
3 slices thick-sliced bacon, cut into thin strips
1 small onion, chopped
3 garlic cloves, minced
2 cups Chicken Stock (page 15) or purchased stock
1 tablespoon balsamic vinegar
Hot red pepper sauce to taste

Place the collard greens and carrot in the cooker and add 3 cups of water. Season to taste with salt and pepper.

Close and lock the lid of the cooker.

STOVETOP: Place the cooker over high heat, and bring it to high pressure. Once high pressure is reached, reduce the heat as much as possible while retaining the high-pressure level. Cook for 8 minutes. Then take the pot off the heat and quick release the pressure according to the instructions provided by the manufacturer. Remove the lid, tilting it away from you, to allow the steam to escape.

OR

ELECTRIC: Set the machine to cook at high pressure for 10 minutes. After 10 minutes, unplug the pot so that it does not go into warming mode. Quick release the pressure according to the instructions provided by the manufacturer. Remove the lid, tilting it away from you, to allow the steam to escape.

Drain the vegetables in a colander, pressing with the back of a spoon, to extract as much liquid as possible.

Heat a 12-inch skillet over medium-high heat. Add the bacon and cook for 5 to 7 minutes, or until crisp. Remove the bacon from the skillet with a slotted spoon and drain it on paper towels. Set it aside.

Add the onion and garlic to the skillet and cook, stirring frequently, for 3 minutes, or until the onion is translucent. Add the collard greens and stock to the pan and bring to a boil over medium heat, stirring occasionally. Reduce the heat to low and simmer the mixture, uncovered, for 8 to 10 minutes, or until the greens are very tender. Turn off the heat and stir in the vinegar. Season to taste with salt, pepper, and hot red pepper sauce, and serve hot, sprinkling each serving with some of the bacon.

VARIATION

★ **Vegetarian Braised Collard Greens:** Omit the bacon and cook the onion and garlic in 2 tablespoons of olive oil. Substitute Vegetable Stock (page 17) for the Chicken Stock and add ⅛ teaspoon of liquid smoke to the stock.

Kale with Pancetta, page 251

Kale with Pancetta

Kale is the pundit of the produce aisle for good reason. It is a nutritional powerhouse, and it's as versatile as it is healthy. You can eat it raw or cooked, which you can't do with collard greens, and in the pressure cooker it's quick to make, too. Serve the kale with Veal Marsala Stew (pages 190) or Duck Legs in Red Wine Sauce (page 114).

SERVES **4 to 6**

SIZE **6-quart or larger pressure cooker**

TIME **2 to 3 minutes at high pressure; then allow the pressure to release naturally**

The kale can be made, up to stirring in the lemon juice and Parmesan, 1 day in advance and refrigerated, tightly covered. Reheat it to a simmer before finishing the dish.

2 pounds kale
2 tablespoons olive oil
¼ pound pancetta, cut into ⅓-inch dice
1 large onion, diced
3 garlic cloves, minced
2 tablespoons chopped fresh parsley
2 teaspoons fresh thyme leaves
1 bay leaf

2 tablespoons unsalted butter
¾ cup Chicken Stock (page 15) or purchased stock
2 tablespoons freshly squeezed lemon juice
½ cup freshly grated Parmesan cheese
Salt and freshly ground black pepper to taste

Discard the stems and center ribs from the kale leaves and wash the leaves well. Slice the leaves into 2-inch ribbons and set them aside.

Heat the oil in the cooker over medium heat or use the browning function of an electric cooker. Add the pancetta and cook, stirring occasionally, for 6 to 8 minutes, or until crisp. Remove the pancetta from the cooker and set it aside. Discard all but 2 tablespoons of fat from the cooker.

Add the onion and garlic to the cooker and cook, stirring frequently, for 3 minutes, or until the onion is translucent. Stir in the parsley, thyme, bay leaf, butter, and stock, and bring to a boil. Add the kale and pancetta to the cooker, stuffing it down into the boiling stock to wilt it.

Close and lock the lid of the cooker.

(continued on the following page)

(*continued from the previous page*)

STOVETOP: Place the cooker over high heat, and bring it to high pressure. Once high pressure is reached, reduce the heat as much as possible while retaining the high-pressure level. Cook for 2 minutes. Then take the pot off the heat and allow it to return to normal pressure naturally. Remove the lid, tilting it away from you, to allow the steam to escape.

OR

ELECTRIC: Set the machine to cook at high pressure for 3 minutes. After 3 minutes, unplug the pot so that it does not go into warming mode. Allow allow the pressure to return to normal naturally. Remove the lid, tilting it away from you, to allow the steam to escape.

Remove and discard the bay leaf. Stir the lemon juice and Parmesan into the kale, season to taste with salt and pepper, and serve hot.

NOTE Leafy greens vie with leeks as the most difficult vegetables to get clean. The best way to clean kale, collards, and chard is to rinse the leaves under cold running water and then swirl them around in a large bowl of cold tap water. Pull the leaves up out of the bowl rather than draining them in a colander or the grit will get right back on them.

White Vegetable Puree

Along with potatoes, this mashed vegetable mélange includes sweet leeks and parsnips and flavorful cauliflower. Serve it with Boeuf Bourguignon (page 132) or Chicken Provençal (page 92).

SERVES **4 to 6**

SIZE **6-quart or larger pressure cooker**

TIME **5 to 6 minutes at high pressure with quick pressure release**

The mixture is best if made just before serving; however, it can be left in the pressure cooker and reheated over low heat, stirring occasionally, until hot.

NOTE I think potatoes really need water to cook properly no matter what method you use to cook them. However, the other vegetables in this dish can be steamed successfully in the pressure cooker, and that means they don't add excess moisture to the dish.

1½ **pounds russet potatoes, peeled and cut into ½-inch slices**
1 **leek, white part only, sliced and rinsed well**
1 **large parsnip, peeled and sliced**
1 **cup cauliflower florets**
6 **tablespoons (¾ stick) unsalted butter**

½ to ¾ **cup heavy cream**
Salt and freshly ground black pepper to taste

GARNISH
2 **tablespoons snipped fresh chives**

Place the potatoes, 1 teaspoon of salt, and 1 cup of water in the cooker. Place the leek, parsnip, and cauliflower in a steamer basket and set it on top of the potatoes. Close and lock the lid of the cooker.

STOVETOP: Place the cooker over high heat and bring it to high pressure. Once high pressure is reached, reduce the heat as much as possible while retaining the high-pressure level. Cook for 5 minutes. Then take the pot off the heat and quick release the pressure according to the instructions provided by the manufacturer. Remove the lid, tilting it away from you, to allow the steam to escape.

OR

ELECTRIC: Set the machine to cook at high pressure for 6 minutes. After 6 minutes, unplug the pot so that it does not go into warming mode. Quick release the pressure according to the instructions provided by the manufacturer. Remove the lid, tilting it away from you, to allow the steam to escape.

Remove the steamer basket and drain the potatoes, shaking them in a colander. Return the potatoes to the cooker and cook over medium heat or use the browning function of an electric cooker for 1 minute. Add the contents of the steamer basket along with the butter, and mash the mixture with a potato masher. Then add ½ cup of the cream and continue to mash. Add additional cream, if necessary, to reach the desired consistency. Season to taste with salt and pepper, and serve immediately, sprinkling chives over the top.

German Potato Salad

Although I associate potato salad with the grilled foods of summer, this one is the exception, because I make it all year. This warm salad has a complex flavor from the combination of salty bacon, sweet apple juice, and sharp mustard. Serve it with Lemon Herb Cod en Papillote (page 60) or Creole Bison Meatloaf (page 146).

SERVES **4 to 6**

SIZE **6-quart or larger pressure cooker**

TIME **5 to 6 minutes at high pressure with quick pressure release**

The salad can be made up to 2 days in advance and refrigerated, tightly covered. Reheat it to warm in a microwave oven or over low heat and do not stir in the bacon or dill until just before serving.

2 pounds red potatoes, scrubbed and cut into ¾-inch dice
Salt and freshly ground black pepper to taste
½ cup cider vinegar, divided
6 slices thick-sliced bacon, cut into 1-inch pieces
½ small red onion, diced
1 tablespoon all-purpose flour
½ cup apple juice
1 tablespoon grainy mustard
1 tablespoon granulated sugar
2 tablespoons chopped fresh dill

Place the potatoes, 1 teaspoon of salt, 2 tablespoons of the vinegar, and 1 cup of water in the cooker.

Close and lock the lid of the cooker.

STOVETOP: Place the cooker over high heat, and bring it to high pressure. Once high pressure is reached, reduce the heat as much as possible while retaining the high-pressure level. Cook for 5 minutes. Then take the pot off the heat and quick release the pressure according to the instructions provided by the manufacturer. Remove the lid, tilting it away from you, to allow the steam to escape.

OR

ELECTRIC: Set the machine to cook at high pressure for 6 minutes. After 6 minutes, unplug the pot so that it does not go into warming mode. Quick release the pressure according to the instructions provided by the manufacturer. Remove the lid, tilting it away from you, to allow the steam to escape.

Drain the potatoes in a colander and set aside.

Cook the bacon in the cooker over medium-high heat or use the browning function of an electric cooker for 5 to 7 minutes, or until crisp. Remove the bacon from the cooker with a slotted spoon, drain it on paper towels, and set it aside. Discard all but 3 tablespoons of bacon grease from the cooker. Add the onion to the cooker and cook for 2 minutes at medium heat or use the browning function of an electric cooker. Stir in the flour and cook for 1 minute, stirring constantly.

Whisk the remaining vinegar, apple juice, mustard, and sugar into the cooker and bring the liquid to a boil. Simmer the dressing for 1 minute.

Return the potato cubes to the cooker and turn off the heat under the cooker. Allow the potatoes to sit for 2 minutes, stir in the bacon and dill, season to taste with salt and pepper, and serve while warm.

NOTE If you want to make this into a vegetarian dish, omit the bacon and use 3 tablespoons of olive oil to sauté the onion. Although you can use turkey bacon, if you don't eat red meat, it does not render very much fat, and so you still may need to add some oil as well.

German Potato Salad,
page 254

Mashed Yams with Ginger

The zesty flavor of fresh ginger enlivens the earthy sweetness of the vivid orange yams in this dish. A small amount of aromatic spices balances the sweetness and richness of the other ingredients. Serve the yams with Chinese Red-Cooked Chicken with Plums (page 98) or Asian Pulled Pork Tacos (page 168).

SERVES **4 to 6**

SIZE **6-quart or larger pressure cooker**

TIME **6 to 7 minutes at high pressure with quick pressure release**

2 **pounds sweet potatoes, peeled and cut into ½-inch slices**
Salt and freshly ground black pepper to taste
3 **tablespoons thinly sliced fresh ginger**

4 **tablespoons (½ stick) unsalted butter**
3 **tablespoons pure maple syrup**
3 **tablespoons heavy cream**
¼ **teaspoon ground cinnamon**
Pinch of freshly grated nutmeg

Place the yams, 1 teaspoon of salt, the ginger, and 1 cup of water in the cooker.

Close and lock the lid of the cooker.

STOVETOP: Place the cooker over high heat, and bring it to high pressure. Once high pressure is reached, reduce the heat as much as possible while retaining the high-pressure level. Cook for 6 minutes. Then take the pot off the heat and quick release the pressure according to the instructions provided by the manufacturer. Remove the lid, tilting it away from you, to allow the steam to escape.

OR

ELECTRIC: Set the machine to cook at high pressure for 7 minutes. After 7 minutes, unplug the pot so that it does not go into warming mode. Quick release the pressure according to the instructions provided by the manufacturer. Remove the lid, tilting it away from you, to allow the steam to escape.

Drain the yams, shaking them in a colander to release extra moisture. Return them to the cooker and cook over medium heat or use the browning function of an electric cooker for 1 minute, or until the yams look dry. Add the butter and mash the yams with a potato masher.

Combine the maple syrup, cream, cinnamon, and nutmeg in a small bowl and stir well. Pour the mixture into the yams and mash until smooth. Season to taste with salt and pepper, and serve immediately.

The yams can be made up to 2 days in advance and refrigerated, tightly covered. Reheat them in a microwave oven or over low heat.

NOTE The yams we buy in supermarkets aren't really yams—they're a different variety of sweet potatoes. Yams, which originally came from Asia and Africa, have lighter skins than sweet potatoes and usually have white or yellow flesh. Sweet potatoes, with their orange skins and vividly colored flesh, have been known as yams for decades. Sweet potatoes with deep orange flesh contain more starch, and so they become fluffier when you mash them.

VARIATION

★ **Mashed Yams and Squash:** Decrease the amount of sweet potatoes to 1 pound and add 1 pound of peeled and thinly sliced acorn or butternut squash to the pressure cooker.

Sweet Potato Salad with Mustard Dressing

Sweet potatoes make a wonderful cold salad, and they need very little adornment since their natural flavor is so extraordinary. The simple mustard vinaigrette provides a great flavor contrast.

SERVES **6 to 8**

SIZE **4-quart or larger pressure cooker**

TIME **6 to 7 minutes at high pressure; then allow the pressure to release naturally**

The salad can be made up to 1 day in advance and refrigerated, tightly covered with plastic wrap.

NOTE Vinaigrette dressings fall into the scientific category of temporary emulsions. They come together and then immediately separate, because we all know that water and oil don't mix. That's why I can never understand why recipes give instructions to whisk the oil laboriously into the vinegar. It's important to dissolve granular seasonings such as salt and sugar in liquid, because they don't dissolve in oil—just add the oil and shake away. Any leftovers can be stored right in the jar.

2 pounds sweet potatoes, scrubbed, cut into 3-inch cubes
3 tablespoons white wine vinegar
2 tablespoons Dijon mustard
Salt and freshly ground black pepper to taste

1 shallot, finely chopped
2 garlic cloves, minced
½ cup olive oil
½ cup diced red onion
½ cup chopped red bell pepper
¼ cup chopped cornichons or sweet pickle slices

Fit the pressure cooker with a steamer and arrange the sweet potato cubes in it. Add 1½ cups water. Close and lock the lid of the cooker.

STOVETOP: Place the cooker over high heat, and bring it to high pressure. Once high pressure is reached, reduce the heat as much as possible while retaining the high-pressure level. Cook for 6 minutes. Then take the pot off the heat and allow it to return to normal pressure naturally. Remove the lid, tilting it away from you, to allow the steam to escape.

OR

ELECTRIC: Set the machine to cook at high pressure for 7 minutes. After 7 minutes, unplug the pot so that it does not go into warming mode. Allow the pressure to return to normal naturally. Remove the lid, tilting it away from you, to allow the steam to escape.

Remove the sweet potato cubes from the cooker and peel them when they are cool enough to handle. Cut the sweet potatoes into bite-size pieces and place them in a mixing bowl.

Combine the vinegar, mustard, salt, pepper, shallot, and garlic in a jar with a tight-fitting lid and shake well to combine. Add the oil and shake well again.

Add the dressing to the potatoes, along with the onion, bell pepper, and cornichons, and gently combine the salad. The salad can be served at room temperature or chilled.

Poached Pears
in Red Wine, page 272

CHAPTER 9

Extras

The recipes in this chapter are a true potpourri of delicious tastes that are made even more delicious you use a pressure cooker. In the case of hummus, you won't believe the difference it makes to cook your own garbanzo beans with seasonings.

I know that other cookbooks tout the wonders of dishes such as cheesecake, custard, and bread pudding made in a pressure cooker, but after many, many experiments I decided that certain categories of desserts should still be a reason to light the oven. However, after I discovered the wonders of pressure-cooked risotto, I knew that rice pudding was a natural candidate for the pressure cooker, and so you'll find a few versions here.

There aren't many fresh fruits that take kindly to a trip in the pressure cooker, but there are a few.

COOKING TIMES (IN MINUTES)
FOR FRUIT IN THE PRESSURE COOKER

FRUIT	STOVETOP	ELECTRIC	RELEASE METHOD
APPLES, SLICED	2 TO 3	3 TO 4	QUICK
APRICOTS, WHOLE	1	2	QUICK
LEMONS, WEDGES	3	5	NATURAL
ORANGES	3	5	NATURAL
PEACHES, HALVES	1	2	QUICK
PEARS, HALVES	3	4	QUICK
PEARS, WHOLE	4	5	QUICK
PLUMS, HALVES	2	3	NATURAL

Marinara Sauce

Marinara is the utility infielder of sauces. It's a stalwart that can be spread on top of cutlets for chicken Parmesan or spread on unbaked crust for pizza. After a considerable time in the pressure cooker, it achieves the silky consistency of a sauce that simmers on the stove for hours.

MAKES **4 cups**

SIZE **6-quart or larger pressure cooker**

TIME **25 to 30 minutes at high pressure; then allow the pressure to release naturally**

The sauce can be refrigerated for up to 5 days or frozen for up to 3 months.

NOTE Adding sugar or wine to a sauce made with canned or not-yet-ripe sweet tomatoes is an old trick from southern Italy that balances the acidity of the tomatoes.

VARIATIONS

⋆ **Herbed Marinara Sauce:** Add 2 bay leaves to the cooker, along with the tomatoes, and discard them when the sauce is cooked. Add ¼ cup chopped fresh basil, 3 tablespoons of chopped fresh parsley, and 2 tablespoons of chopped fresh oregano to the sauce after the pressure is released, and simmer it for 2 minutes.

⋆ **Puttanesca Sauce:** Increase the garlic to 6 cloves, add 2 tablespoons of capers and 2 tablespoons of anchovy paste along with the tomatoes, add ⅔ cup of chopped kalamata olives to the sauce after the pressure is released, and omit salt as a seasoning.

3 tablespoons olive oil
1 large sweet onion such as Vidalia or Bermuda, diced
3 garlic cloves, minced
1 large carrot, diced
¼ to ½ teaspoon crushed red pepper flakes (optional)
½ cup dry red wine
1 (28-ounce) can crushed tomatoes in tomato puree, preferably San Marzano
1 (14.5-ounce) can diced tomatoes, undrained
2 teaspoons granulated sugar
Salt and freshly ground black pepper to taste

Heat the olive oil in the cooker over medium heat or use the browning function of an electric cooker. Add the onion, garlic, carrot, and red pepper flakes, if using. Cook, stirring frequently, for 3 minutes, or until the onion is translucent. Stir in the wine and boil for 3 minutes. Add the crushed tomatoes, diced tomatoes, and sugar.

Close and lock the lid of the cooker.

STOVETOP: Place the cooker over high heat, and bring it to high pressure. Once high pressure is reached, reduce the heat as much as possible while retaining the high-pressure level. Cook for 25 minutes. Then take the pot off the heat and allow it to return to normal pressure naturally. Remove the lid, tilting it away from you to allow the steam to escape.

OR

ELECTRIC: Set the machine to cook at high pressure for 30 minutes. After 30 minutes, unplug the pot so that it does not go into warming mode and allow the pressure to return to normal naturally. Remove the lid, tilting it away from you, to allow the steam to escape.

Season to taste with salt and pepper, and serve hot.

Hummus

It's obvious from the size of the section in every supermarket devoted to Middle Eastern hummus that it is the onion dip of the twenty-first century. This simple puree of garbanzo beans, sesame paste, lemon, and garlic—a recipe that goes back to thirteenth-century Egypt—could not be easier to make, and you can personalize it to match your taste.

MAKES **5 cups**

SIZE **6-quart or larger pressure cooker**

TIME **13 to 15 minutes at high pressure; then allow the pressure to release naturally**

The dip can be made up to 3 days in advance and refrigerated, tightly covered. Allow it to reach room temperature before serving. If you don't want to take the time to allow the beans to soak, cook them for 35 minutes in a stove-top pressure cooker or 40 minutes in an electric pot.

⅔ pound dried garbanzo beans
6 garlic cloves, divided
1 bay leaf
1 sprig fresh thyme
⅔ cup olive oil, divided

⅔ cup well-stirred tahini
⅓ cup freshly squeezed lemon juice or to taste
2 teaspoons grated lemon zest
Salt and freshly ground black pepper to taste

Rinse the beans in a colander and place them in a mixing bowl covered with cold salted water. Allow the beans to soak for a minimum of 6 hours, or overnight. Or place the beans into a saucepan of salted water and bring to a boil over high heat. Boil 1 minute. Turn off the heat, cover the pan, and soak the beans for 1 hour. After using either of these soaking methods, drain the beans, discard the soaking water, and cook or refrigerate the beans as soon as possible.

Peel the garlic cloves. Leave 3 whole and mince the remainder. Set them aside separately.

Place the beans in the cooker with the 3 whole garlic cloves, the bay leaf, the thyme, 2 tablespoons of the olive oil, and 2 quarts of water.

Close and lock the lid of the cooker.

STOVETOP: Place the cooker over high heat, and bring it to high pressure. Once high pressure is reached, reduce the heat as much as possible while retaining the high-pressure level. Cook for 13 minutes. Then take the pot off the heat and allow it to return to normal pressure naturally. Remove the lid, tilting it away from you, to allow the steam to escape.

OR

ELECTRIC: Set the machine to cook at high pressure for 15 minutes. After 15 minutes, unplug the pot so that it does not go into warming mode. Allow the pressure to return to normal naturally. Remove the lid, tilting it away from you, to allow the steam to escape.

Remove and discard the bay leaf and thyme sprig; the garlic cloves will have melted into the bean water. Drain the beans, reserving 1 cup of the cooking liquid. Refrigerate the beans until cold.

Combine the beans, tahini, remaining oil, remaining garlic, and lemon juice in a food processor fitted with the steel blade or in a blender. Puree until smooth. Add some of the reserved bean liquid if the dip is too thick. Scrape the mixture into a mixing bowl.

Stir in the lemon zest and season to taste with salt and pepper. Serve chilled.

NOTE Tahini, pronounced *tah-HEE-knee*, is a paste made from sesame seeds; it plays a role in many Middle Eastern dishes. Regardless of the brand, the oil tends to separate and rise to the top of the container. It's very important to stir the mixture thoroughly before measuring it. If the container is too full to stir the tahini without spilling it, whisk it in a mixing bowl.

VARIATIONS

⋆ **Lemon Hummus:** Add 3 tablespoons of additional lemon juice, plus an additional 1 teaspoon of lemon zest.

⋆ **Red Pepper Hummus:** Add ¼ cup of pureed roasted red bell pepper and 1 tablespoon of smoked Spanish paprika.

⋆ **Horseradish Hummus:** Add 2 tablespoons of prepared horseradish.

⋆ **Garlic-Lovers Hummus:** Add up to 3 more garlic cloves or up to 3 tablespoons of pureed roasted garlic.

⋆ **Spicy Hummus:** Add up to 1 teaspoon of crushed red pepper flakes or 1 tablespoon of hot red pepper sauce or sriracha sauce.

⋆ **Spinach Parmesan Hummus:** Add ½ cup of chopped cooked spinach and ¼ cup of freshly grated Parmesan cheese.

Baba Ganoush

The traditional way of making this popular Middle Eastern eggplant dip is to grill the eggplants or bake them in a very hot oven. But once you've discarded the charred skin, there's only a slightly smoky nuance to the dish. The same thing can be achieved in a fraction of the time by browning the eggplant in a pressure cooker.

SERVES **4 to 6**

SIZE **6-quart or larger pressure cooker**

TIME **3 to 4 minutes at high pressure with quick pressure release**

The baba ganoush can be made up to 2 days in advance and refrigerated, tightly covered. Allow it to reach room temperature before serving it.

3 medium Italian eggplants (about 2 pounds total), peeled
¼ teaspoon baking soda
½ cup olive oil, divided
4 garlic cloves, peeled
Salt and freshly ground black pepper to taste

⅓ cup freshly squeezed lemon juice or more to taste
¼ cup well-stirred tahini

GARNISH

3 tablespoons chopped fresh parsley
°Warm pita bread for serving

Cut each eggplant into 8 pieces and sprinkle the pieces with the baking soda. Heat 3 tablespoons of the oil in the cooker over medium-high heat or use the browning function of an electric cooker. Add as many eggplant slices as will comfortably fit in the cooker and brown them well on one side. Remove the eggplant by using tongs and brown the remaining pieces on one side. Add the garlic cloves to the cooker and sprinkle with salt and pepper. Add ½ cup of water to a stovetop cooker or ¾ cup to an electric cooker.

Close and lock the lid of the cooker.

STOVETOP: Place the cooker over high heat, and bring it to high pressure. Once high pressure is reached, reduce the heat as much as possible while retaining the high-pressure level. Cook for 3 minutes. Then take the pot off the heat and quick release the pressure according to the instructions provided by the manufacturer. Remove the lid, tilting it away from you, to allow the steam to escape.

OR

ELECTRIC: Set the machine to cook at high pressure for 4 minutes. After 4 minutes, unplug the pot so that it does not go into warming mode. Quick release the pressure according to the instructions provided by the manufacturer. Remove the lid, tilting it away from you, to allow the steam to escape.

Pour the contents of the cooker into a colander and shake it vigorously for 30 seconds to remove as much liquid as possible. Transfer the contents to a mixing bowl and whisk in the lemon juice and tahini. Slowly whisk in the remaining oil as if you were making mayonnaise. Season the mixture to taste with salt and pepper, sprinkle with parsley, and serve with pita at room temperature.

NOTE The amount of water added to the cooker in the recipe above for Baba Ganoush may be less than the minimum amount recommended by the manufacturer, but I promise I'm not going to lead you astray. About 90 percent of the weight of an eggplant is water; that is why the volume decreases so much when you cook it. The water added to the cooker starts the process—as soon as the steams begins, more than enough water will be drawn out of the eggplant to cook it successfully.

VARIATION

⋆ **Eggplant and Olive Spread**: Follow the recipe but omit the additional salt. Stir ½ cup of chopped oil-cured black olives into the spread before serving.

Mango Chutney

When people think of chutney, the mixture of fruits and spices in this recipe is what comes to mind. Mango chutney is a wonderful accompaniment to curries, but it's also a perfect condiment to serve with roasted pork or poultry.

MAKES **5 cups**

SIZE **6-quart or larger pressure cooker**

TIME **4 to 5 minutes at high pressure; then allow the pressure to release naturally**

The chutney can be refrigerated for up to 2 weeks.

NOTE If it matters how the apples in the dish look, the time-honored way of peeling, coring, and then slicing each half or quarter is still the best method. But if the apples are going to be hidden, there's a faster way: Peel an apple and keep turning it in your hand as you cut off slices. Soon all you'll be left with is the core, which you can discard.

- 2 tablespoons vegetable oil
- 1 medium onion, diced
- ½ red bell pepper, seeds and ribs removed, chopped
- 2 garlic cloves, minced
- ¼ cup chopped fresh ginger
- 1 tablespoon garam masala
- ½ teaspoon ground cinnamon
- ¼ teaspoon freshly grated nutmeg
- ¼ to ½ teaspoon crushed red pepper flakes or to taste (optional)
- 3 Granny Smith apples, peeled, cored, and chopped
- 2 large mangoes, peeled and chopped
- 1 cup granulated sugar
- ½ cup firmly packed light brown sugar
- ¾ cup cider vinegar
- ½ cup raisins
- 1 tablespoon freshly squeezed lemon juice
- Salt and freshly ground black pepper to taste

Heat the oil in the cooker over medium-high heat or use the browning function of an electric cooker. Add the onion, bell pepper, garlic, and ginger, and cook, stirring frequently, for 3 minutes, or until the onion is translucent. Stir in the garam masala, cinnamon, nutmeg, and red pepper flakes, if using. Cook for 1 minute, stirring constantly. Add remaining ingredients and stir well. Close and lock the lid of the cooker.

STOVETOP: Place the cooker over high heat, and bring it to high pressure. Once high pressure is reached, reduce the heat as much as possible while retaining the high-pressure level. Cook for 4 minutes. Then take the pot off the heat and allow it to return to normal pressure naturally. Remove the lid, tilting it away from you, to allow the steam to escape.

OR

ELECTRIC: Set the machine to cook at high pressure for 5 minutes. After 5 minutes, unplug the pot so that it does not go into warming mode. Allow the pressure to return to normal naturally. Remove the lid, tilting it away from you, to allow the steam to escape.

Cook for 3 minutes over medium heat or use the browning function of an electric cooker. Pack the chutney into canning jars or refrigerate.

Green Tomato Chutney

This chutney saves the day at the end of the gardening season, and is a great condiment to serve on burgers and sausages as well as with pork and poultry.

MAKES **5 cups**

SIZE **6-quart or larger pressure cooker**

TIME **7 to 8 minutes at high pressure; then allow the pressure to release naturally**

The chutney can be refrigerated for up to 2 weeks.

NOTE When you're cooking in a pressure cooker, the sugar in a recipe counts as part of the liquid, so don't worry if it seems that this recipe doesn't contain enough steam-making ingredients.

1 tablespoon vegetable oil
1 medium onion, diced
2 garlic cloves, minced
½ teaspoon ground coriander
¼ teaspoon ground allspice
¼ to ½ teaspoon crushed red pepper flakes
¼ teaspoon ground cinnamon
Pinch of ground cloves
3 pounds firm green tomatoes, cored and diced
¾ cup golden raisins
1 cup firmly packed light brown sugar
¾ cup cider vinegar
1 tablespoon finely chopped crystallized ginger
1 teaspoon yellow mustard seeds
1 bay leaf
Salt and freshly ground black pepper to taste

Heat the oil in the cooker over medium heat or use the browning function of an electric cooker. Add the onion and garlic, and cook, stirring frequently, for 3 minutes, or until the onion is translucent. Add the coriander, allspice, red pepper flakes, cinnamon, and cloves. Cook for 1 minute, stirring constantly. Add the tomatoes, raisins, sugar, vinegar, ginger, mustard seeds, and bay leaf. Stir well. Close and lock the lid of the cooker.

STOVETOP: Place the cooker over high heat, and bring it to high pressure. Once high pressure is reached, reduce the heat as much as possible while retaining the high-pressure level. Cook for 7 minutes. Then take the pot off the heat and allow it to return to normal pressure naturally. Remove the lid, tilting it away from you, to allow the steam to escape.

OR

ELECTRIC: Set the machine to cook at high pressure for 8 minutes. After 8 minutes, unplug the pot so that it does not go into warming mode. Allow the pressure to return to normal naturally. Remove the lid, tilting it away from you, to allow the steam to escape.

Cook for 3 minutes over medium heat or use the browning function of an electric cooker. Season to taste with salt and pepper. Pack the chutney into canning jars or refrigerate.

Spiked Applesauce

Homemade applesauce is a treat that can be enjoyed all year, although I tend to make it most often in the fall, when apples are available from local orchards. The combination of heady dark rum and brown sugar is a wonderful way to flavor this applesauce.

SERVES **4 to 6**

SIZE **6-quart or larger pressure cooker**

TIME **4 to 5 minutes at high pressure with quick pressure release**

The applesauce can be made up to 4 days in advance and refrigerated, tightly covered.

NOTE In general, you want to use soft apples that fall apart easily when you're making applesauce and hard apples that hold their shape for baking pies and tarts. I like to combine both types of apples for flavor and texture. McIntosh, Rome, Cortland, and Gala are the traditional choices for making applesauce, whereas Granny Smith and Golden Delicious are most often used for pies.

VARIATIONS

★ **Applesauce with Dried Cranberries:** Omit the rum, substitute granulated sugar for the brown sugar, and add ½ cup of dried cranberries.

★ **Applesauce with Crème de Cassis:** Omit the brown sugar, rum, and cinnamon stick, and add ½ cup of crème de cassis and 2 tablespoons of red currant jelly.

1 lemon
2 pounds McIntosh apples, peeled, cored, and cut into 1½-inch chunks
1 pound Granny Smith apples, peeled, cored, and cut into 1½-inch chunks
⅓ cup firmly packed dark brown sugar
¼ cup dark rum
1 tablespoon unsalted butter
1 (3-inch) cinnamon stick
Pinch of salt

Grate the zest off the lemon and squeeze the juice into a mixing bowl. Add the McIntosh and Granny Smith apples and brown sugar. Toss to coat the apples to prevent discoloration and allow them to sit for 10 minutes. Transfer the mixture to the pressure cooker and stir in the rum, butter, cinnamon stick, and salt.

Close and lock the lid of the cooker.

STOVETOP: Place the cooker over high heat, and bring it to high pressure. Once high pressure is reached, reduce the heat as much as possible while retaining the high-pressure level. Cook for 4 minutes. Then take the pot off the heat and quick release the pressure according to the instructions provided by the manufacturer. Remove the lid, tilting it away from you, to allow the steam to escape.

OR

ELECTRIC: Set the machine to cook at high pressure for 5 minutes. After 5 minutes, unplug the pot so that it does not go into warming mode. Quick release the pressure according to the instructions provided by the manufacturer. Remove the lid, tilting it away from you, to allow the steam to escape.

Remove and discard the cinnamon stick, and stir the applesauce. Serve warm or at room temperature.

Brandied Dried Fruit and Walnut Compote

Think of this luscious addition to any fall or winter meal as a road map more than a recipe. You can use any combination of dried fruits you like. I serve this compote with roast poultry and pork, but I also heat and use it as a topping for ice cream.

SERVES **6 to 8**

SIZE **6-quart or larger pressure cooker**

TIME **5 to 6 minutes at high pressure with quick pressure release**

The compote can be refrigerated, tightly covered, for up to 10 days.

NOTE Whenever you are cutting dried fruit, keep a can of cooking spray handy. If you give your knife an occasional squirt, it will keep the dried fruit from sticking to the blade. The same is true if you're chopping dried fruit in a food processor fitted with a steel blade; you want to lightly spray both the blade and the inside of the work bowl.

½ cup chopped walnuts
⅓ pound pitted prunes, halved if large
⅓ pound dried apricots
½ cup dried cranberries
½ cup golden raisins
1¼ cups apple cider
½ teaspoon ground ginger
2 tablespoons pure maple syrup
2 tablespoons brandy
Pinch of salt

Preheat the oven to 350°F and line a rimmed baking sheet with aluminum foil. Toast the nuts for 5 to 7 minutes, or until lightly browned. Set them aside.

Combine the prunes, apricots, cranberries, raisins, cider, ginger, maple syrup, brandy, and salt in the cooker.

Close and lock the lid of the cooker.

STOVETOP: Place the cooker over high heat, and bring it to high pressure. Once high pressure is reached, reduce the heat as much as possible while retaining the high-pressure level. Cook for 5 minutes. Then take the pot off the heat and quick release the pressure according to the instructions provided by the manufacturer. Remove the lid, tilting it away from you, to allow the steam to escape.

OR

ELECTRIC: Set the machine to cook at high pressure for 6 minutes. After 6 minutes, unplug the pot so that it does not go into warming mode. Quick release the pressure according to the instructions provided by the manufacturer. Remove the lid, tilting it away from you, to allow the steam to escape.

Place the cooker over medium-high heat or use the browning function of an electric cooker, and cook the mixture for 3 to 5 minutes, or until the juice becomes syrupy. Serve at room temperature or chilled.

Poached Pears in Red Wine

Poached pears are a timeless winter treat, and what you'll find when you make them in a pressure cooker is that the added ingredients flavor each bite of the fruit, not just the outer coating. I've also made this recipe and used the fruit as layers in a trifle.

SERVES **4 to 6**

SIZE **6-quart or larger pressure cooker**

TIME **4 to 5 minutes at high pressure with quick pressure release**

The pears can be cooked up to 3 days in advance and refrigerated, tightly covered.

NOTE If you use an electric cooker, you might want to dirty a second pot and reduce the sauces in a saucepan on the stove. The amount of heat generated by the browning function varies greatly from brand to brand. A few minutes will do the trick to thicken liquid with cornstarch even at a simmer. When a great deal of reduction is required, if the liquid doesn't come to a boil within 3 minutes, transfer it to a saucepan.

1 (750-ml) bottle red wine, such as Merlot or Pinot Noir
½ cup granulated sugar
1 vanilla bean, split in half lengthwise
1 (3-inch) cinnamon stick
2 whole cloves
2 star anise pods
½ orange, thinly sliced
4 to 6 firm but almost ripe pears, preferably Bosc

GARNISH

4 to 6 sprigs fresh mint leaves
Sweetened whipped cream or sweetened mascarpone for serving

Combine the wine, sugar, vanilla bean, cinnamon stick, cloves, star anise, and orange in the cooker and stir well.

Peel the pears, leaving the stems attached. Cut a small slice off the bottom so that the pears sit flat. Arrange the pears in the cooker and add enough water so that the pears are covered.

Close and lock the lid of the cooker.

STOVETOP: Place the cooker over high heat, and bring it to high pressure. Once high pressure is reached, reduce the heat as much as possible while retaining the high-pressure level. Cook for 4 minutes. Then take the pot off the heat and quick release the pressure according to the instructions provided by the manufacturer. Remove the lid, tilting it away from you, to allow the steam to escape.

OR

ELECTRIC: Set the machine to cook at high pressure for 5 minutes. After 5 minutes, unplug the pot so that it does not go into warming mode. Quick release the pressure according to the instructions provided by the manufacturer. Remove the lid, tilting it away from you, to allow the steam to escape.

> **VARIATION**
>
> ⋆ **Poached Pears with Ginger and Honey:** Substitute a fruity white wine such as a Moscato for the red wine. Omit the cloves, star anise pods, and orange. Add ¼ cup of honey and 2 tablespoons of thinly sliced fresh ginger to the cooker.

Remove the pears from the cooker with a slotted spoon and place them in a storage container. Strain the cooking liquid through a sieve, rinse out the cooker, and return the wine mixture to the cooker. Bring to a boil over high heat or use the browning function of an electric cooker. Boil until the liquid is reduced to 2 cups. Cool the pears and the liquid to at least room temperature, or chill them.

To serve, place a pear in a shallow bowl and top with a sprig of mint. Drizzle with some of the sauce and pass around the whipped cream or mascarpone.

Old-Fashioned Creamy Rice Pudding

Rice pudding falls into the nursery food category of desserts, but Arborio rice gives this creamy pudding some textural interest, because the rice remains al dente within the luscious matrix.

SERVES **4 to 6**

SIZE 6-quart or larger pressure cooker

TIME 6 to 8 minutes at high pressure; then allow the pressure to release naturally

The pudding can be made up to 2 days in advance and refrigerated, tightly covered.

NOTE If you add beaten eggs to a simmering pot of liquid, you'll get scrambled eggs. The process of heating beaten eggs in a hot liquid (usually milk) to thicken it is called tempering. Make sure the eggs are whisked very well; clumps of white or yolk will not blend evenly. Then take the pan of hot liquid off the heat and whisk about one-fourth of it into the eggs. Now, while whisking constantly, add the heated egg mixture back into the pan. Then turn the heat on very low and cook until the liquid thickens, but if you see bubbles start to form, turn off the heat.

Vegetable oil spray
3 tablespoons unsalted butter
1 cup Arborio rice
3 cups whole milk, divided
½ cup granulated sugar
½ cup raisins
2 teaspoons pure vanilla extract
¼ teaspoon salt
1 (3-inch) cinnamon stick
2 large eggs
1 large egg yolk

GARNISH
Ground cinnamon

Spray the inside of the cooker and the inside of the lid with vegetable oil spray.

Melt the butter in the cooker over medium-low heat or use the browning function in an electric cooker. Stir in the rice and cook for 1 minute, stirring constantly. Stir in 2 cups of the milk, the sugar, raisins, vanilla, salt, and cinnamon stick.

Close and lock the lid of the cooker.

STOVETOP: Place the cooker over high heat, and bring it to high pressure. Once high pressure is reached, reduce the heat as much as possible while retaining the high-pressure level. Cook for 6 minutes. Then take the pot off the heat and allow it to return to normal pressure naturally. Remove the lid, tilting it away from you, to allow the steam to escape.

— OR —

ELECTRIC: Set the machine to cook at high pressure for 8 minutes. After 8 minutes, unplug the pot so that it does not go into warming mode. Allow the pressure to return to normal naturally. Remove the lid, tilting it away from you, to allow the steam to escape.

Combine the remaining 1 cup of milk, eggs, and egg yolk in a mixing bowl and whisk well. Slowly beat about 1 cup of the hot rice mixture into the eggs so that they warm up gradually and then return the contents of the mixing bowl to the cooker. Place the cooker over low heat or use the "keep warm" function of an electric cooker and stir constantly, reaching all parts of the bottom of the pan, until the mixture reaches about 170°F on an instant-read thermometer; at this point it begins to emit steam, thickens slightly, and coats the back of a spoon. This takes between 2 and 4 minutes. Do not allow the mixture to boil, or the eggs will scramble. Remove and discard the cinnamon stick.

Chill the pudding. To serve, spoon out the pudding and sprinkle each serving with cinnamon.

VARIATIONS

★ **Maple Walnut Rice Pudding:** Substitute pure maple syrup for the granulated sugar, omit the raisins and cinnamon stick, and stir ¾ cup of chopped toasted walnuts or pecans into the finished pudding.

★ **Rum Raisin Rice Pudding:** Plump the raisins in ½ cup of dark rum and then add the raisins and any remaining rum to the cooker. Omit the cinnamon stick.

★ **Mexican Chocolate Rice Pudding:** Reduce the sugar to ⅓ cup and add 3 tablespoons of unsweetened cocoa powder to the cooker. Add 1 cup of bittersweet chocolate chips to the finished pudding and stir until they melt. Garnish each serving with toasted slivered almonds.

Coconut Tangerine Rice Pudding

It's difficult to know what to serve for dessert after an Asian-inspired dinner; this explains why a platter of fresh fruit is served so often. But this creamy pudding has a range of flavors that are compatible with Asian food, from creamy coconut to zesty tangerine juice and even a touch of aromatic five-spice powder.

SERVES **4 to 6**

SIZE **6-quart or larger pressure cooker**

TIME **6 to 8 minutes at high pressure; then allow the pressure to release naturally**

The pudding can be made up to 2 days in advance and refrigerated, tightly covered.

Vegetable oil spray
½ cup sweetened flaked coconut
3 tablespoons unsalted butter
1 cup Arborio rice
1 (14-ounce) can light coconut milk, divided
2 teaspoons grated tangerine zest

2⅓ cups freshly squeezed tangerine juice
¼ teaspoon salt
⅓ cup granulated sugar
½ teaspoon Chinese five-spice powder
2 large eggs
1 large egg yolk

Spray the inside of the cooker and the inside of the lid with vegetable oil spray.

Preheat the oven to 350 degrees and cover a rimmed baking sheet with aluminum foil. Spread the coconut out on the baking sheet and bake it in the center of the oven for 6 to 10 minutes, stirring it after 5 minutes, or until it is browned. Set aside.

Melt the butter in the cooker over medium-low heat or use the browning function of an electric cooker. Stir in the rice and cook for 1 minute, stirring constantly.

Reserve ½ cup of the coconut milk. Stir the remaining coconut milk, tangerine zest, tangerine juice, salt, sugar, and five-spice powder into the rice.

Close and lock the lid of the cooker.

STOVETOP: Place the cooker over high heat, and bring it to high pressure. Once high pressure is reached, reduce the heat as much as possible while retaining the high-pressure level. Cook for 6 minutes. Then take the pot off the heat and allow it to return to normal pressure naturally. Remove the lid, tilting it away from you, to allow the steam to escape.

OR

ELECTRIC: Set the machine to cook at high pressure for 8 minutes. After 8 minutes, unplug the pot so that it does not go into warming mode. Allow the pressure to return to normal naturally. Remove the lid, tilting it away from you, to allow the steam to escape.

Combine the reserved coconut milk, eggs, and egg yolk in a mixing bowl and whisk well. Slowly beat about 1 cup of the hot rice mixture into the eggs so that they warm up gradually; then return the contents of the mixing bowl to the cooker. Place the cooker over low heat or use the "keep warm" function of an electric cooker and stir constantly, reaching all parts of the bottom of the pan, until the mixture reaches about 170°F on an instant-read thermometer; at this point it begins to emit steam, thickens slightly, and coats the back of a spoon. This takes between 2 and 4 minutes. Do not allow the mixture to boil, or the eggs will scramble.

Stir ⅓ cup of the toasted coconut into the rice pudding and then chill the pudding. To serve, spoon the pudding into bowls and sprinkle each serving with some of the remaining coconut.

NOTE Keep an eye on the flaked coconut when you're toasting it in the oven. Because of the fat content of the coconut meat—and the sugar that is added to it— the flakes tend to turn from brown to burnt in the wink of an eye.

VARIATION

★ Substitute orange juice and orange zest for the tangerine juice and zest.

Indian Pudding

Recipes for Indian Pudding—sometimes called Hasty Pudding—date back to the early eighteenth century, when Native Americans introduced European settlers to corn. This dessert pudding, sweetened with a combination of brown sugar and maple syrup, is the epitome of winter comfort food, and, because it's made with cornmeal, it's gluten-free, too.

SERVES **6 to 8**

SIZE **4-quart or larger pressure cooker**

TIME **5 to 6 minutes at high pressure; then allow the pressure to release naturally**

Any leftover pudding can be refrigerated for up to 3 days, tightly covered. However, you will have to whisk in milk as it reheats to achieve the same consistency.

NOTE Using vegetable oil spray is a wonderful way to pretreat pots and casseroles and make cleanup easier, but it's hard to keep the spray from splattering onto nearby counters. One answer is to spray the pan inside the dishwasher, assuming it's empty or has dirty dishes in it. Then it doesn't matter if the oil spatters; it will get cleaned up the next time you use the dishwasher.

VARIATION

★ Omit the cinnamon and nutmeg and add ¼ cup of chopped crystallized ginger to the pressure cooker.

3 cups skim milk
¾ cup firmly packed dark brown sugar
½ cup pure maple syrup
½ teaspoon pure vanilla extract
¾ teaspoon ground cinnamon
¼ teaspoon freshly grated nutmeg
¼ teaspoon salt
¾ cup polenta or coarse yellow cornmeal
¼ pound (1 stick) unsalted butter, cut into small pieces
1 cup heavy cream
Vanilla ice cream or sweetened whipped cream for serving

Spray the inside of the pressure cooker with vegetable oil spray.

Combine the milk, brown sugar, maple syrup, vanilla, cinnamon, nutmeg, and salt in the cooker and stir well. Heat over medium-high heat or use the browning function of an electric cooker and bring the liquid to a simmer, stirring occasionally. Whisk in the polenta in a thin stream, moving the whisk in only one direction. Then close and lock the lid of the cooker.

STOVETOP: Place the cooker over high heat, and bring it to high pressure. Once high pressure is reached, reduce the heat as much as possible while retaining the high-pressure level. Cook for 5 minutes. Then take the pot off the heat and allow it to return to normal pressure naturally. Remove the lid, tilting it away from you, to allow the steam to escape.

OR

ELECTRIC: Set the machine to cook at high pressure for 6 minutes. After 6 minutes, unplug the pot so that it does not go into warming mode. Allow the pressure to return to normal naturally. Remove the lid, tilting it away from you, to allow the steam to escape.

Unlock the lid and add the butter and cream to the cooker. Beat the pudding with a heavy whisk until it is smooth and the butter has melted in. Serve hot, topped with ice cream or whipped cream.

Metric Conversion Charts

The recipes that appear in this cookbook use the standard United States method for measuring liquid and dry or solid ingredients (teaspoons, tablespoons, and cups). The information on this chart is provided to help cooks outside the U.S. successfully use these recipes. All equivalents are approximate.

METRIC EQUIVALENTS FOR DIFFERENT TYPES OF INGREDIENTS

STANDARD CUP	FINE POWDER (e.g. flour)	GRAIN (e.g. rice)	GRANULAR (e.g. sugar)	LIQUID SOLIDS (e.g. butter)	LIQUID (e.g. milk)
¾	105 g	113 g	143 g	150 g	180 ml
⅔	93 g	100 g	125 g	133 g	160 ml
½	70 g	75 g	95 g	100 g	120 ml
⅓	47 g	50 g	63 g	67 g	80 ml
¼	35 g	38 g	48 g	50 g	60 ml
⅛	18 g	19 g	24 g	25 g	30 ml

USEFUL EQUIVALENTS FOR LIQUID INGREDIENTS BY VOLUME

¼ tsp	=							1 ml
½ tsp	=							2 ml
1 tsp	=							5 ml
3 tsp	=	1 tbls	=			½ fl oz	=	15 ml
		2 tbls	=	⅛ cup	=	1 fl oz	=	30 ml
		4 tbls	=	¼ cup	=	2 fl oz	=	60 ml
		5⅓ tbls	=	⅓ cup	=	3 fl oz	=	80 ml
		8 tbls	=	½ cup	=	4 fl oz	–	120 ml
		10⅔ tbls	=	⅔ cup	=	5 fl oz	=	160 ml
		12 tbls	=	¾ cup	=	6 fl oz	=	180 ml
		16 tbls	=	1 cup	=	8 fl oz	=	240 ml
		1 pt	=	2 cups	=	16 fl oz	=	480 ml
		1 qt	=	4 cups	=	32 fl oz	=	960 ml
						33 fl oz	=	1000 ml = 1 L

USEFUL EQUIVALENTS FOR DRY INGREDIENTS BY WEIGHT

(To convert ounces to grams, multiply the number of ounces by 28.35.)

1 oz	=	¹/₁₆ lb	=	28.3 g
4 oz	=	¼ lb	=	113 g
8 oz	=	½ lb	=	227 g
12 oz	=	¾ lb	=	340 g
16 oz	=	1 lb	=	454 g

Acknowledgments

While testing recipes and writing a cookbook is a solitary venture, transforming it into a tangible object to hold in your hands is always a group effort. My thanks to the following people:

To Jennifer Williams, my editor at Sterling Epicure, for all her wisdom and guidance.

To Chris Bain, photo director at Sterling, for his vision, and to production editor Scott Amerman who kept the project on track.

To cover designer Jo Obarowski and interior designer Christine Heun whose work makes this book a delight to hold.

To Bill Milne for his inspired photography and use of his luscious painted canvas backdrops.

To Diane Vezza, the food stylist, who made all these dishes stunning, and to Joan Parkin, who assisted her and overcame her own fear of pressure cookers in the process.

To Ed Claflin, my agent, for his constant support, encouragement, and humor.

To my dear family for their love and support, especially to Nancy and Walter Dubler; Ariela Dubler; Jesse Furman; Ilan, Mira, and Lev Dubler-Furman; Joshua Dubler; Lisa Cerami; Zahir and Charlie Cerami; and David Krimm and Peter Bradley.

To my many friends who critiqued my work as any number of dishes emerged from three pressure cookers every day, especially to Constance Brown, Kenn Speiser, Gail Ciampa, Fox Wetle, Richard Besdine, Vicki Veh, Kim Montour, Nick Brown, Karen Davidson, Bruce Tillinghast, Edye de Marco, Sylvia Brown, and Bob Oates.

And to Patches and Rufous, my wonderful feline companions, who kept me company from their perches in the office and always hoped there would be more fish and seafood recipes.

Index

Note: Page numbers in italics indicate photos.